Microsoft® Access® 2010

Step by Step

Joyce Cox
Joan Lambert

PUBLISHED BY
Microsoft Press
A Division of Microsoft Corporation
One Microsoft Way
Redmond, Washington 98052-6399

Library of Congress Control Number: 2010928521

Printed and bound in the United States of America.

1 2 3 4 5 6 7 8 9 WCT 5 4 3 2 1 0

A CIP catalogue record for this book is available from the British Library.

Microsoft Press books are available through booksellers and distributors worldwide. For further information about international editions, contact your local Microsoft Corporation office or contact Microsoft Press International directly at fax (425) 936-7329. Visit our Web site at www.microsoft.com/mspress. Send comments to mspinput@microsoft.com.

Microsoft and the trademarks listed at http://www.microsoft.com/about/legal/en/us/IntellectualProperty/Trademarks/EN-US.aspx are trademarks of the Microsoft group of companies. All other marks are property of their respective owners.

The example companies, organizations, products, domain names, e-mail addresses, logos, people, places, and events depicted herein are fictitious. No association with any real company, organization, product, domain name, e-mail address, logo, person, place, or event is intended or should be inferred.

This book expresses the author's views and opinions. The information contained in this book is provided without any express, statutory, or implied warranties. Neither the authors, Microsoft Corporation, nor its resellers, or distributors will be held liable for any damages caused or alleged to be caused either directly or indirectly by this book.

Acquisitions Editor: Juliana Aldous
Developmental Editor: Devon Musgrave
Project Editor: Joel Panchot
Editorial Production: Online Training Solutions, Inc.
Cover: Girvin

Body Part No. X16-95385

Contents

Part 1   Simple Database Techniques

What do you think of this book? We want to hear from you!

Microsoft is interested in hearing your feedback so we can continually improve our books and learning resources for you. To participate in a brief online survey, please visit:

> **microsoft.com/learning/booksurvey**

7   Create Custom Forms   179

8   Create Queries   209

9   Create Custom Reports   241

What do you think of this book? We want to hear from you!

Microsoft is interested in hearing your feedback so we can continually improve our books and learning resources
for you. To participate in a brief online survey, please visit:

microsoft.com/learning/booksurvey

Introducing Microsoft Access 2010

Microsoft Access 2010 is a powerful relational database program that includes hundreds of tools you can use to quickly start tracking, sharing, and reporting information, even if you are new to database development. Users have access to a large library of professionally designed templates; wizards that automatically create tables, forms, queries, and reports; and extensive local and online help resources.

Access supports sharing data with other sources, including other Microsoft Office 2010 programs, Microsoft SQL Server, Windows SharePoint Services, and documents in XML, HTML, XPS, and PDF formats. Advanced features allow you to create sophisticated executable database applications that your employees and customers can use to gather and view data without needing to know anything at all about database design or development.

This book gives you straightforward instructions for using Access to create databases. It takes you from knowing little or nothing about Access—or, for that matter, about databases—to a level of expertise that will enable you to create complex databases for use by one person or by many people.

New Features

If you're upgrading to Access 2010 from a previous version, you're probably more interested in the differences between the old and new versions and how they will affect you than you are in the basic functionality of Access. To help you identify the entire scope of changes from the version of Access you're familiar with, we've listed here the new features introduced in Access 2010, as well as in Access 2007.

If You Are Upgrading from Access 2007

If you have been using Access 2007, you might be wondering how Microsoft could have improved on what seemed like a pretty comprehensive set of features and tools. In addition to enhancing many of the new features introduced with Access 2007, Access 2010 includes the following new features:

- **The Backstage view** Finally, all the tools you need to work with your files, as opposed to their content, really are accessible from one location. You display the Backstage view by clicking the File tab, which replaces the Microsoft Office Button at the left end of the ribbon.

- **Customizable ribbon** The logical next step in the evolution of the command center introduced with Access 2007: Create your own tabs and groups to suit the way you work.

- **Unifying themes** Adding pizzazz to database objects such as forms and reports is just a matter of applying a professional-looking theme from a gallery of options.

- **Web capabilities** Companies that have employees and clients in different geographic locations can publish databases to Access Services, thereby making those databases accessible over the Internet in a Web browser.

- **Navigation forms** Offering the sophisticated browsing techniques people are accustomed to using on Web sites, these new forms provide an essential navigation tool for Web databases, and can also increase the usability of non-Web databases.

- **New database templates** Getting started with the creation of common types of databases has never been easier. The databases that come with Access are supplemented by those made available by a community of database developers through Microsoft Office Online.

- **Application parts** You can now add predefined database objects to an existing database. In addition to 10 types of forms, several Quick Start parts are available. For example, adding the Contacts part adds one table and associated queries, forms, and reports.

- **Enhanced Layout view and layout controls** It is now easier to make design changes in Layout view while actively viewing the underlying data.

- **Enhanced Expression Builder** The layout of the Expression Builder dialog box has been refined to make building an expression more intuitive. In addition, a feature called *IntelliSense* has been incorporated to display options based on what you type and to provide syntax guidance.

- **Improved conditional formatting** You can now use data bars to add at-a-glance insight into the data in Number fields.

- **Ability to export to PDF and XPS files** When you want to make a report or other database object available to people but don't want them to be able to manipulate it, you can export the object in either PDF or XPS format. You can optimize the file size for printing or publishing online.

If You Are Upgrading from Access 2003

Access 2010 builds on Access 2007, which introduced a long list of new and improved features that made it easier than ever to create databases to track, share, manage, and audit information, including the following:

- **The ribbon** The new user interface organizes the most common commands for any database object into tabs and groups so that the appropriate commands are immediately accessible for the current object.

- **Quick Access Toolbar** Customize a portion of the toolbar to include commands you regularly use, regardless of which object is currently active.

- **Navigation pane** The customizable Navigation pane replaces the Database window from Access 2003. You can display or hide all tables, queries, forms, reports, macros, and modules, or create a custom group that displays only the objects you want to work with at the moment. You can even hide the Navigation pane to make more room on the screen for your database object.

- **View Shortcuts toolbar** This context-sensitive toolbar at the lower-right corner of the program window provides single-click switching among the supported views of the current database object. Quickly switch between Datasheet view, Design view, PivotTable view, PivotChart view, Form view, Layout view, Report view, and other views appropriate to the current object.

- **Tabbed documents** Open multiple database objects and switch between them quickly by clicking tabs on a tab bar.

- **Template library** Quickly locate and download professionally designed templates for common database projects.

- **Improved sorting and filtering** Easily sort all records in a table based on one or more fields, or filter a table or form to display or hide records matching multiple criteria.

- **Layout view** Redesign a form or report while viewing it.

- **Stacked and Tabular layouts** Group controls in a form or report layout so you can easily manipulate the entire group as one unit.

- **Automatic calendar** The Date/Time data type includes an optional calendar control. Click the calendar, and select the date you want.

- **Rich Text** Memo fields now support most common formatting options, including fonts, color, and character formatting. The formatting is stored with the database.

- **Create tab** Quickly create a new table, form, query, report, macro, SharePoint list, or other Access object.

- **Totals function** Add a totals row to a query, and select from a list of formulas to automatically calculate aggregate values for forms and reports.

- **Field List** Drag and drop fields from one or more related or unrelated tables onto your active table.

- **Attachment data type** Attach photos and other files to a database record.

- **Embedded macros** Macros embedded in a form or report offer a higher level of security in database applications.

- **Microsoft Access Help** Easily search end-user and developer help content from within Access.

- **Improved information sharing** Easily import and export data between Access and other Office applications or XML, HTML, PDF, and dBase files; collect information through e-mail surveys in Microsoft Office Outlook and automatically update your database with the responses; create or link a database with a SharePoint list; or publish your database to a SharePoint library and allow users to update and extract information.

- **Improved report design** Quickly create a professional-looking report, complete with logo, header, and footer; and use Report view, combined with filters, to browse only selected records in the report.

- **Group, Sort, and Total pane** This feature makes it much easier to group and sort data in reports, and add totals from a drop-down list.

- **Enhanced security** Adding password protection to a database now causes Access to automatically encrypt the database when it closes, and decrypt it when it opens.

Let's Get Started!

There are so many new and improved features to this already feature-rich program that there are bound to be some exciting discoveries for even the most advanced users. If you are new to Access, you will find many automated features that let you painlessly create databases and add queries, forms, and professional-looking reports to track and share your data. We look forward to showing you around Microsoft Access 2010.

Modifying the Display of the Ribbon

The goal of the Microsoft Office 2010 working environment is to make working with Office files—including Microsoft Word documents, Excel workbooks, PowerPoint presentations, Outlook e-mail messages, and Access databases—as intuitive as possible. You work with an Office file and its contents by giving commands to the program in which the document is open. All Office 2010 programs organize commands on a horizontal bar called the *ribbon*, which appears across the top of each program window whether or not there is an active document.

Ribbon tabs   Ribbon groups

A typical program window ribbon.

Commands are organized on task-specific tabs of the ribbon, and in feature-specific groups on each tab. Commands generally take the form of buttons and lists. Some appear in galleries in which you can choose from among multiple options. Some groups have related dialog boxes or task panes that contain additional commands.

Throughout this book, we discuss the commands and ribbon elements associated with the program feature being discussed. In this section, we discuss the general appearance of the ribbon, things that affect its appearance, and ways of locating commands that aren't visible on compact views of the ribbon.

See Also For detailed information about the ribbon in Microsoft Access, see "Working in Access 2010" in Chapter 1, "Explore an Access 2010 Database."

Tip Some older commands no longer appear on the ribbon, but are still available in the program. You can make these commands available by adding them to the Quick Access Toolbar. For more information, see "Customizing the Quick Access Toolbar" in Chapter 13, "Customize Access."

Dynamic Ribbon Elements

The ribbon is dynamic, meaning that the appearance of commands on the ribbon changes as the width of the ribbon changes. A command might be displayed on the ribbon in the form of a large button, a small button, a small labeled button, or a list entry. As the width of the ribbon decreases, the size, shape, and presence of buttons on the ribbon adapt to the available space.

For example, when sufficient horizontal space is available, the buttons on the Review tab of the Word program window are spread out and you're able to see more of the commands available in each group.

The Review tab of the Word program window at 1024 pixels wide.

If you decrease the width of the ribbon, small button labels disappear and entire groups of buttons are hidden under one button that represents the group. Click the group button to display a list of the commands available in that group.

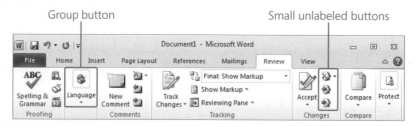

The Review tab of the Word program window at 675 pixels wide.

When the window becomes too narrow to display all the groups, a scroll arrow appears at its right end. Click the scroll arrow to display hidden groups.

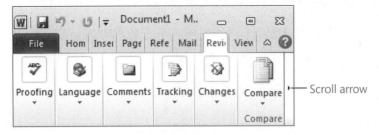   Scroll arrow

The Review tab of the Word program window at 340 pixels wide.

Changing the Width of the Ribbon

The width of the ribbon is dependent on the horizontal space available to it, which depends on these three factors:

- **The width of the program window** Maximizing the program window provides the most space for ribbon elements. You can resize the program window by clicking the button in its upper-right corner or by dragging the border of a non-maximized window.

  On a computer running Windows 7, you can maximize the program window by dragging its title bar to the top of the screen.

- **Your screen resolution** Screen resolution is the amount of information your screen displays, expressed as *pixels wide by pixels high*. The greater the screen resolution, the greater the amount of information that will fit on one screen. Your screen resolution options are dependent on your monitor. At the time of writing, possible screen resolutions range from 800 × 600 to 2048 × 1152. In the case of the ribbon, the greater the number of pixels wide (the first number), the greater the number of buttons that can be shown on the ribbon, and the larger those buttons can be.

On a computer running Windows 7, you can change your screen resolution from the Screen Resolution window of Control Panel.

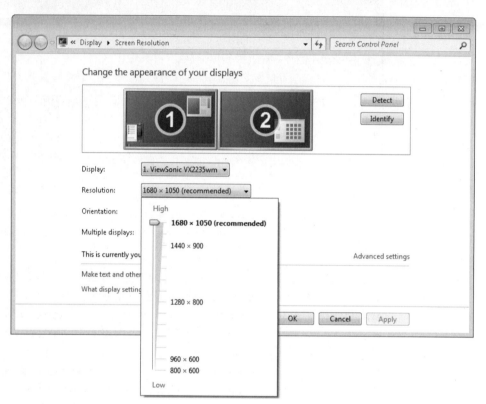

You set the resolution by dragging the pointer on the slider.

● **The density of your screen display** You might not be aware that you can change the magnification of everything that appears on your screen by changing the screen magnification setting in Windows. Setting your screen magnification to 125% makes text and user interface elements larger on screen. This increases the legibility of information, but it means that less information fits onto each screen.

On a computer running Windows 7, you can change the screen magnification from the Display window of Control Panel.

See Also For more information about display settings, refer to *Windows 7 Step by Step* (Microsoft Press, 2009), *Windows Vista Step by Step* (Microsoft Press, 2006), or *Windows XP Step by Step* (Microsoft Press, 2002) by Joan Lambert Preppernau and Joyce Cox.

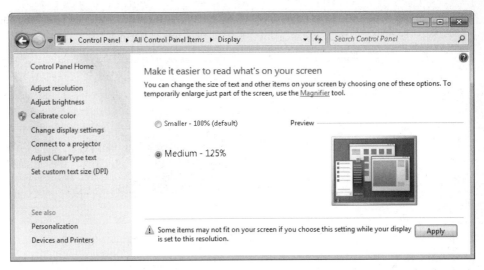

You can choose one of the standard display magnification options or create another by setting a custom text size.

The screen magnification is directly related to the density of the text elements on screen, which is expressed in dots per inch (dpi) or points per inch (ppi). (The terms are interchangeable, and in fact are both used in the Windows dialog box in which you change the setting.) The greater the dpi, the larger the text and user interface elements appear on screen. By default, Windows displays text and screen elements at 96 dpi. Choosing the Medium - 125% display setting changes the dpi of text and screen elements to 120 dpi. You can choose a custom setting of up to 500 percent magnification, or 480 dpi, in the Custom DPI Setting dialog box.

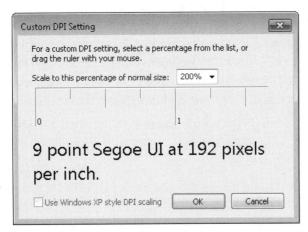

You can choose a magnification of up to 200 percent from the lists, or choose a greater magnification by dragging the ruler from left to right.

Adapting Exercise Steps

The screen images shown in the exercises in this book were captured at a screen resolution of 1024 × 768, at 100% magnification, and with the default text size (96 dpi). If any of your settings are different, the ribbon on your screen might not look the same as the one shown in the book. For example, you might see more or fewer buttons in each of the groups, the buttons you see might be represented by larger or smaller icons than those shown, or the group might be represented by a button that you click to display the group's commands.

When we instruct you to give a command from the ribbon in an exercise, we do it in this format:

- On the **Insert** tab, in the **Illustrations** group, click the **Chart** button.

If the command is in a list, we give the instruction in this format:

- On the **Page Layout** tab, in the **Page Setup** group, click the **Breaks** button and then, in the list, click **Page**.

The first time we instruct you to click a specific button in each exercise, we display an image of the button in the page margin to the left of the exercise step.

If differences between your display settings and ours cause a button on your screen to not appear as shown in the book, you can easily adapt the steps to locate the command. First, click the specified tab. Then locate the specified group. If a group has been collapsed into a group list or group button, click the list or button to display the group's commands. Finally, look for a button that features the same icon in a larger or smaller size than that shown in the book. If necessary, point to buttons in the group to display their names in ScreenTips.

If you prefer not to have to adapt the steps, set up your screen to match ours while you read and work through the exercises in the book.

Features and Conventions of This Book

This book has been designed to lead you step by step through all the tasks you're most likely to want to perform in Microsoft Access 2010. If you start at the beginning and work your way through all the exercises, you will gain enough proficiency to be able to manage complex databases through Access. However, each topic is self contained. If you have worked with a previous version of Access, or if you completed all the exercises and later need help remembering how to perform a procedure, the following features of this book will help you locate specific information:

- **Detailed table of contents** Scane the listing of the topics and sidebars within each chapter.

- **Chapter thumb tabs** Easily locate the beginning of each chapter by looking at the colored blocks on the odd-numbered pages.

- **Topic-specific running heads** Within a chapter, quickly locate a topic by looking at the running heads at the top of odd-numbered pages.

- **Glossary** Look up the meaning of a word or the definition of a concept.

- **Keyboard Shortcuts** If you prefer to work from the keyboard rather than with a mouse, find all the shortcuts in one place.

- **Detailed index** Look up specific tasks and features in the index, which has been carefully crafted with the reader in mind.

You can save time when reading this book by understanding how the Step by Step series shows exercise instructions, keys to press, buttons to click, and other information. These conventions are listed in the following table.

Convention	Meaning
SET UP	This paragraph preceding a step-by-step exercise indicates the practice files that you will use when working through the exercise. It also indicates any requirements you should attend to or actions you should take before beginning the exercise.
CLEAN UP	This paragraph following a step-by-step exercise provides instructions for saving and closing open files or programs before moving on to another topic. It also suggests ways to reverse any changes you made to your computer while working through the exercise.
1 2	Blue numbered steps guide you through hands-on exercises in each topic.
1 2	Black numbered steps guide you through procedures in sidebars and expository text.
See Also	This paragraph directs you to more information about a topic in this book or elsewhere.
Troubleshooting	This paragraph alerts you to a common problem and provides guidance for fixing it.
Tip	This paragraph provides a helpful hint or shortcut that makes working through a task easier.
Important	This paragraph points out information that you need to know to complete a procedure.
Keyboard Shortcut	This paragraph provides information about an available keyboard shortcut for the preceding task.
Ctrl+B	A plus sign (+) between two keys means that you must press those keys at the same time. For example, "Press Ctrl+B" means that you should hold down the Ctrl key while you press the B key.
	Pictures of buttons appear in the margin the first time the button is used in an exercise.
Black bold	In exercises that begin with SET UP information, the names of program elements, such as buttons, commands, windows, and dialog boxes, as well as files, folders, or text that you interact with in the steps, are shown in bold black type.
Blue bold	In exercises that begin with SET UP information, text that you should type is shown in bold blue type.

Using the Practice Files

Before you can complete the exercises in this book, you need to copy the book's practice files to your computer. These practice files, and other information, can be downloaded from the book's detail page, located at:

go.microsoft.com/fwlink/?LinkId=192153

Display the detail page in your Web browser and follow the instructions for downloading the files.

Important The Microsoft Access 2010 program is not available from this Web site. You should purchase and install that program before using this book.

The following table lists the practice files for this book.

Chapter	File
Chapter 1: Explore an Access 2010 Database	GardenCompany01_start.accdb
Chapter 2: Create Databases and Simple Tables	None
Chapter 3: Create Simple Forms	GardenCompany03_start.accdb Logo.png
Chapter 4: Display Data	GardenCompany04_start.accdb
Chapter 5: Create Simple Reports	GardenCompany05_start.accdb
Chapter 6: Maintain Data Integrity	GardenCompany06_start.accdb
Chapter 7: Create Custom Forms	GardenCompany07_start.accdb Hydrangeas.jpg
Chapter 8: Create Queries	GardenCompany08_start.accdb
Chapter 9: Create Custom Reports	GardenCompany09_start.accdb

(continued)

Chapter	File
Chapter 10: Import and Export Data	Customers.xlsx Employees.txt GardenCompany10_start.accdb ProductsAndSuppliers.accdb Shippers.xlsx
Chapter 11: Make Databases User Friendly	GardenCompany11_start.accdb Icon.ico Logo.png
Chapter 12: Protect Databases	GardenCompany12_start.accdb
Chapter 13: Customize Access	GardenCompany13_start.accdb

Getting Help

Every effort has been made to ensure the accuracy of this book. If you do run into problems, please contact the sources listed in the following sections.

Getting Help with This Book

If your question or issue concerns the content of this book or its practice files, please first consult the book's errata page, which can be accessed at:

go.microsoft.com/fwlink/?LinkID=192153

This page provides information about known errors and corrections to the book. If you do not find your answer on the errata page, send your question or comment to Microsoft Press Technical Support at:

mspinput@microsoft.com

Getting Help with Access 2010

If your question is about Microsoft Access 2010, and not about the content of this book, your first recourse is the Access Help system. This system is a combination of tools and files stored on your computer when you installed Access and, if your computer is connected to the Internet, information available from the Microsoft Office Online Web site. You can find general or specific Help information in the following ways:

- To find out about an item on the screen, you can display a ScreenTip. For example, to display a ScreenTip for a button, point to the button without clicking it. The ScreenTip gives the button's name, the associated keyboard shortcut if there is one, and sometimes a description of what the button does when you click it.

- In the Access program window, you can click the Microsoft Access Help button (a question mark in a blue circle) at the right end of the ribbon to display the Access Help window.

- At the right end of the title bars of some dialog boxes is a Help button (also a question mark) that you can click to display the Access Help window. Sometimes, topics related to the functions of that dialog box are already identified in the window.

To practice getting help, you can work through the following exercise.

SET UP You don't need any practice files to complete this exercise. Start Access, and then follow the steps.

1. At the right end of the ribbon, click the **Microsoft Access Help** button.

   The Access Help window opens.

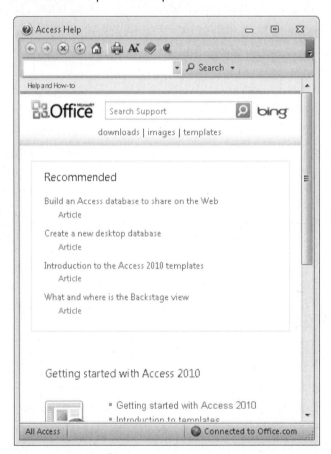

Your Help window might look different from this one because the material on the Office Online Web site is constantly being updated.

Tip You can maximize the window or adjust its size by dragging the handle in the lower-right corner. You can change the size of the font by clicking the Change Font Size button on the toolbar.

2. Toward the bottom of the window, below the bulleted list under **Browse Access 2010 support**, click **see all**.

Troubleshooting The See All link is available only if the Search option is set to one of the Content From Office.com choices. If your Search option is set to one of the Content From This Computer choices, the complete list is already displayed. To switch among the available Search options, click the Search arrow and then click your choice in the list.

The window changes to display a list of help topics.

3. In the list of topics, click **Activating Access**.

Access Help displays a list of topics related to activating Microsoft Office programs. You can click any topic to display the corresponding information.

4. On the toolbar, click the **Show Table of Contents** button, and then scroll down the pane that appears on the left.

Like the table of contents in a book, the Help table of contents is organized in sections. If you're connected to the Internet and the Search option is set to one of the Content From Office.com choices, Access displays sections, topics, and training available from the Office Online Web site as well as the Help information stored on your computer.

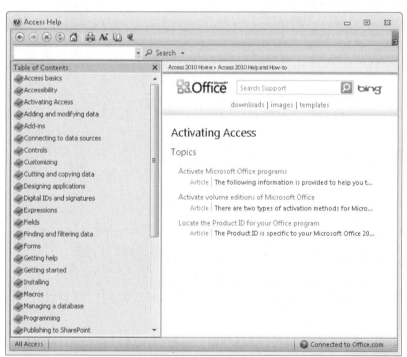

Clicking any section (represented by a book icon) displays that section's topics (represented by help icons).

5. In the **Table of Contents** pane, click a few sections and topics. Then click the **Back** and **Forward** buttons to move among the topics you have already viewed.

6. At the right end of the **Table of Contents** title bar, click the **Close** button.

7. At the top of the **Access Help** window, click the **Search** box, type relationships, and then press the Enter key.

The Access Help window displays topics related to the word you typed.

Next and Back buttons appear below the search term to make it easier to search for the topic you want.

Tip If you enter a term in the Search box and then click the adjacent Search arrow, you can specify the type of help you are looking for or where you want to look for it.

8. In the results list, click the **Guide to table relationships** topic.

   The selected topic appears in the Access Help window.

9. Below the first paragraph of the topic, click **Database design basics**.

   Access jumps to the related topic about database design. This type of hyperlink is identified by blue text. You might also see a Show All button that displays hidden auxiliary information available in the topic. (The button changes to Hide All when the hidden information is displayed.)

   Tip You can click the Print button on the toolbar to print a topic. Only the displayed information is printed.

 CLEAN UP Click the Close button in the upper-right corner of the Access Help window.

More Information

If your question is about Access 2010 or another Microsoft software product and you cannot find the answer in the product's Help system, please search the appropriate product solution center or the Microsoft Knowledge Base at:

support.microsoft.com

In the United States, Microsoft software product support issues not covered by the Microsoft Knowledge Base are addressed by Microsoft Product Support Services. Location-specific software support options are available from:

support.microsoft.com/gp/selfoverview/

Part 1
Simple Database Techniques

Chapter at a Glance

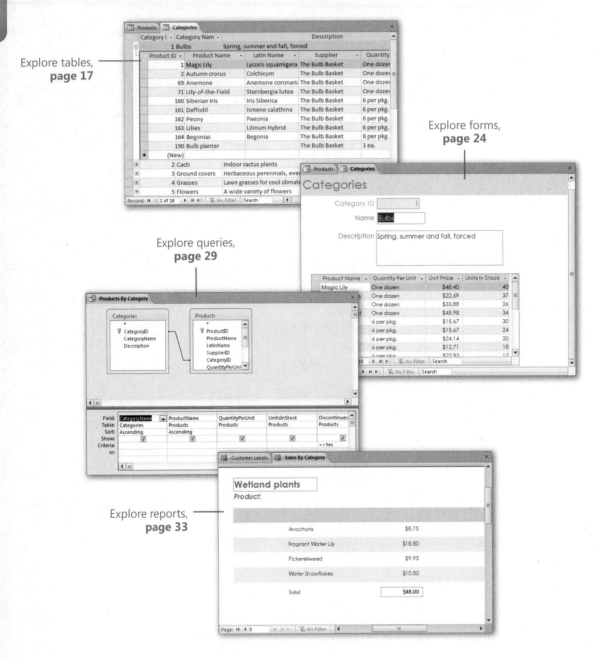

Explore tables,
page 17

Explore forms,
page 24

Explore queries,
page 29

Explore reports,
page 33

1 Explore an Access 2010 Database

In this chapter, you will learn how to

✔ Work in Access 2010.

✔ Understand database concepts.

✔ Explore tables.

✔ Explore forms.

✔ Explore queries.

✔ Explore reports.

✔ Preview and print Access objects.

Microsoft Access 2010 is part of Microsoft Office 2010, so the basic interface—such as the Quick Access Toolbar, the ribbon, the Backstage view, and dialog boxes—should be familiar if you have used other Office 2010 programs. However, Access has more dimensions than many of those programs, so it might seem more complex until you become familiar with it.

Tip If you are upgrading from an earlier version of Access, you should review "Introducing Microsoft Access 2010" at the beginning of this book to learn about differences between earlier versions and Access 2010.

Throughout this book, you'll be working with databases that contain information about the employees, products, suppliers, and customers of a fictional company. As you complete the exercises in this book, you will develop an assortment of tables, forms, queries, and reports, which are called *database objects*. These objects can be used to enter, edit, and manipulate the information in a database in many ways.

In this chapter, you'll explore the Access program window and learn about the concepts and structure of data storage in Access, including types of databases, types of database objects, and relationships between objects. You'll look at objects in a working database, learning about interesting features of Access as well as functionality that you'll explore in more depth in later chapters.

> **Practice Files** Before you can complete the exercises in this chapter, you need to copy the book's practice files to your computer. The practice file you'll use to complete the exercises in this chapter is in the Chapter01 practice file folder. A complete list of practice files is provided in "Using the Practice Files" at the beginning of this book.

Working in Access 2010

As with all programs in Office 2010, the most common way to start Access is from the Start menu displayed when you click the Start button at the left end of the Windows Taskbar. When you start Access without opening a database, the program window opens in the Backstage view, with the New page active. In the Backstage view, commands related to managing Access and Access databases (rather than their objects) are organized as buttons and pages, which you display by clicking the page tabs in the left pane. You can display the Backstage view at any time by clicking the colored File tab in the upper-left corner of the program window.

Clicking the File tab displays the Backstage view, where you can manage database files and customize the program.

From the New page of the Backstage view, you can create a blank database; or you can create a new database based on a template that comes with Access, on a template downloaded from the Office.com Web site, or on a custom template saved on your computer or on your network. From the Backstage view, you can also open a database you worked in recently, or navigate to any database on your computer and open it.

When you create or open a database, it is displayed in the program window.

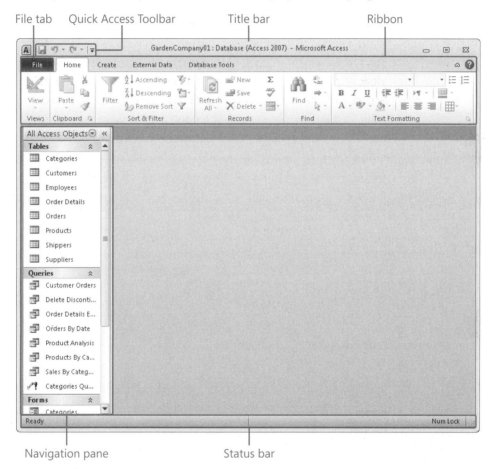

An Access database in the program window

Troubleshooting The appearance of buttons and groups on the ribbon changes depending on the width of the program window. For information about changing the appearance of the ribbon to match our screen images, see "Modifying the Display of the Ribbon" at the beginning of this book.

The database interface is designed to closely reflect the way people generally work with a database or database object. For those of you who are not familiar with this interface, which was first introduced with Microsoft Office Access 2007, here is a quick survey of the program window elements:

- The title bar displays the name of the active database. The designation *(Access 2007)* after the database name indicates that the database is in the .accdb format introduced with Access 2007. At the left end of the title bar is the Access icon, which you click to display commands to move, size, and close the program window. The Minimize, Restore Down/Maximize, and Close buttons at the right end of the title bar serve the same functions as in all Windows programs.

  See Also Windows 7 introduced many fun and efficient new window-management techniques. For information about ways to work with the Access program window on a Windows 7 computer, refer to *Windows 7 Step by Step,* by Joan Lambert Preppernau and Joyce Cox (Microsoft Press, 2009).

- By default, the Quick Access Toolbar appears to the right of the Access icon at the left end of the title bar, and displays the Save, Undo, and Redo buttons. You can change the location of the Quick Access Toolbar and customize it to include any command that you use frequently.

  Tip If you create and work with complicated databases, you might achieve greater efficiency if you add the commands you use frequently to the Quick Access Toolbar and display it below the ribbon, directly above the workspace. For information, see "Customizing the Quick Access Toolbar" in Chapter 13, "Customize Access."

- Below the title bar is the ribbon. All the commands for working with your Access database content are available from this central location so that you can work efficiently with the program.

- Across the top of the ribbon is a set of tabs. Clicking the File tab displays the Backstage view. Clicking any other tab displays a set of related commands represented by buttons and lists. The Home tab is active by default.

  Tip Don't be alarmed if your ribbon has tabs not shown in our screens. You might have installed programs that add their own tabs to the Access ribbon.

- On each tab, commands are organized into named groups. Depending on your screen resolution and the size of the program window, the commands in a group might be displayed as labeled buttons, as unlabeled icons, or as one or more large buttons that you click to display the commands within the group.

- If a button label isn't visible, you can display the command name and its keyboard shortcut (if it has one) in a ScreenTip by pointing to the button.

  See Also For more information about keyboard shortcuts, see "Keyboard Shortcuts" at the end of this book.

  Tip To control the display of ScreenTips, display the Backstage view, click Options to open the Access Options dialog box, and change settings in the User Interface Options area of the General page. You can also change the language of ScreenTip content on the Language page. For more information, see "Changing Default Program Options" in Chapter 13, "Customize Access."

- Some buttons include an integrated or separate arrow. If a button and its arrow are integrated, clicking the button will display options for refining the action of the button. If the button and its arrow are separate, clicking the button will carry out the default action indicated by the button's current icon. You can change the default action by clicking the arrow and then clicking the action you want.

- Related but less common commands are not represented as buttons in a group. Instead they are available in a dialog box or task pane, which you display by clicking the dialog box launcher located in the lower-right corner of the group.

- To the right of the ribbon tab names, below the Minimize/Maximize/Close buttons, is the Minimize The Ribbon button. Clicking this button hides the commands but leaves the tab names visible. You can then click any tab name to temporarily display its commands. Clicking anywhere other than the ribbon hides the commands again. When the full ribbon is temporarily visible, you can click the button at its right end, shaped like a pushpin, to make the display permanent. When the full ribbon is hidden, you can click the Expand The Ribbon button to permanently redisplay it.

  Keyboard Shortcut Press Ctrl+F1 to minimize or expand the ribbon.

- Clicking the Access Help button at the right end of the ribbon displays the Access Help window, in which you can use standard techniques to find information.

  Keyboard Shortcut Press F1 to display the Access Help window.

  See Also For information about the Access Help system, see "Getting Help" at the beginning of this book.

- On the left side of the program window, the Navigation pane displays lists of database objects. By default, it displays all the objects in the database by type of object, but you can filter the list by clicking the pane's title bar and then clicking the category or group of objects you want to display. You can collapse and expand the groups in the list by clicking the chevrons in the section bars. If the Navigation pane is in your way, you can click the Shutter Bar Open/Close button in its upper-right corner to minimize it. To redisplay the Navigation pane, click the Shutter Bar Open/Close button again. You can drag the right border of the pane to the left or right to make it wider or narrower.

Keyboard Shortcut Press F11 to display or hide the Navigation pane.

● Across the bottom of the program window, the status bar displays information about the current database and provides access to certain program functions. You can control the contents of the status bar by right-clicking it to display the Customize Status Bar menu, on which you can click any item to display or hide it.

● At the right end of the status bar, the View Shortcuts toolbar provides buttons for quickly switching the view of the active database object.

The goal of all these interface features is to make working with a database as intuitive as possible. Commands for tasks you perform often are readily available, and even those you might use infrequently are easy to find.

In this exercise, you'll take a tour of the command structure in the Access 2010 program window.

SET UP You need the GardenCompany01_start database located in your Chapter01 practice file folder to complete this exercise, but don't open it yet. Just follow the steps.

1. On the **Start** menu, click **All Programs**, click **Microsoft Office**, and then click **Microsoft Access 2010**.

    Access starts and displays the program window in the Backstage view. From this view, you manage your Access database files, but you don't work with the content of databases. For example, you can create a database, but not a database object. We'll talk about the tasks you can perform in the Backstage view in other chapters of this book.

2. In the left pane of the Backstage view, click **Open**. Then in the **Open** dialog box, navigate to your **Chapter01** practice file folder, and double-click the **GardenCompany01_start** database.

    The database opens in the program window. A security warning appears below the ribbon.

3. In the security warning bar, click **Enable Content**.

    Important Be sure to read the sidebar "Enabling Macros and Other Database Content" later in this chapter to learn about Access security options.

    Let's save the database so that you can explore it without fear of overwriting the original practice file.

4. Click the **File** tab to display the Backstage view, click **Save Database As**, and then in the **Save As** dialog box, save the database in your **Chapter01** practice file folder with the name **GardenCompany01**.

    Tip In this book, we assume you will save files in your practice file folders, but you can save them wherever you want. When we refer to your practice file folders in the instructions, simply substitute the save location you chose.

    In the program window, the title bar tells you that you can work with this database in Access 2007 as well as Access 2010. On the left, the Navigation pane displays a list of all the objects in this database. Spanning the top of the window, the ribbon includes five tabs: File, Home, Create, External Data, and Database Tools. The Home tab is active by default. Because no database object is currently open, none of the buttons on the Home tab are available.

    Tip Databases created with Access 2010 use the file storage format introduced with Access 2007, and their files have the .accdb extension. You can open database files created in earlier versions of Access (which have an .mdb extension) in Access 2010. You can then either work with and save them in the old format or work with and save them in the new format. If you convert them, you can no longer open them in versions prior to Access 2007. For more information about the ACCDB format, search for accdb in Access Help.

5. In the **Navigation** pane title bar, click **All Access Objects**, and then under **Filter By Group** in the menu, click **Tables**.

    The Navigation pane now lists only the tables in the database.

6. In the **Navigation** pane, under **Tables**, double-click **Categories**.

    The Categories table opens on a tabbed page. Because a table is displayed, two Table Tools contextual tabs (Fields and Table) appear on the ribbon. These contextual tabs are displayed only when you are working with a table.

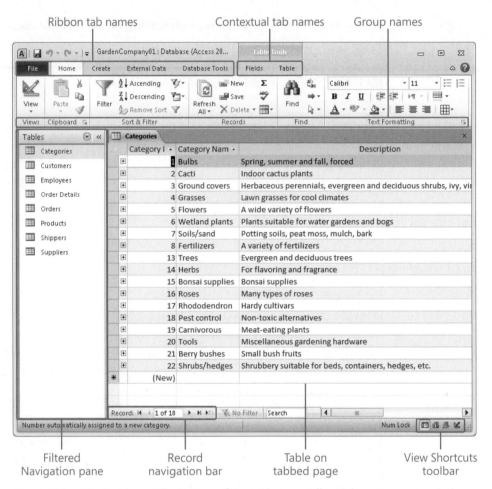

The record navigation bar at the bottom of the table page tells you how many records the table contains and which one is active, and enables you to move among records.

Buttons representing commands related to working with database content are organized on the Home tab in six groups: Views, Clipboard, Sort & Filter, Records, Find, and Text Formatting. Only the buttons for commands that can be performed on the currently selected database object—in this case, a table—are active.

7. On the **Home** tab, click the **Text Formatting** dialog box launcher.

   The Datasheet Formatting dialog box opens.

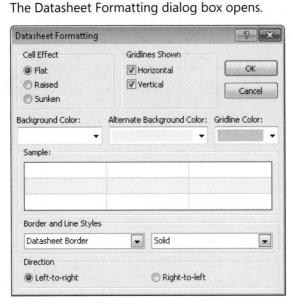

From this dialog box, you can access settings not available as buttons in the Text Formatting group, such as Gridline Color and Border And Line Styles.

8. In the **Datasheet Formatting** dialog box, click **Cancel**.

9. Click the **Create** tab.

   Buttons representing commands related to creating database objects are organized on this tab in six groups: Templates, Tables, Queries, Forms, Reports, and Macros & Code.

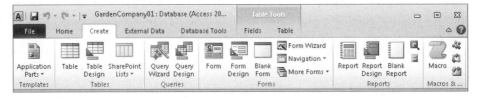

The Create tab.

10. Double-click the **Create** tab.

Double-clicking the active tab hides the ribbon and provides more space for the current database object.

The ribbon is hidden.

11. Click the **External Data** tab.

The ribbon temporarily drops down, with the External Data tab active. Buttons representing commands related to moving information between a database and other sources are organized on this tab in four groups: Import & Link, Export, Collect Data, and Web Linked Lists.

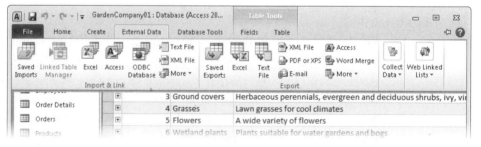

Clicking any tab—in this case, the External Data tab—displays the ribbon temporarily.

Tip To make the graphics in this book readable, we are working in a program window that is smaller than full-screen. As a result, the Collect Data and Web Linked Lists groups are represented in this graphic as buttons. For more information, see "Modifying the Display of the Ribbon" at the beginning of this book.

12. Click anywhere in the open table.

    The ribbon disappears again.

13. Double-click the **Database Tools** tab.

    Double-clicking a tab permanently displays the ribbon and activates that tab. Buttons representing commands related to managing, analyzing, and ensuring data reliability are organized on the Database Tools tab in six groups: Tools, Macro, Relationships, Analyze, Move Data, and Add-Ins.

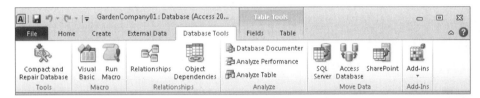

The Database Tools tab.

14. To the right of the **Categories** table page tab, click the **Close** button to close the table without closing the database.

    Clicking this button closes the active object.

15. Click the **File** tab to display the Backstage view, and then click **Close Database**.

    When you close a database without exiting Access, the New page of the Backstage view is displayed so that you can open another database or create a new one.

    Note that if you don't close the active database before opening another one, Access prompts you to save your changes and closes the active database for you. You cannot have two databases open simultaneously in a single instance of Access. If you want to have two databases open at the same time, you must start a new instance of Access.

    Tip You can close Access entirely by clicking the Close button in the upper-right corner of the program window, or by clicking Exit in the Backstage view.

✖ **CLEAN UP** Retain the GardenCompany01 database for use in later exercises.

Enabling Macros and Other Database Content

Some databases contain Microsoft Visual Basic for Applications (VBA) macros that can run code on your computer. In most cases, the code is there to perform a database-related task, but hackers can also use macros to spread a virus to your computer.

When you open a database that is not stored in a trusted location or signed by a trusted publisher, Access displays a security warning below the ribbon.

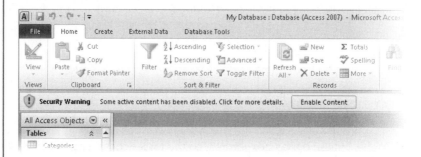

The security warning.

While the security warning is displayed, the macros in the database are disabled. You can enable macros in three ways:

- By enabling the macros in the database for use in the current database session.
- By adding the database publisher to the list of trusted publishers. This option is available only if the publisher's digital signature is attached to the database. Access will then automatically enable macro content in any database that is also signed by that publisher.
- By placing the database in a trusted location. Access automatically enables macro content in any database saved in that location. The trusted locations you specify within Access are not also trusted by other Office programs.

To enable macros for the current database session only:

- In the Security Warning area, click Enable Content.

To add the publisher of a digitally signed database to the trusted publishers list:

1. In the Security Warning area, click Some Active Content Has Been Disabled. Click For More Details.

2. On the Information About *<Database Name>* page, click the Enable Content button, and then click Advanced Options.

3. In the Microsoft Office Security Options dialog box, click Trust All From Publisher, and then click OK.

   Note that the Trust All From Publisher option is available only if the database is digitally signed.

To add the location of a database to the trusted locations list:

1. Display the Backstage view, and then click Options.

2. In the left pane of the Access Options dialog box, click Trust Center, and then click Trust Center Settings.

3. In the left pane of the Trust Center, click Trusted Locations.

4. On the Trusted Locations page, click Add New Location.

5. In the Microsoft Office Trusted Location dialog box, click Browse.

6. In the Browse dialog box, browse to the folder containing the current database, and then click OK.

7. In the Microsoft Office Trusted Location dialog box, select the Subfolders Of This Location Are Also Trusted check box if you want to do so, and then click OK in each of the open dialog boxes.

If you prefer, you can change the way Access handles macros in all databases:

1. Display the Trust Center, and then in the left pane, click Macro Settings.

2. Select the option for the way you want Access to handle macros:

   ○ **Disable All Macros Without Notification** If a database contains macros, Access disables them and doesn't display the security warning to give you the option of enabling them.

   ○ **Disable All Macros With Notification** Access disables all macros and displays the security warning.

   ○ **Disable All Macros Except Digitally Signed Macros** Access automatically enables digitally signed macros.

   ○ **Enable All Macros** Access enables all macros (not recommended).

3. Click OK to close the Trust Center, and then click OK to close the Access Options dialog box.

Understanding Database Concepts

Simple database programs, such as the Database component of Microsoft Works, can store information in only one table. These simple databases are often called *flat file databases*, or just *flat databases*. More complex database programs, such as Access, can store information in multiple related tables, thereby creating what are referred to as *relational databases*. If the information in a relational database is organized correctly, you can treat these multiple tables as a single storage area and pull information electronically from different tables in whatever order meets your needs.

A table is just one of the object types you work with in Access. Other object types include forms, queries, reports, macros, and modules.

Of all these object types, only one—the table—is used to store information. The rest are used to enter, manage, manipulate, analyze, retrieve, or display the information stored in a table—in other words, to make the information as accessible and therefore as useful as possible.

Over the years, Microsoft has put a lot of effort into making Access not only one of the most powerful consumer database programs available, but also one of the easiest to learn and use. Because Access is part of Office 2010, you can use many of the same techniques you use with Microsoft Word and Microsoft Excel. For example, you can use familiar commands, buttons, and keyboard shortcuts to open and edit the information in Access tables. And you can easily share information between Access and Word, Excel, or other Office programs.

In its most basic form, a database is the electronic equivalent of an organized list of information. Typically, this information has a common subject or purpose, such as the list of employees shown in the following table.

ID	Last name	First name	Title	Hire date
1	Anderson	Nancy	Sales Rep	May 1, 2003
2	Carpenter	Chase	Sales Manager	Aug 14, 2001
3	Emanuel	Michael	Sales Rep	Apr 1, 1999
4	Furse	Karen	Buyer	May 3, 2004

This list is arranged in a table of columns and rows. Each column represents a field—a specific type of information about an employee: last name, first name, hire date, and so on. Each row represents a record—all the information about a specific employee.

If a database did nothing more than store information in a table, it would be no more useful than a paper list. But because the database stores information in an electronic format, you can manipulate the information in powerful ways to extend its utility.

For example, suppose you want to find the phone number of a person who lives in your city. You can look up this information in the telephone book, because its information is organized for this purpose. If you want to find the phone number of someone who lives further away, you can go to the public library, which probably has a telephone book for each major city in the country. However, if you want to find the phone numbers of all the people in the country with your last name, or if you want to find the phone number of your grandmother's neighbor, these printed phone books won't do you much good, because they aren't organized in a way that makes that information easy to find.

When the information published in a phone book is stored in a database, it takes up far less space, it costs less to reproduce and distribute, and, if the database is designed correctly, the information can be retrieved in many ways. The real power of a database isn't in its ability to store information; it is in your ability to quickly retrieve exactly the information you want from the database.

Exploring Tables

Tables are the core database objects. Their purpose is to store information. The purpose of every other database object is to interact in some manner with one or more tables. An Access database can contain thousands of tables, and the number of records each table can contain is limited more by the space available on your hard disk than by anything else.

Tip For detailed information about Access specifications, such as the maximum size of a database or the maximum number of records in a table, search for *"Access 2010 specifications"* (including the quotation marks) in Access help.

Every Access object has two or more views. For tables, the two most common views are Datasheet view, in which you can see and modify the table's data, and Design view, in which you can see and modify the table's structure. To open a table in Datasheet view, either double-click its name in the Navigation pane, or right-click its name and then click Open. To open a table in Design view, right-click its name and then click Design View. When a table is open in Datasheet view, clicking the View button in the Views group on the Home tab switches to Design view; when it is open in Design view, clicking the button switches to Datasheet view. To switch to either of the two remaining table views (PivotTable view or PivotChart view), you click the View arrow and then click the view you want in the list. You can also switch the view by clicking one of the buttons on the View Shortcuts toolbar in the lower-right corner of the program window.

When you view a table in Datasheet view, you see the table's data in columns (fields) and rows (records). The first row contains column headings (field names). In this format, the table is often simply referred to as a *datasheet*.

Field names

Category ID	Category Name	Description
1	Bulbs	Spring, summer and fall, forced
2	Cacti	Indoor cactus plants
3	Ground covers	Herbaceous perennials, evergreen and deciduous shrubs
4	Grasses	Lawn grasses for cool climates
5	Flowers	A wide variety of flowers
6	Wetland plants	Plants suitable for water gardens and bogs
7	Soils/sand	Potting soils, peat moss, mulch, bark
8	Fertilizers	A variety of fertilizers
13	Trees	Evergreen and deciduous trees
14	Herbs	For flavoring and fragrance
15	Bonsai supplies	Bonsai supplies
16	Roses	Many types of roses
17	Rhododendron	Hardy cultivars
18	Pest control	Non-toxic alternatives
19	Carnivorous	Meat-eating plants
20	Tools	Miscellaneous gardening hardware
21	Berry bushes	Small bush fruits

Record: 1 of 18   No Filter   Search

Field   Record

Field names, fields, and records in a table.

If two tables have one or more field names in common, you can embed the datasheet from one table in another. By using an embedded datasheet, called a *subdatasheet*, you can see the information in more than one table at the same time. For example, you might want to embed an Orders datasheet in a Customers table so that you can see the orders each customer has placed.

In this exercise, you'll open existing database tables and explore the table structure in different views.

SET UP You need the GardenCompany01 database you worked with in the preceding exercise to complete this exercise. Open the GardenCompany01 database, ensure that tables are listed in the Navigation pane, and then follow the steps.

1. In the **Navigation** pane, double-click **Products**. Then at the right end of the **Navigation** pane title bar, click the **Shutter Bar Close** button so that you can see more of the table's fields.

The Products table is displayed in Datasheet view.

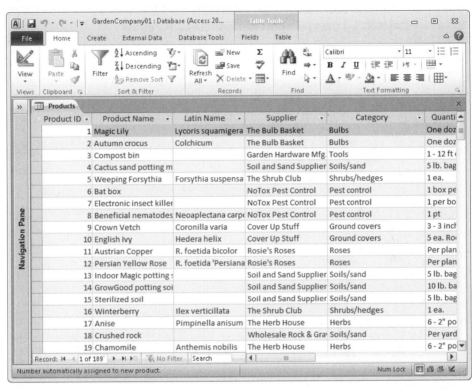

Each row in this table contains information about a product and each column contains one field from each record.

2. In the row of field names at the top of the table, point to the right border of the **Product Name** field name, and when the pointer changes to a double-headed arrow, double-click the border.

    Access adjusts the width of the field to accommodate its longest entry. Notice that Product 1, Magic Lily, and Product 2, Autumn crocus, are assigned to the Bulbs category.

3. Double-click the right border of the **Category** field name to adjust that field's width.

    Tip You can also resize a table column by pointing to the border and dragging it to the left or right.

4. In the **Navigation** pane, click the **Shutter Bar Open** button, and then double-click **Categories**.

    Tip From now on, open the Navigation pane whenever you need to work with a different object, but feel free to close it if you want to see more of the data.

The Categories table opens on a new tabbed page in Datasheet view. The Categories page is active, but the Products page is still open and available if you need it.

5. At the left end of the record for the **Bulbs** category, click the **Expand** button.

The Bulbs category expands to reveal a subdatasheet containing all the records from the Products table that are assigned to the Bulbs category. This is possible because a relationship has been established between the two tables.

Subdatasheet

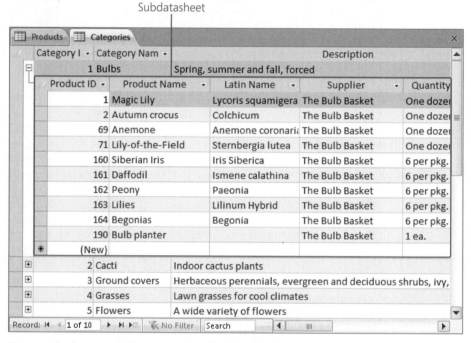

Category I ▾	Category Nam ▾	Description	
1	Bulbs	Spring, summer and fall, forced	

Product ID ▾	Product Name ▾	Latin Name ▾	Supplier ▾	Quantity
1	Magic Lily	Lycoris squamigera	The Bulb Basket	One dozen
2	Autumn crocus	Colchicum	The Bulb Basket	One dozen
69	Anemone	Anemone coronaria	The Bulb Basket	One dozen
71	Lily-of-the-Field	Sternbergia lutea	The Bulb Basket	One dozen
160	Siberian Iris	Iris Siberica	The Bulb Basket	6 per pkg.
161	Daffodil	Ismene calathina	The Bulb Basket	6 per pkg.
162	Peony	Paeonia	The Bulb Basket	6 per pkg.
163	Lilies	Lilinum Hybrid	The Bulb Basket	6 per pkg.
164	Begonias	Begonia	The Bulb Basket	6 per pkg.
190	Bulb planter		The Bulb Basket	1 ea.
*	(New)			

	2	Cacti	Indoor cactus plants
	3	Ground covers	Herbaceous perennials, evergreen and deciduous shrubs, ivy,
	4	Grasses	Lawn grasses for cool climates
	5	Flowers	A wide variety of flowers

Record: 1 of 10 No Filter Search

You can display records from two related tables simultaneously.

See Also For information about relationships, see "Creating Relationships Between Tables" in Chapter 2, "Create Databases and Simple Tables."

6. To the left of the record for the **Bulbs** category, click the **Collapse** button to hide the subdatasheet.

7. Click the **Close** button at the right end of the tab bar (not the Close button in the upper-right corner of the program window) to close the **Categories** table.

8. Close the **Products** table, and when Access asks whether you want to save your changes to this table, click **Yes**.

In steps 2 and 3, you changed the look of the table by changing the widths of columns. If you want those changes to be in effect the next time you open the table, you must save them.

9. In the **Navigation** pane, double-click the **Orders** table.

This table contains order-fulfillment information.

The record navigation bar at the bottom of the window indicates that this table contains 87 records, and that the active record is number 1 of 87.

 10. On the record navigation bar, click the **Next Record** button several times.

The selection moves down the OrderID field, because that field is active.

Keyboard Shortcut Press the Up Arrow or Down Arrow key to move the selection one record at a time. Press the Page Up or Page Down key to move one screen at a time. Press Ctrl+Home or Ctrl+End move the selection to the first or last field in the table.

11. Click the record navigation bar, select the current record number, type **40**, and then press the Enter key.

The selection moves directly to record 40.

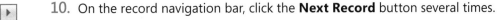 12. On the **View Shortcuts** toolbar, click the **Design View** button.

The Orders table structure is displayed in Design view, and the Table Tools Design contextual tab appears on the ribbon.

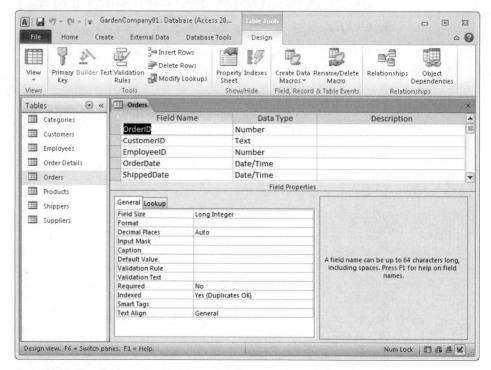

Datasheet view displays the data stored in the table, whereas Design view displays the underlying table structure.

See Also For information about table structure, see "Refining Table Structure" in Chapter 2, "Create Databases and Simple Tables."

 CLEAN UP Close the Orders table. Retain the GardenCompany01 database for use in later exercises.

Tabbed Pages vs. Overlapping Windows

By default, Access 2010 displays database objects on tabbed pages in the program window. If you prefer to display each object in a separate window rather than on a separate page, you can do so.

To switch to overlapping windows:

1. Click the File tab to display the Backstage view, and then click Options.

   The Access Options dialog box opens.

2. Display the Current Database page, and then in the Application Options area, under Document Window Options, click Overlapping Windows.

3. Click OK.

A message tells you that you must close and reopen the current database to put this change into effect.

4. Click OK. Then close and reopen the database.

When database objects are displayed on tabbed pages, a Close button appears at the right end of the tab bar. When objects are displayed in overlapping windows, the window of each object has its own set of Minimize, Restore Down/Maximize, and Close buttons at the right end of its title bar.

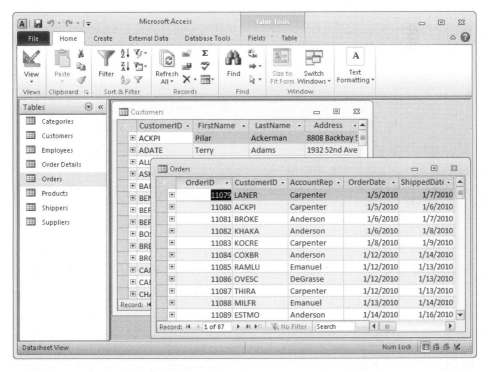

Two forms displayed in overlapping windows.

You can move object windows by dragging their title bars, and you can size them by dragging their frames. You can also arrange windows by using the options available when you click the Switch Windows button in the Window group. (This group is added to the Home tab when you select Overlapping Windows in the Access Options dialog box.)

Exploring Forms

Access tables are dense lists of raw information. Working directly with tables in a database you create for your own use might be quite simple for you, but it might be overwhelming for people who don't know much about databases. To make it easier to enter, display, and print information, you can design forms.

A form acts as a friendly interface for a table. Through a form, you can display and edit the records of the underlying table, or create new records. Most forms provide an interface to only one table, but if you want to use one form to interact with multiple tables that are related through one or more common fields, you can embed subforms within a main form.

Forms are essentially collections of controls that either accept information or display information. You can create forms by using a wizard, or you can create them from scratch by manually selecting and placing the controls. Access provides the types of controls that are standard in Windows dialog boxes, such as labels, text boxes, option buttons, and check boxes. With a little ingenuity, you can create forms that look and work much like the dialog boxes in all Windows programs.

As with tables, you can display forms in several views. The following are the three most common views:

- **Form** A view in which you display and enter data.

- **Layout** A view in which you can work with the elements of the form to refine the way it looks and behaves while also being able to see the data from the underlying table.

- **Design** A view that gives you more precise control over the look, placement, and behavior of elements of the form but that hides the underlying data.

See Also For more information about forms, see Chapter 3, "Create Simple Forms," and Chapter 7, "Create Custom Forms."

In this exercise, you'll explore forms, subforms, and the available form controls.

 SET UP You need the GardenCompany01 database you worked with in the preceding exercise to complete this exercise. Open the GardenCompany01 database, and then follow the steps.

1. In the **Navigation** pane, click the title bar to display the category list, and then under **Filter By Group**, click **Forms**.

    This group includes all the forms that have been saved as part of this database.

2. In the **Navigation** pane, double-click **Products**.

The Products form opens on a tabbed page.

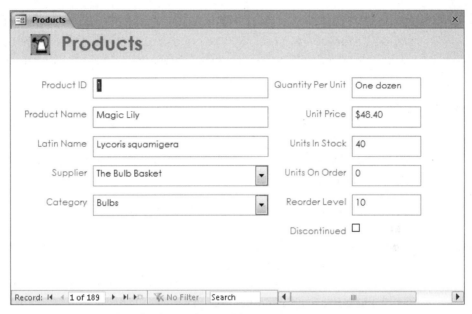

This form is the interface for the Products table.

3. Click the arrow adjacent to the **Supplier** box.

Access displays a list of all the company's suppliers.

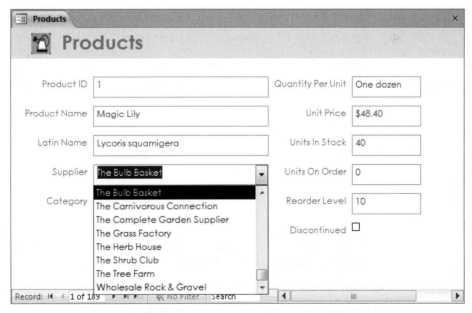

This is an example of a list box control.

4. In the **Navigation** pane, double-click **Categories**.

The Categories form opens on its own tabbed page. This form includes a main form and a subform. The main form displays information from the Categories table, and the subform, which looks like a datasheet, displays information for the current record from the Products table.

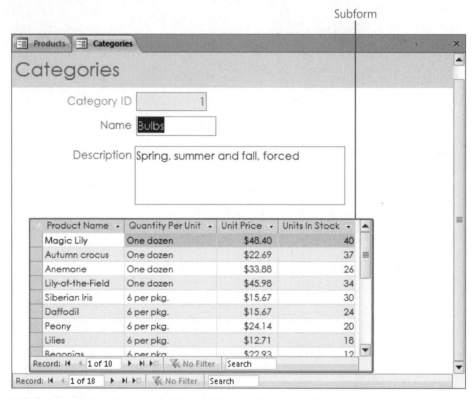

This form is the interface for the Categories and Products tables.

5. On the record navigation bar, click the **Next Record** button a few times to display the next few records.

Notice that the subform changes with each click to display the products in each category.

6. In the **Navigation** pane, double-click **Customers**.

The Customers form opens in Form view.

The purpose of this form is to edit or create customer records.

7. On the **Home** tab, in the **Views** group, click the **View** button.

For forms, clicking the View button switches between Form view and Layout view.

8. In the **Views** group, click the **View** arrow, and then click **Design View**.

Access displays the Customers form in Design view, and adds three Form Design Tools contextual tabs (Design, Arrange, and Format) to the ribbon. The contextual tabs are available only when you are working on the design of the form in either Layout view or Design view.

In this view, you can add controls to a form.

9. Switch between Form view, Layout view, and Design view, noticing the differences in the program window.

10. On the **Design** contextual tab, in the **Controls** group, display the **Controls** gallery.

   Depending on the size of your program window, you might have to click the Controls button or the More button to display this gallery.

You can use these controls to assemble custom forms for your database.

See Also For information about form controls, see "Adding Controls" in Chapter 7, "Create Custom Forms."

11. Click away from the gallery to close it.

12. Right-click the tab of the **Customers** form, and then click **Close All**.

    All the open database objects close.

 **CLEAN UP** Retain the GardenCompany01 database for use in later exercises.

Exploring Queries

You can locate specific information stored in a table, or in multiple tables, by creating a query that specifies the criteria you want to match. Queries can be quite simple. For example, you might want a list of all products in a specific category that cost less than $10. Queries can also be quite complex. For example, you might want to locate all out-of-state customers who have purchased gloves within the last three months. For the first example, you might be able to sort and filter the data in the Products table fairly quickly to come up with a list. For the second example, sorting and filtering would be very tedious. It would be far simpler to create a query that extracts all records in the Customers table with billing addresses that are not in your state and whose customer IDs map to records that appear in the Orders table within the last three months and that include item IDs mapping to records classified as gloves in the Products table.

You can create queries by using a Query wizard, and you can also create them from scratch. The most common type is the select query, which extracts matching records from one or more tables. Less common are queries that perform specific types of actions.

Processing a query, commonly referred to as *running a query* or *querying the database*, displays a datasheet containing the records that match your search criteria. You can use the query results as the basis for further analysis, create other Access objects (such as reports) from the results, or export the results in another format, such as an Excel spreadsheet.

If you create a query that you are likely to want to run more than once, you can save it. It then becomes part of the database and appears in the list when you display the Queries group in the Navigation pane. To run the query at any time, you simply double-click it in the Navigation pane. Each time you run the query, Access evaluates the records in the specified table or tables and displays the current subset of records that match the criteria defined in the query.

Don't worry if this all sounds a bit complicated at the moment. When you approach queries logically, they soon begin to make perfect sense.

See Also   For more information about queries, see Chapter 8, "Create Queries."

In this exercise, you'll explore two existing queries.

SET UP   You need the GardenCompany01 database you worked with in the preceding exercise to complete this exercise. Open the GardenCompany01 database, and then follow the steps.

1. In the **Navigation** pane, display the **Queries** group.

   The group includes all the queries that have been saved as part of this database.

2. In the **Navigation** pane, right-click the **Delete Discontinued Products** query, and then click **Object Properties**.

   Access displays the properties of the query, including a description of its purpose.

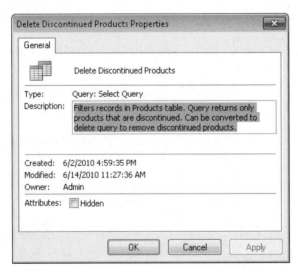

The icon at the top of the General tab indicates that this is a select query.

3. In the **Delete Discontinued Products Properties** dialog box, click **Cancel**.

4. Right-click the **Products By Category** query, and then click **Open**.

Access runs the query.

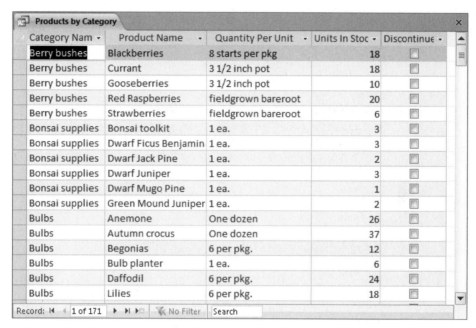

Category Nam ▾	Product Name ▾	Quantity Per Unit ▾	Units In Stoc ▾	Discontinue ▾
Berry bushes	Blackberries	8 starts per pkg	18	☐
Berry bushes	Currant	3 1/2 inch pot	18	☐
Berry bushes	Gooseberries	3 1/2 inch pot	10	☐
Berry bushes	Red Raspberries	fieldgrown bareroot	20	☐
Berry bushes	Strawberries	fieldgrown bareroot	6	☐
Bonsai supplies	Bonsai toolkit	1 ea.	3	☐
Bonsai supplies	Dwarf Ficus Benjamin	1 ea.	3	☐
Bonsai supplies	Dwarf Jack Pine	1 ea.	2	☐
Bonsai supplies	Dwarf Juniper	1 ea.	3	☐
Bonsai supplies	Dwarf Mugo Pine	1 ea.	1	☐
Bonsai supplies	Green Mound Juniper	1 ea.	2	☐
Bulbs	Anemone	One dozen	26	☐
Bulbs	Autumn crocus	One dozen	37	☐
Bulbs	Begonias	6 per pkg.	12	☐
Bulbs	Bulb planter	1 ea.	6	☐
Bulbs	Daffodil	6 per pkg.	24	☐
Bulbs	Lilies	6 per pkg.	18	☐

Record: ◄ ◄ 1 of 171 ► ►I ►▶ 🍷 No Filter Search

This datasheet displays the results of running the Products By Category query.

The record navigation bar indicates that 171 records are displayed; the Products table actually contains 189 records. To find out why 18 of the records are missing, you need to look at this query in Design view.

5. On the **View Shortcuts** toolbar, click the **Design View** button.

Access displays the query in the Query Designer, and the Query Tools Design contextual tab appears on the ribbon.

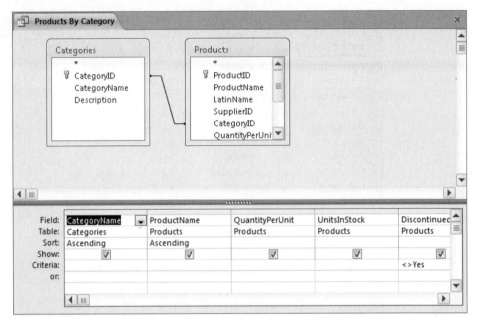

The Query Designer.

Two boxes in the top pane of the Query Designer list the fields in the tables this query is designed to work with. The line between the boxes indicates that before the query was created, a relationship was established between the two tables based on the fact that the CategoryID field is present in both of them. The relationship enables this query to draw information from both tables.

See Also For more information about relationships, see "Creating Relationships Between Tables" in Chapter 2, "Create Databases and Simple Tables."

The query is defined in the design grid in the bottom pane of the Query Designer. Each column of the grid refers to one field from one of the tables above. Notice that <> Yes (not equal to Yes) is entered in the Criteria row for the Discontinued field. This query finds all the records that don't have a value of Yes in that field (in other words, all the records that have not been discontinued).

6. As an experiment, in the **Criteria** row of the **Discontinued** field, replace **<>** with **=**. Then on the **Design** contextual tab, in the **Results** group, click the **Run** button.

Tip You can also run a query by switching to Datasheet view.

This time, the query finds all the records that have been discontinued. The 18 discontinued products account for the difference between the number of records in the Products table and the number of records displayed by the original query.

Run

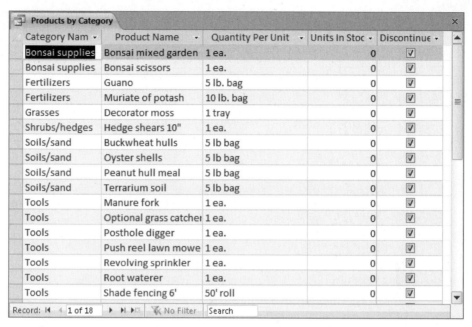

The new query results.

7. Close the **Products By Category** query. When a message asks whether you want to save your changes to the query, click **No**.

✖ **CLEAN UP** Retain the GardenCompany01 database for use in later exercises.

Exploring Reports

You can display the information recorded in your tables in nicely formatted, easily accessible reports, either on your computer screen or on paper. A report can include items of information selected from multiple tables and queries, values calculated from information in the database, and formatting elements such as headers, footers, titles, and headings.

You can look at reports in four views:

● **Report view** In this view, you can scroll through the information in the report without being distracted by the page breaks that will be inserted when it is printed.

● **Print Preview** In this view, you see your report exactly as it will look when printed.

● **Layout view** This view displays the data in the report (similar to Print Preview) but enables you to edit the layout.

● **Design view** In this view, you can manipulate the design of a report in the same way that you manipulate a form.

See Also For more information about reports, see Chapter 5, "Create Simple Reports," and Chapter 9, "Create Custom Reports."

In this exercise, you'll preview a report as it will appear when printed. You'll also examine another report in Design view.

 SET UP You need the GardenCompany01 database you worked with in the preceding exercise to complete this exercise. Open the GardenCompany01 database, and then follow the steps.

1. In the **Navigation** pane, display the **Reports** group.

   The group includes all the reports that have been created and saved as part of this database.

2. In the **Navigation** pane, right-click **Customer Labels**, and then click **Print Preview**.

   Troubleshooting If a message tells you that some data may not be displayed because of column widths and spacing, for the purposes of this exercise, simply press OK to continue.

   The Customer Labels report opens, displaying a full page of labels in a view that is much like Print Preview in other Office programs. The ribbon now displays only the Print Preview tab.

   Tip Access provides a wizard that can help you create a mailing label report. You can also create labels like these by using the Customers table as a data source for the Word 2010 mail merge tool.

3. Move the pointer over the report, where it changes to a magnifying glass. Then with the pointer over the middle label at the top of the report, click the mouse button.

   The zoom percentage changes to 100%, as indicated on the Zoom Level button in the lower-right corner of the window. You can click this button to switch back and forth between the current and previous zoom levels.

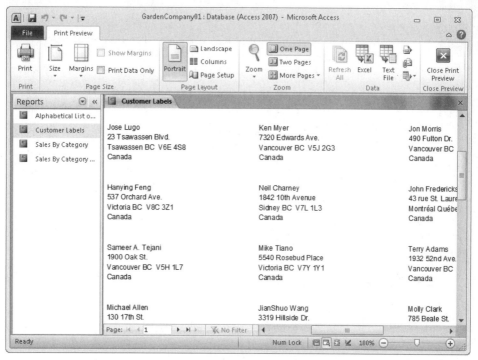

This report prints customer names and addresses in a mailing label format.

If the report is too small to read in Print Preview, you can adjust the zoom percentage by clicking the Zoom In button (the plus sign) at the right end of the Zoom slider in the lower-right corner of the window, or by dragging the Zoom slider. You can also click the Zoom arrow in the Zoom group on the Print Preview tab and then click a specific percentage.

4. In the **Navigation** pane, right-click the **Sales By Category** report, and then click **Print Preview**.

5. Use any method to zoom the page to 100 percent.

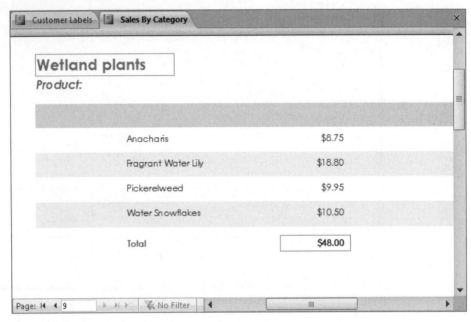

6. On the page navigation bar in the lower-left corner of the page, click the **Last Page** button.

   This report generates nine pages of information by combining data from the Categories table and the Products table.

The magnified Sales By Category report.

7. Click the **Previous Page** button a few times to view a few more pages of the report.

8. On the **View Shortcuts** toolbar, click the **Design View** button.

Access switches to Design view and displays four Report Design Tools contextual tabs (Design, Arrange, Format, and Page Setup) on the ribbon. In this view, the report looks similar to a form.

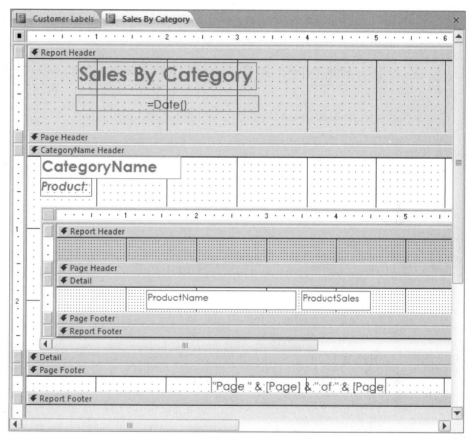

You create reports by using the same techniques you use to create forms.

 **CLEAN UP** Close the open reports. Retain the GardenCompany01 database for use in the last exercise.

Previewing and Printing Access Objects

Because Access is a Windows application, it interacts with your printer through standard Windows dialog boxes and drivers. This means that any printer that you can use from other programs can be used from Access, and any special features of that printer, such as color printing or duplex printing, are available in Access.

The commands for printing database objects are available from the Print page of the Backstage view. From this page, you can do the following:

● Print the active object with the default settings.

● Display the Print dialog box, where you can select the printer you want to use, as well as adjust various other settings appropriate to the active object and the current view.

● Display the active object in Print Preview.

In this exercise, you'll explore the printing options for a table and a form.

 SET UP You need the GardenCompany01 database you worked with in the preceding exercise to complete this exercise. Open the GardenCompany01 database, and then follow the steps.

1. In the **Navigation** pane, display the **All Access Objects** category.

2. In the **Tables** group, double-click the **Employees** table to open it in Datasheet view.

   This table contains information about nine employees. Some of the columns are too narrow to display all their data, and even with the program window maximized, depending on your screen resolution, some of the fields might not fit on the screen.

3. Adjust the widths of all the columns so that all the values in the fields are visible.

   Access will not print data that is not visible.

4. Click the File tab to display the Backstage view.

5. In the left pane, click **Print**.

    The Print page displays the available print options.

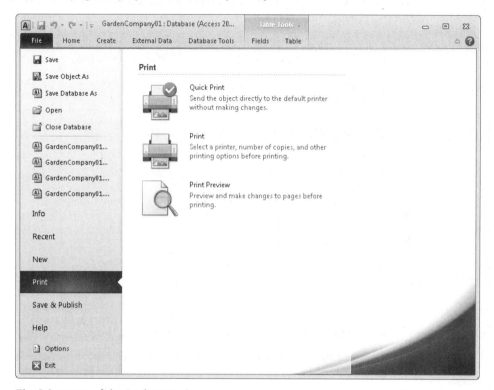

The Print page of the Backstage view.

6. In the right pane, click **Print Preview**.

    The first page of the Employees table is displayed in Print Preview.

    Tip This is the only way to preview a table, a query results datasheet, or a form. There is no Print Preview command available when you right-click one of these objects, and there is no Print Preview button on the View Shortcuts toolbar or in the View button list, as there is for reports.

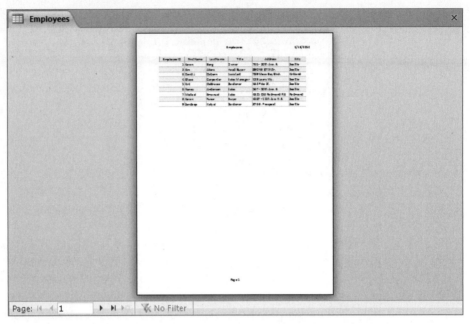

The Employees table in the default Portrait orientation.

7. On the navigation bar at the bottom of the window, click the **Next Page** button. Then click the **First Page** button to move back to page 1.

If you print this datasheet with the current settings, it will print as two short, vertically oriented pages.

8. On the **Print Preview** tab, in the **Page Layout** group, click the **Landscape** button. Then click the **Next Page** button.

In Landscape orientation, the datasheet still fits on two pages, with only one field on the second page.

9. In the **Page Size** group, click the **Margins** button, and then click **Narrow**.

On the page navigation bar, the buttons are now gray, indicating that the Employee list fits on one page.

Tip You can set custom margins by clicking the Page Setup button in the Page Layout group and then adjusting the Top, Bottom, Left, and Right settings on the Print Options page of the Page Setup dialog box.

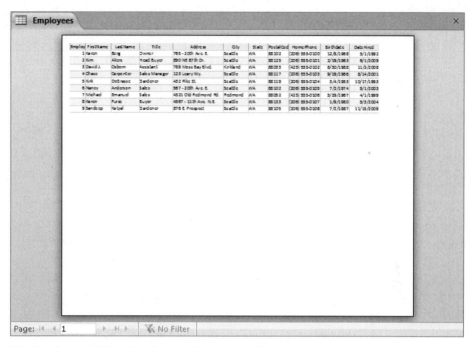

The Employees table in Landscape orientation with narrow margins.

Print

10. In the **Print** group, click the **Print** button.

    The Print dialog box opens.

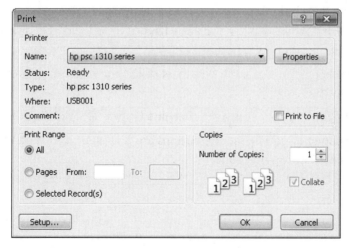

In this dialog box, you can select the printer and set print options such as the pages or records to print, and the number of copies.

Close Print
Preview

11. Click **Cancel** to close the **Print** dialog box, and then in the **Close Preview** group, click the **Close Print Preview** button.

12. In the **Navigation** pane, under **Reports**, double-click **Alphabetical List of Products**.

The report opens in Report view.

13. Display the Backstage view, click **Print**, and then click **Print Preview**.

Access displays a preview of the information that will be printed.

 Two Pages   14. On the **Print Preview** tab, in the **Zoom** group, click the **Two Pages** button.

Access displays the first two pages in the report side by side.

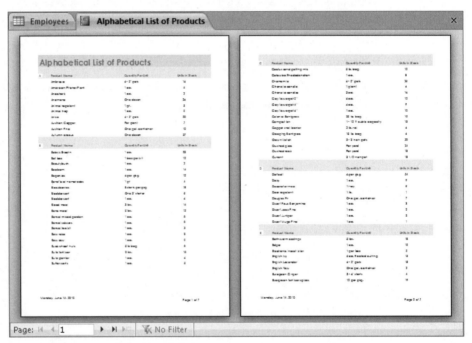

You can preview more than one page at a time.

15. On the **View Shortcuts** toolbar, click the **Report View** button to return to that view.

CLEAN UP Save your changes to the Employees table, and close both the table and the report. Then close the GardenCompany01 database.

Key Points

- The basic Access interface objects work much the same as in other Office or Windows programs.

- A database is the computer equivalent of an organized list of information.

- Tables are the core database objects. Access data is organized in tables made up of columns and rows, called *fields* and *records*.

- In a relational database, tables can be related based on common fields, enabling the retrieval of information from more than one table at the same time.

- The purpose of the other database objects—forms, reports, queries, macros, and modules—is to interact with one or more tables.

- Every Access object has two or more views. For example, you view data in a table in Datasheet view and define how the data is structured in Design view.

- If you want to print a database object, be sure the information you need is visible on the screen before you print.

Chapter at a Glance

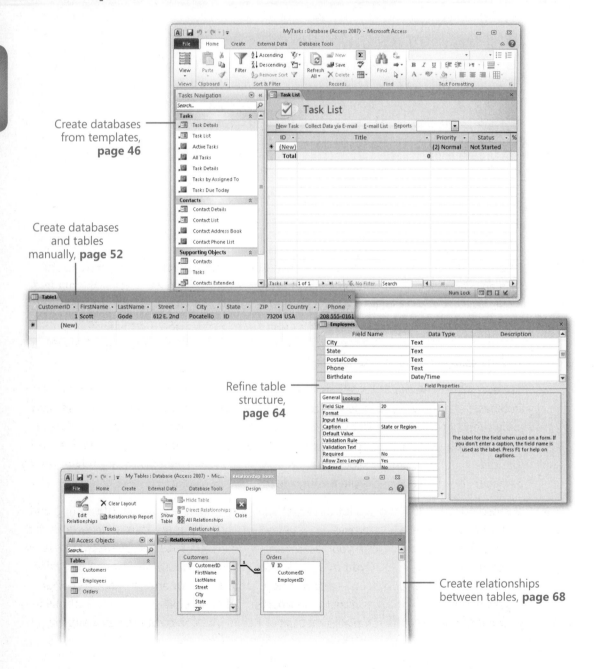

Create databases from templates, **page 46**

Create databases and tables manually, **page 52**

Refine table structure, **page 64**

Create relationships between tables, **page 68**

2 Create Databases and Simple Tables

Creating the container for a database is easy. But an empty database is no more useful than an empty document or worksheet. It is only when you fill a database with data in tables (known as populating a database) that it starts to serve a purpose. As you add forms, queries, and reports, it becomes a useful tool. If you customize it by adding a startup page and organizing the various objects into categories and groups, it moves into the realm of being a database application.

Not every database has to be refined to the point that it can be classified as an application. Databases that only you or a few experienced database users will work with can remain fairly simple. But if you expect someone without database knowledge to enter data or generate their own reports, spending a little extra time in the beginning to create a solid foundation will save a lot of work later. Otherwise, you'll find yourself continually repairing damaged files or walking people through seemingly easy tasks.

Microsoft Access 2010 takes a lot of the difficult and mundane work out of creating and customizing a database by providing database applications in the form of templates that you modify and populate with your own information. Access 2010 also provides templates for common elements that you might want to plug into a database. These application parts consist of sets of objects—a table and related forms, queries, or reports—that together provide a complete, functioning part of a database. All you have to do is fill in your data. If none of the templates meet your needs, you can create tables manually.

In this chapter, you'll create a database from a template and create a table manually. Then you'll adjust the display of a data table to fit your needs. By the end of this chapter, you'll have a database containing a few tables and you'll understand a bit about how the tables in the databases you will use for the exercises in the remaining chapters of the book were created.

> **Practice Files** You don't need any practice files to complete the exercises in this chapter. For more information about practice file requirements, see "Using the Practice Files" at the beginning of this book.

Creating Databases from Templates

A few years ago (the distant past, in computer time), creating a database structure involved first analyzing your needs and then laying out the database design on paper. You would decide what information you needed to track and how to store it in the database. Creating the database structure could be a lot of work, and after you created it and entered data, making changes could be difficult. Templates have changed this process, and committing yourself to a particular database structure is no longer the big decision it once was.

A template is a pattern that you use to create a specific type of database. Access 2010 comes with templates for several databases typically used in business and education, and when you are connected to the Internet, many more are available from the Microsoft Office Online Web site at office.microsoft.com. By using pre-packaged templates, you can create a database application in far less time than it used to take to sketch the design on paper, because someone has already done the design work for you.

Using an Access template might not produce exactly the database application you want, but it can quickly create something that you can customize to fit your needs. However, you can customize a database only if you know how to manipulate its basic building blocks: tables, forms, queries, and reports. Due to the complexity of these templates, you probably shouldn't try to modify them until you're comfortable working with database objects in Design view and Layout view. By the time you finish this book, you will know enough to be able to confidently work with the sophisticated pre-packaged application templates that come with Access.

In this exercise, you'll create a database application based on the Tasks template. This template is typical of those provided with Microsoft Access 2010, in that it looks nice and demonstrates a lot of the neat things you can do in a database.

SET UP You don't need any practice files to complete this exercise. Close any open databases, and then with the New page of the Backstage view displayed, follow the steps.

1. In the **Available Templates** area, click **Sample Templates**.

   Access displays a list of the templates that shipped with the program and are installed on your computer.

2. Click the **Tasks** template icon.

   In the right pane, you can assign a name to the database and browse to the location where you want to store the database.

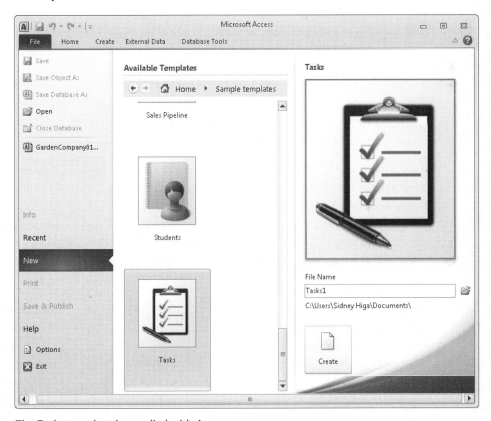

The Tasks template is supplied with Access.

3. In the **File Name** box, type **MyTasks**.

   Tip Naming conventions for Access database files follow those for Windows files. File names cannot contain the following characters: \ / : * ? " < > |. By default, file name extensions are hidden, and you shouldn't type the extension in the File Name box. (The extension for an Access 2010 database file is .accdb. For information about this file format, which was introduced with Access 2007, search for *accdb* in Access Help.)

4. Click the adjacent **Browse** button, and then in the **File New Database** dialog box, navigate to your **Chapter02** practice file folder.

You use the same navigational techniques in this dialog box that you would use in any Open or Save dialog box.

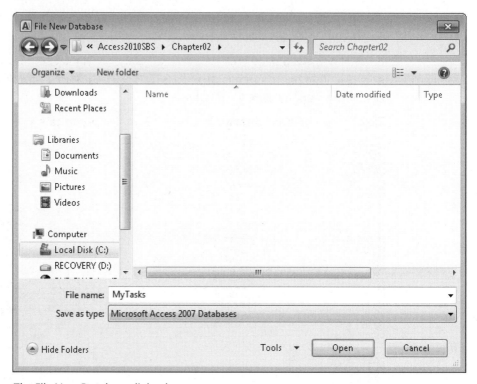

The File New Database dialog box.

5. With **Microsoft Access 2007 Databases** selected in the **Save as type** box, click **OK**.

The path to the specified folder is displayed below the File Name box.

Tip By default, Access creates new databases in your Documents folder. You can change the location when you create each database, as you did here, or you can change the default save folder. To specify a different default folder, click the File tab to display the Backstage view, click Options, and then on the General page of the Access Options dialog box, under Creating Databases, click the Browse button to the right of Default Database Folder. In the Default Database Path dialog box, browse to the folder you want to be the default, and then click OK in each of the open dialog boxes.

6. Click the **Create** button.

Access briefly displays a progress bar, and then the new database opens, with the Task List form displayed in Layout view.

> **Tip** Below the form name is a toolbar with commands created by embedded macros. These commands are an example of what makes this a database application rather than a simple database. The topic of macros is beyond the scope of this book. For information, search for *macros* in Access Help.

7. If the **Navigation** pane is closed, click the **Shutter Bar Open** button at the right end of its title bar to open it. Then if any of the groups are collapsed, click their chevrons to open them.

The Navigation pane displays a custom Tasks Navigation category.

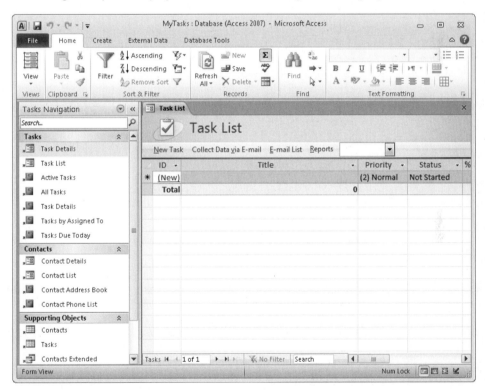

The custom category has custom Tasks, Contacts, and Supporting Objects groups.

> **Troubleshooting** The appearance of buttons and groups on the ribbon changes depending on the width of the program window. For information about changing the appearance of the ribbon to match our screen images, see "Modifying the Display of the Ribbon" at the beginning of this book.

8. In the **Navigation** pane, click the **Tasks Navigation** title bar, and then in the category and group list, click **Object Type** to list all the objects in this database.

9. In the **Tables** group, double-click **Contacts**.

The empty Contacts table is displayed. You could now start entering data in this table.

10. Right-click the **Contacts** tab, and click **Close All**.

11. On the **Create** tab of the ribbon, in the **Templates** group, click the **Application Parts** button.

The Application Parts gallery appears.

The Application Parts gallery.

You can add various types of forms and several sets of related tables and other database objects to this or any other database. These ready-made objects give you a jump start on creating a fully functional database application.

12. Click away from the gallery to close it.

13. Continue exploring the objects that are part of the **MyTasks** database on your own.

 **CLEAN UP** Close the MyTasks database.

Web Databases

Several of the templates in the Sample Templates gallery and many of the templates available from the Microsoft Office Online Web site are designated as Web databases. A Web database is one that is compatible with the new Web publishing capabilities of Access 2010.

If Access Services are installed on your organization's Microsoft SharePoint server, you can now publish a database to Access Services. Publishing converts tables to SharePoint lists stored on the server and makes it possible to work with the database either in Access or in a Web browser.

You can create a Web database based on a Web template or build a new one from scratch by choosing Blank Web Database on the New page of the Backstage view. You can also publish a regular database as a Web database, although the tables in the database must conform to Web database requirements for publication to be successful. Because of these requirements, if you work for an organization where future deployment of Access Services is a possibility, you might want to consider creating a Web database to ensure that your database can be published to Access Services in the future.

In a Web database, you can create two kinds of objects:

- **Web objects** These can be created and viewed in either a Web browser or Access.
- **Non-Web objects** These can be created and viewed only in Access.

When you are working with a Web database from a browser, you are working with the database on the server. When you are working with it from Access, you are working with a local copy of the database that is synchronized with the database on the server. For both types of objects, you can make design changes only in Access and only when connected to the server.

These days, more and more companies have employees and clients in different geographic locations, and more and more people are working away from company offices. Web databases make it possible for people to access company databases from wherever they are and from any computer, whether or not it has Access installed.

Creating Databases and Tables Manually

Suppose you need to store different types of information for different types of people. For example, you might want to maintain information about employees, customers, and suppliers. In addition to the standard information—such as names, addresses, and phone numbers—you might want to track these other kinds of information:

- Employee identification numbers, hire dates, marital status, deductions, and pay rates
- Customer orders and account status
- Supplier contacts, current order status, and discounts

You could start with a template, add fields for all the different items of information to a single Contacts table, and then fill in only the relevant fields for each type of contact. However, cramming all this information into one table would soon get pretty messy. It's better to create a new database based on the Blank Database template and then manually create separate tables for each type of contact: employee, customer, and supplier.

When you create a new blank database or insert a new table into an existing database, the table is displayed on a tabbed page in Datasheet view with one empty row that is ready to receive data. Because the active object is a table, Access adds the Table Tools contextual tabs to the ribbon so that you can work with the table.

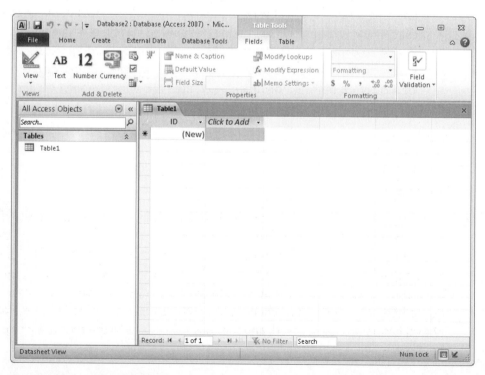

A new table in a new database.

If you close the table at this point, it will disappear, because it contains no data and it has no structure. The simplest way to make the table part of the database is to create at least one record by entering data, which simultaneously defines the table's structure.

Tip You can also define the structure of the table without entering data. For information about table structure, see "Refining Table Structure" later in this chapter. For information about adding new blank fields to a table, see "Restricting the Type of Data" in Chapter 6, "Maintain Data Integrity."

Obviously, to create a record, you need to know how to enter information in Datasheet view.

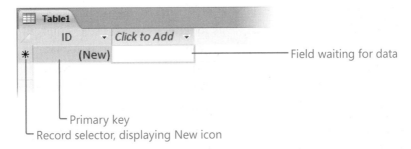

The first record in a new table, before data is entered.

Every table has an empty row that is ready to receive a new record, as indicated by the New icon (the asterisk) in the record selector at the left end of the row. By default, the first field in each new table is an ID field designed to contain an entry that will uniquely identify the record. Also by default, this field is designated as the table's *primary key*. No two records in this table can have the same value in this primary key field. Behind the scenes, the data type of this field is set to AutoNumber, so Access will enter a sequential number in this field for you.

Tip As you'll see in a later exercise, the primary key field does not have to be the default AutoNumber type. If you need to you create your own primary key field, then anything meaningful and unique will work.

See Also For information about data types, see "Refining Table Structure" later in this chapter.

The first field you need to be concerned about is the active field labeled *Click To Add*. You enter the first item of information for the new record in the first cell in this field, and then press the Tab or Enter key to move to the first cell in the field to the right. Access then assigns the value 1 to the ID field, assigns the name Field1 to the second field, and moves the Click To Add label to the third field. The icon in the record selector at the left end of the record changes to two dots and a pencil to indicate that this record has not yet been saved, and the New icon moves to the record selector of the next row.

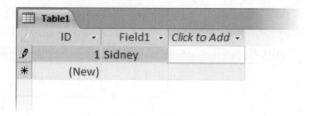

The first record in a new table, after data has been entered in the first field.

When creating a new table in Datasheet view, you need to save the first record after entering the first item of data. If you don't, Access increments the ID value for each field you add to that record. For example, if you add seven fields, Access assigns the value 7 to the ID field of the first record. To avoid this problem, you simply click the icon in the record selector after you enter your first value in the first record. This saves the record with the value 1 assigned to the ID field, and subsequent records will be numbered sequentially.

Having entered the first item of data and saved the record, you continue entering items of information in consecutive cells and pressing Tab or Enter. When you finish entering the last item for the first record, you click anywhere in the row below to tell Access that the record is complete.

After you complete the first record of a new table, you will probably want to change the default field names to something more meaningful. To rename a field, you simply double-click its field name and then type the name you want.

At any time while you are entering data in a new table, you can save the table by clicking the Save button on the Quick Access Toolbar and naming the table. If you try to close the table without explicitly saving it, Access prompts you to save the table. If you click No, Access discards the table and any data you have entered.

After you have saved the table for the first time, Access automatically saves each record when you move away from it. You don't have to worry about losing your changes, but you do have to remember that most data entries can be undone only by editing the record.

Databases almost always contain more than one table. You can create additional empty tables by clicking the Table button in the Tables group on the Create tab of the ribbon. If you need to create a table that is similar in structure to an existing one, you can copy and paste the existing table to create a new one. When you paste the table, Access gives you the option of naming the table and of specifying whether you want the new table to have the existing table's structure or both its structure and its data.

For some kinds of tables, Access provides Quick Start fields that you can use to add common sets of fields or kinds of fields to a table. The Quick Start options take the work out of defining these fields and can be very useful when you know exactly what type of field you need.

In this exercise, you'll create a blank database, enter information into the first record of its default table, assign field names, add another record, and save and close the table. Then you'll copy that table to create a second one. Finally, you'll create a new table and experiment with Quick Start fields.

 SET UP You don't need any practice files to complete this exercise. Close any open databases, and then with the New page of the Backstage view displayed, follow the steps.

1. In the center pane of the **New** page, in the **Available Templates** area, click **Blank Database**.

 2. In the right pane, click the **File Name** box, and type **MyTables**. Then click the **Browse** button, navigate to your **Chapter02** practice file folder, and click **OK**.

    Tip You can't create a blank database without saving it. If you don't provide a file name and location, Access saves the file with the name *Database* followed by a sequential number in the default location (your Documents folder, unless you have changed it).

3. In the right pane, click the **Create** button.

    Access creates the blank database in the specified location, opens the database, and displays a new blank table named *Table1*.

4. With the empty field below **Click to Add** selected, type **Scott**, and then press Tab to move to the next field.

    The icon in the record selector changes to indicate that this record has not yet been saved. The value 1 appears in the ID field, the name of the second column changes to Field1, and the Click To Add label moves to the third column.

5. Click the icon in the record selector to save the record before you move on.

    Tip Clicking the record selector is necessary only after you enter the first value in a new table. This action sets the ID field value to 1.

6. Click the cell under **Click to Add**, and type the following information into the next seven cells, pressing Tab after each entry:

> Gode
>
> 612 E. 2nd
>
> Pocatello
>
> ID
>
> 73204
>
> USA
>
> 208 555-0161

As the cursor moves to the next cell, the name of the field in which you just entered data changes to *Field* followed by a sequential number.

The first complete record.

Tip Don't be concerned if your screen does not look exactly like ours. In this graphic, we've scrolled the page and adjusted the widths of the columns so that you can see all the fields. For information about adjusting columns, see "Manipulating Table Columns and Rows" later in this chapter.

7. Double-click the **ID** field name (not the ID value in Field5), and then type **CustomerID** to rename it.

Tip Field names can include spaces, but the spaces can affect how queries have to be constructed, so it is best not to include them. For readability, capitalize each word and then remove the spaces, or use underscores instead of spaces.

8. Repeat step 7 for the other fields, changing the field names to the following:

Field1	FirstName	**Field4**	City	**Field7**	Country
Field2	LastName	**Field5**	State	**Field8**	Phone
Field3	Street	**Field6**	ZIP		

The table now has intuitive field names.

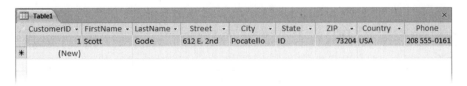

The renamed fields.

Tip Again, don't worry if your screen doesn't look exactly like this graphic, because we've made adjustments so that you can see all the fields.

9. Add another record containing the following field values to the table, pressing Tab to move from field to field:

FirstName	John	**City**	Montreal	**Country**	Canada
LastName	Frederickson	**State**	Quebec	**Phone**	514 555-0167
Street	43 rue St. Laurent	**ZIP**	(press Tab to skip this field)		

10. At the right end of the tab bar, click the **Close** button.

11. When Access asks whether you want to save the design of the table, click **Yes**.

    Important Clicking No will delete the new table and its data from the database.

    Access displays the Save As dialog box.

You must save the table before closing it.

12. In the **Table Name** box, type **Customers**, and then click **OK**.

    Access closes the table, which is now listed in the Tables group on the Navigation bar.

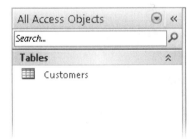

The database now contains one table.

Tip You can rename a table by right-clicking it in the Navigation pane and then clicking Rename. You can delete a table by right-clicking it, clicking Delete, and then confirming the deletion in the message box that appears. (You can also delete a table by selecting it in the Navigation bar and then clicking the Delete button in the Records group on the Home tab or pressing the Delete key.)

13. In the **Navigation** pane, click the **Customers** table to select it.

14. On the **Home** tab, in the **Clipboard** group, click the **Copy** button. Then click the **Paste** button.

Keyboard Shortcut Press Ctrl+C to copy data. Press Ctrl+V to paste data.

See Also For more information about keyboard shortcuts, see "Keyboard Shortcuts" at the end of this book.

The Paste Table As dialog box opens.

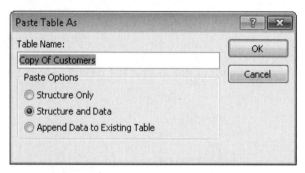

If you need to create a table that is similar to an existing table, it is sometimes easier to customize a copy than to create it from scratch.

15. In the **Table Name** box, type **Employees**. In the **Paste Options** area, click **Structure Only** to capture the fields from the **Customers** table but none of the customer information. Then click **OK**.

The new Employees table appears in the Navigation pane.

Tip You can also use the Copy and Paste commands to append the information in the selected table to another existing table. In that case, in the Paste Table As dialog box, type the name of the destination table in the Table Name box, click Append Data To Existing Table, and then click OK.

16. Double-click **Employees** to open it in Datasheet view so that you can view its fields. Then close the table again.

17. On the **Create** tab, in the **Tables** group, click the **Table** button.

    Access creates a new table containing an ID field and a Click To Add field placeholder.

18. With the **Click to Add** field active, on the **Fields** contextual tab, in the **Add & Delete** group, click the **More Fields** button.

    The More Fields gallery appears.

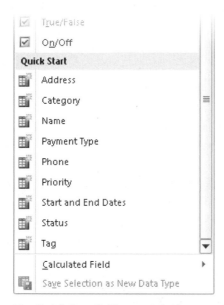

The Quick Start fields are at the bottom of the More Fields gallery.

19. If necessary scroll to the bottom of the gallery, and then under **Quick Start**, click **Name**.

    Access inserts ready-made LastName and FirstName fields.

20. Repeat steps 18 and 19 to add the **Address** fields from the **Quick Start** list.

    Access inserts ready-made Address, City, State Province, ZIP Postal, and Country Region fields.

21. Close the table, saving it with the name **Shippers** when prompted.

CLEAN UP Retain the MyTables database for use in later exercises.

Database Design

In a well-designed database, each item of data is stored only once. If you're capturing the same information in multiple places, that is a sure sign that you need to analyze the data and figure out a way to put the duplicated information in a separate table.

For example, an Orders table should not include information about the customer placing each order, for two significant reasons. First, if the same customer orders more than once, all his or her information has to be repeated for each order, which inflates the size of the table and the database. Second, if the customer moves, his or her address will need to be updated in the record for every order placed.

The way to avoid this type of problem is to put customer information in a Customers table and assign each customer a unique identifier, such as a sequential number or unique string of letters, in the primary key field. Then in the Orders table, you can identify the customer by the unique ID. If you need to know the name and address of the customer who placed a particular order, you can have Access use the unique ID to look up that information in the Customers table.

The process of ensuring that a set of information is stored in only one place is called *normalization*. This process tests a database for compliance with a set of normalization rules that ask questions such as "If I know the information in the primary key field of a record, can I retrieve information from one and only one record?" For example, knowing that a customer's ID is 1002 means you can pull the customer's name and address from the Customers table, whereas knowing that a customer's last name is Jones does not mean that you can pull the customer's name and address from the table, because more than one customer might have the last name Jones.

The topic of normalization is beyond the scope of this book. If you need to design a database that will contain several tables, you should search for *Database design basics* in Access Help to learn more about the normalization process.

Manipulating Table Columns and Rows

In Chapter 1, "Explore an Access 2010 Database," we showed you how to quickly adjust the width of table columns to efficiently display their data. In addition to adjusting column width, sometimes you might want to rearrange a table's fields to get a better view of the data. For example, if you want to look up a phone number but the names and phone numbers are several fields apart, you will have to scroll the page to get the information you need. You might want to rearrange or hide a few fields to be able to simultaneously see the ones you are interested in.

You can manipulate the columns and rows of an Access table without affecting the under-lying data in any way. You can size rows and size, hide, move, and freeze columns. You can save your table formatting so that the table will look the same the next time you open it, or you can discard your changes without saving them.

In this exercise, you'll open a table and manipulate its columns and rows.

 SET UP You need the MyTables database you worked with in the preceding exercise to complete this exercise. Open the MyTables database, and then follow the steps.

1. In the **Navigation** pane, double-click the **Customers** table to open it in Datasheet view.

2. In the field name row, point to the right border of the **Street** field name, and when the pointer changes to a double-headed arrow, drag to the right until you can see all of the street addresses.

3. Double-click the right border of any column that seems too wide or too narrow to adjust the column to fit its contents.

   This technique is particularly useful in a large table where you can't easily determine the length of a field's longest entry.

4. Point to the border between any two record selectors, and drag downward.

   When you release the mouse button, Access increases the height of all rows in the table.

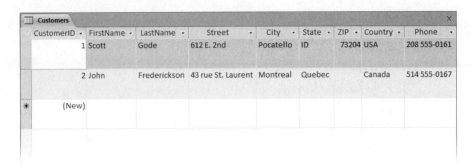

You cannot adjust the height of a single row.

 5. On the **Home** tab, in the **Records** group, click the **More** button, and then click **Row Height**.

The Row Height dialog box opens.

You can set the rows to the precise height you want.

6. In the **Row Height** dialog box, select the **Standard Height** check box, and then click **OK**.

Access resets the height of the rows to the default setting.

7. Click anywhere in the **FirstName** field. Then in the **Records** group, click the **More** button, and click **Hide Fields**.

The FirstName field disappears, and the fields to its right shift to the left.

Tip If you select several fields before clicking Hide Fields, they all disappear. You can select adjacent fields by clicking the field name of the first one, holding down the Shift key, and then clicking the field name of the last one. The two fields and any fields in between are selected.

8. To restore the hidden field, in the **Records** group, click the **More** button, and then click **Unhide Fields**.

The Unhide Columns dialog box opens.

You can select and clear check boxes to control which fields are visible.

> **Tip** If you want to hide several columns that are not adjacent, you can display the Unhide Columns dialog box and clear their checkboxes.

9. In the **Unhide Columns** dialog box, select the **FirstName** check box, and then click **Close**.

    Access redisplays the FirstName field.

10. If you can see all of the fields in the table, for the purposes of this exercise, adjust the size of the program window until some of the fields are no longer visible.

11. Point to the **CustomerID** field name, hold down the mouse button, and drag through the **FirstName** and **LastName** field names. With the three columns selected, click the **More** button in the **Records** group, and then click **Freeze Fields**.

12. Scroll the page to the right until the **Phone** field is adjacent to the **LastName** field.

    The first three columns remain in view as you scroll.

13. In the **Records** group, click **More,** and then click **Unfreeze All Fields** to restore the fields to their normal condition.

    > **Tip** The commands to hide, unhide, freeze, and unfreeze columns are also available from the shortcut menu that appears when you right-click a field name.

14. Click the **Phone** field name to select that field. Then drag the field to the left, releasing the mouse button when the thick black line appears to the right of the **LastName** field.

15. Close the **Customers** table, clicking **Yes** to save the changes you have made to the column widths and order. If you see a warning that this action will clear the Clipboard, click **Yes**.

✖ CLEAN UP Retain the MyTables database for use in later exercises.

Refining Table Structure

Although you can create the structure of a database in Datasheet view, some structural refinements can be carried out only in Design view. When you are familiar with tables, you might even want to create your tables from scratch in Design view, where you have more control over the fields. You can open a new table in Design view by clicking the Table Design button in the Tables group on the Create tab.

When you open an existing table in Design view, the tabbed page shows the underlying structure of the table.

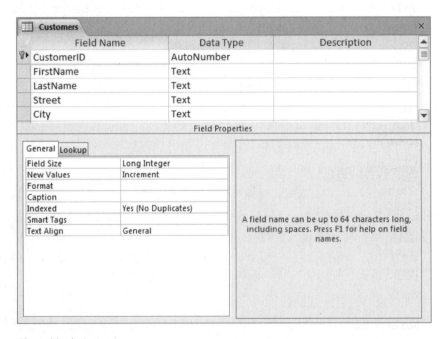

The table design page.

- **Selector** You can click the shaded box at the left end of a row to select the entire field. You can then insert a row above the selected one, delete the row (thereby deleting the field), or drag the row up or down to reposition its field in the table.

  The selector also identifies the primary key field of the table by displaying the Primary Key icon (a key with a right-pointing arrow).

  Tip If you don't want a table to have a primary key (for example, if none of the fields will contain a unique value for every record), select the field designated as the primary key, and on the Design contextual tab, in the Tools group, click the Primary Key button to toggle it off. If you want to designate a different field as the primary key, select the new field, and click the Primary Key button to toggle it on. (You don't have to remove the primary key from the current field first; it will happen automatically.)

- **Field Name column** This column contains the names you specified when you created the table. You can edit the names by using regular text-editing techniques. You can add a new field by typing its name in the first empty cell in this column.

- **Data Type column** This column specifies the type of data that the field can contain. By default, the ID field in a new table is assigned the AutoNumber data type, and all other fields are assigned the Text data type. With the exception of fields with the OLE Object and Attachment data types, you can change the type of any field by clicking its Data Type entry, clicking the arrow that appears, and clicking a new data type in the list.

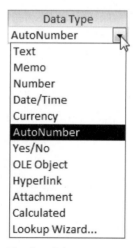

The list of data types.

  See also For more information about data types, see "Restricting the Type of Data" in Chapter 6, "Maintain Data Integrity."

- **Description column** This column contains an optional description of the field.

The Field Properties area at the bottom of the design page displays the properties of the field selected in the top part. Different properties are associated with different data types. They can determine such things as the number of characters allowed in a field, the value inserted if the user doesn't type an entry, and whether an entry is required. Properties can also assess whether an entry is valid and can force the user to select from a list of values rather than typing them (with the risk of errors).

All fields, no matter what their data type, can be assigned a Caption property that will appear in the place of the field name in tables or in other database objects. For example, you might want to use captions to display the names of fields with spaces, such as First Name for the FirstName field.

See Also For information about using properties to control the accuracy of data entry, see Chapter 6, "Maintain Data Integrity." For a comprehensive list of data types and properties, search on *data types* in Access Help.

In this exercise, you'll open a table in Design view, add and delete fields, change a data type, set field sizes, and add a caption.

 SET UP You need the MyTables database you worked with in the preceding exercise to complete this exercise. Open the MyTables database, and then follow the steps.

1. In the **Navigation** pane, right-click the **Employees** table, and then click **Design View**.

   Access opens the table with its structure displayed. Because you created this table by copying the Customers table, you need to make some structural changes.

2. With **CustomerID** highlighted in the **Field Name** column, type **EmployeeID**, and then press the Tab key twice.

3. In the **Description** column, type **Unique identifying number**.

4. Click the **Country** field's selector, and then on the **Design** contextual tab, in the **Tools** group, click the **Delete Rows** button.

5. In the empty row below the **Phone** field, click the **Field Name** cell, and type **Birthdate**. Then click the **Data Type** cell.

   Access assigns the default Text data type to the new field.

6. Click the arrow at the right end of the **Data Type** cell, and in the list, click **Date/Time**.

7. Repeat steps 5 and 6 to add another **Date/Time** field named **DateHired**.

8. Select the **ZIP** field name, change it to **PostalCode**, and then change its data type to **Text**.

Tip If you use only five-digit ZIP codes, the Number data type is fine. But setting it to Text allows you to enter ZIP+4 codes or the letter-number postal codes used in Canada and other countries.

The properties in the Field Properties area at the bottom of the design page change to those that are appropriate for this type of field.

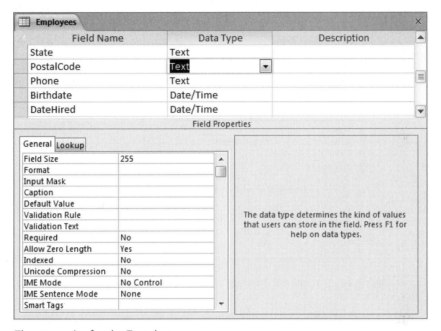

The properties for the Text data type.

9. In the box to the right of **Field Size**, double-click **255**, and type **10**.

You are specifying that this field can contain no more than 10 characters.

10. Change the **Field Size** property of the following fields as shown:

FirstName	50	**City**	50	**Phone**	30
LastName	50	**State**	20		

Tip Sometimes changing the field properties of a table that already contains data can produce unanticipated results. If you make a change to a field property that might cause data to be lost (for example, if you make the Field Size property smaller than one of the field's existing values), Access warns you of this problem when you attempt to save the table. For more information, see Chapter 6, "Maintain Data Integrity."

11. Click the **State** field. Then in the **Field Properties** area, click the **Caption** box, and type **State or Region**.

The Field Name remains State, but in Datasheet view, the column heading will be *State or Region*.

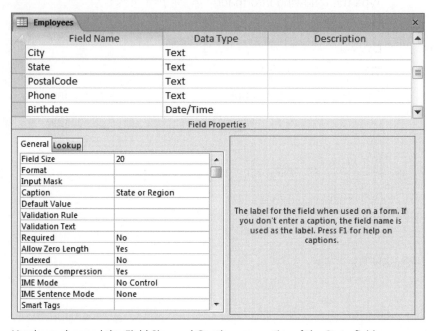

You have changed the Field Size and Caption properties of the State field.

12. On the **Design** tab, in the **Views** group, click the **View** button to switch to Datasheet view.

Access tells you that you must save the table before leaving Design view.

13. In the message box, click **Yes** to save the table.

Access saves the table and displays it in Datasheet view.

14. With the table displayed in Datasheet view, click the **LastName** field name. Then on the **Fields** contextual tab, in the **Add & Delete** group, click the **Text** button.

A new field called *Field1* that has the Text data type is inserted to the right of the LastName field.

Tip You can also create a new field with a specific data type by clicking the Click To Add label to the right of the last field in the field name row. Then in the list that appears, you can click the data type you want.

15. With **Field1** selected, type **Title**, and press Enter.

16. Click the **Title** field name. Then in the **Properties** group, in the **Field Size** box, click **255** to select it, type **50**, and press Enter.

17. Type the following information in the first record:

    FirstName   Karen

    LastName   Berg

    Title   Owner

    The Employees table is now ready for you to start entering data.

The first record of the Employees table.

CLEAN UP Close the Employees table. Retain the MyTables database for use in the last exercise.

Creating Relationships Between Tables

In Access, a relationship is an association between common fields in two tables. You can use this association to link the primary key field in one table to a field that contains the same information in another table. The field in the other table is called the *foreign key*. For example, if customer accounts are assigned to specific sales employees, you can establish a relationship by linking the primary key EmployeeID field in the Employees table with the foreign key EmployeeID field in the Customers table. Each customer account is assigned to only one employee, but each employee can manage many customer accounts, so this type of relationship—the most common—is known as a *one-to-many relationship*.

Similarly, if every order is associated with a customer, you can establish a relationship by linking the primary key CustomerID field in the Customers table and foreign key CustomerID field in the Orders table. Each order is placed by only one customer, but each customer can place many orders. So again, this is a one-to-many relationship.

Less common relationships include:

- **One-to-one** In this type of relationship, each record in one table can have one and only one related record in the other table. This type of relationship isn't commonly used because it is easier to put all the fields in one table. However, you might use two related tables instead of one to break up a table with many fields, or to track information that applies to only some of the records in the first table.

- **Many-to-many** This type of relationship is really two one-to-many relationships tied together through a third table. You might see this relationship in a database that contains Products, Orders, and Order Details tables. The Products table has one record for each product, and each product has a unique ProductID. The Orders table has one record for each order placed, and each record in it has a unique OrderID. However, the Orders table doesn't specify which products were included in each order; that information is in the Order Details table—the table in the middle that ties the other two tables together. Products and Orders each have a one-to-many relationship with Order Details. Products and Orders therefore have a many-to-many relationship with each other. In plain language, this means that every product can appear in many orders, and every order can include many products.

The most common way of creating a relationship between two tables is to add the tables to the Relationships page displayed when you click the Relationships button in the Relationships group on the Database Tools tab. You then drag a field in one table to the common field in the other table and complete the relationship definition in the Edit Relationships dialog box. In this dialog box, you are given the opportunity to impose a restriction called *referential integrity* on the data, which means that an entry will not be allowed in one table unless it already exists in the other table.

After you have created a relationship, you can delete it by deleting the line connecting the tables on the Relationships page. You can clear all the boxes from the page by clicking the Clear Layout button in the Tools group on the Relationship Tools Design contextual tab.

Tip The coverage of relationships in this topic is deliberately simple. However, relationships are what make relational databases tick, and Access provides a number of fairly complex mechanisms to ensure the integrity of the data on either end of the relationship. Some of these mechanisms are covered in Chapter 6, "Maintain Data Integrity." For a good overview, search for *Guide to table relationships* in Access Help.

In this exercise, you'll create relationships between one table and two other tables. Then you'll test the referential integrity of one of the relationships.

SET UP You need the MyTables database you worked with in the preceding exercise to complete this exercise. Open the MyTables database, and then follow the steps.

1. On the **Create** tab, in the **Tables** group, click the **Table** button to create a new table.

   Before we add fields to this table, let's save it.

2. On the Quick Access Toolbar, click the **Save** button, name the table Orders, and click **OK**.

3. To the right of **Click to Add**, click the arrow, and in the data type list, click **Number**. Repeat this step to create a second field with the **Number** data type.

4. Double-click **Field1**, and type CustomerID. Then double-click **Field2**, and type EmployeeID.

   Each order in the Orders table will be placed by one customer and will be handled by one employee. Let's create relationships between the Orders table and the Customers and Employees tables so that we don't create records for orders from customers who don't exist or that seem to have been handled by employees who don't exist.

5. Close the **Orders** table.

   Tip You cannot create a relationship for an open table.

6. On the **Database Tools** tab, in the **Relationships** group, click the **Relationships** button.

   The Show Table dialog box opens so that you can indicate the tables for which you want to create a relationship.

The Tables page of the Show Table dialog box.

Troubleshooting If the dialog box doesn't open automatically, click the Show Table button in the Relationships group on the Design contextual tab.

7. With **Customers** selected on the **Tables** page, click **Add**. Then double-click **Orders**, and click **Close**.

   Access displays the Relationships page and adds a Relationship Tools contextual tab to the ribbon.

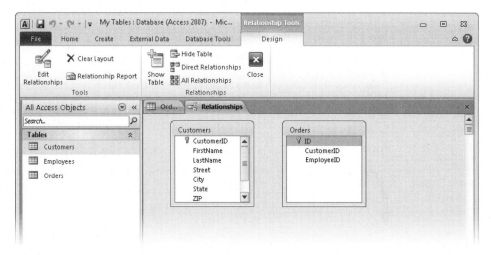

The two boxes list all the fields in their respective tables.

8. In the **Customers** field list, click **CustomerID**, and drag it down and over **CustomerID** in the **Orders** field list, releasing the mouse button when two little boxes, one containing a plus sign, appear below the pointer.

The Edit Relationships dialog box opens.

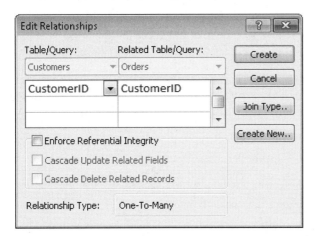

At the bottom of the dialog box, Access indicates that this will be a one-to-many relationship.

9. Select the **Enforce Referential Integrity** check box, and then click **Create**.

Access creates the link between the primary key in the Customers table and the foreign key in the Orders table, and a line now connects the two field lists on the Relationships page.

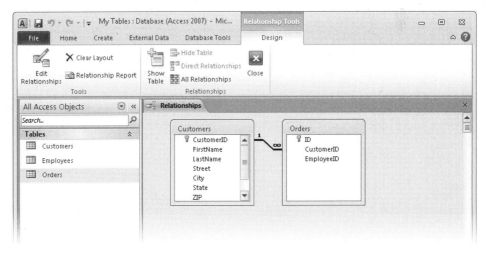

The symbols at each end of the line indicate that each Customer ID value appears only once in the Customers table but can appear many times in the Orders table.

Show
Table

10. On the **Design** contextual tab, in the **Relationships** group, click the **Show Table** button. Then in the **Show Table** dialog box, double-click the **Employees** table, and click **Close**.

   Access adds a box listing all the fields in the Employees table to the Relationships page.

11. On the page, drag the title bars of the three field lists to arrange them so that they are side by side and equidistant.

12. In the **Employees** field list, click the **EmployeeID** field, and drag it down and over the **EmployeeID** field in the **Orders** field list. Then in the **Edit Relationships** dialog box, select the **Enforce Referential Integrity** check box, and click **Create**.

13. After Access draws the relationship line between the primary key and the foreign key, close the Relationships page, clicking **Yes** to save its layout.

14. Open the **Orders** table. Then in the **CustomerID** field of the first record, type **11**, and click below the record to complete it.

   Access displays a message box telling you that you cannot add the new record to the table.

The value in the CustomerID field in the Orders table must match a value in the primary key CustomerID field in the Customer table.

15. Click **OK**. Then change the value to **1**, and click below the record to complete it.

   This time, Access accepts the value because there is a record with the value 1 in the primary key CustomerID field of the Customers table.

 CLEAN UP Close the Orders table, and then close the My Tables database.

Key Points

- Access 2010 includes templates to help you create databases and application parts to help you add related tables and other database objects.

- Rather than storing all information in one table, you can create different tables for each type of information, such as customers, orders, and suppliers.

- You can create a simple table structure by entering data and naming fields in Datasheet view. You can also set the data type and certain properties.

- You can manipulate or hide columns and rows without affecting the data.

- In Design view, you can modify any table, whether you created it manually or as part of a template.

- Data types and properties determine what data can be entered in a field, and how the data will look on the screen. Caution: changing some properties might affect the data.

- You can create a relationship between the primary key field of one table and the foreign key field of another so that you can combine information from both tables.

Chapter at a Glance

Create forms by using the
Form tool, **page 78**

Change the look of
forms, **page 85**

Change the
arrangement
of forms, **page 93**

3 Create Simple Forms

In this chapter, you will learn how to

✔ Create forms by using the Form tool.

✔ Change the look of forms.

✔ Change the arrangement of forms.

A database that contains the day-to-day records of an active company is useful only if it is kept current and if the information stored in it can be found quickly. Although Microsoft Access 2010 is fairly easy to use, entering, editing, and retrieving information in Datasheet view is not a task you would want to assign to someone who's not familiar with Access. Not only would these tasks be tedious and inefficient, but working in Datasheet view leaves far too much room for error, especially if details of complex transactions have to be entered into several related tables. The solution to this problem is to create and use forms.

A form is an organized and formatted view of some or all of the fields from one or more tables. Forms work interactively with the tables in a database. You use controls in the form to enter new information, to edit or remove existing information, or to locate information. The controls you will use most frequently in an Access form are:

- **Text box controls** You can view or enter information in these controls. Think of a text box control as a little window through which you can insert data into the corresponding field of the related table or view information that is already in that field.

- **Label controls** These tell you the type of information you are looking at in the corresponding text box control, or what you are expected to enter in the text box control.

Tip An Access form can also include a variety of other controls, such as list boxes, that transform the form into something very much like a Windows dialog box or wizard page. For information, see "Restricting Data to Values in Lists" in Chapter 6, "Maintain Data Integrity."

In this chapter, you'll discover how easy it is to create forms to view and enter information. You'll also modify forms to suit your needs by changing their appearance and the arrangement of their controls.

> **Practice Files** Before you can complete the exercises in this chapter, you need to copy the book's practice files to your computer. The practice files you'll use to complete the exercises in this chapter are in the Chapter03 practice file folder. A complete list of practice files is provided in "Using the Practice Files" at the beginning of this book.

Creating Forms by Using the Form Tool

Before you begin creating a form, you need to know the following:

- Which table the form should be based on
- How the form will be used

After making these decisions, you can create a form in the following ways:

- By clicking the table you want in the Navigation bar, and then clicking the Form button in the Forms group on the Create tab. This method creates a simple form that uses all the fields in the table.

- By using a wizard. This method enables you to choose which of the table's fields you want to use in the form.

  See Also For information about using wizards to create forms, see "Modifying Forms Created by Using a Wizard" in Chapter 7, "Create Custom Forms."

- Manually in Layout view where you can see the underlying data or Design view where you have more control over form elements.

  See Also For information about manipulating forms in Layout view, see the other two topics in this chapter. For information about manually creating forms in Design view, see "Adding Controls" in Chapter 7, "Create Custom Forms."

  Tip When creating forms for a Web database, you must use Layout view. You can use Layout view or Design view for non-Web databases.

You will usually want to start the process of creating forms that are based on tables by using the Form tool or a wizard—not because the manual process is especially difficult, but because it is simply more efficient to have the tool or a wizard create the basic form for you and then refine that form manually.

In this exercise, you'll use the Form tool to create a form based on a table. You will then enter a couple of records by using the new form and refresh the table to reflect the new entries.

SET UP You need the GardenCompany03_start database located in your Chapter03 practice file folder to complete this exercise. Open the GardenCompany03_start database, and save it as *GardenCompany03*. Then follow the steps.

Important The practice file for this exercise contains tables that look similar to those in the practice file for Chapter 1. However, to simplify the steps, we have removed the relationships between the tables. Be sure to use the practice database for each chapter rather than continuing on with the database from an earlier chapter.

1. In the **Navigation** pane, display **All Access Objects**, and then in the **Tables** group, double-click **Customers**.

   The Customers table opens in Datasheet view.

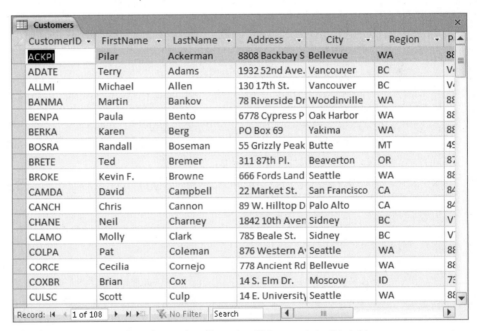

The record navigation bar shows that there are 108 records in this table.

Notice the CustomerID field, which contains a unique identifier for each customer and is the primary key field. In this case, the unique identifier is not an auto-generated number, but the first three letters of the customer's last name combined with the first two letters of his or her first name.

See Also For more information about this type of primary key, see "Restricting Data to Values in Other Tables" in Chapter 6, "Maintain Data Integrity."

2. On the **Create** tab, in the **Forms** group, click the **Form** button.

Access creates a simple form based on the active table and displays the form in Layout view. In this view, you can make adjustments to the layout and content of the form by clicking the buttons on three Form Layout Tools contextual tabs.

Tip You don't have to open a table to create a form based on it. You can simply click the table in the Navigation pane to select it and then click the Form button in the Forms group on the Create tab. But it is sometimes useful to have the table open behind the form so that you can verify the form contents against the table contents.

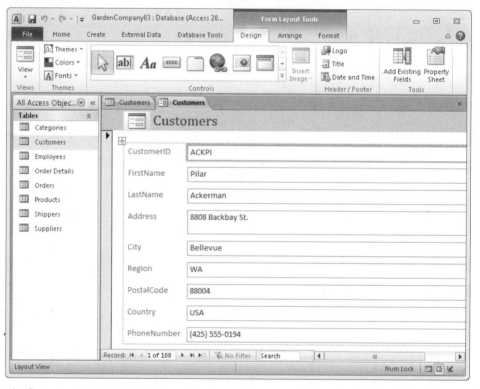

The first record in the table, displayed in Layout view.

Troubleshooting The appearance of buttons and groups on the ribbon changes depending on the width of the program window. For information about changing the appearance of the ribbon to match our screen images, see "Modifying the Display of the Ribbon" at the beginning of this book.

The Form tool has configured all the field names in the table as labels and all the fields as text boxes. In the header at the top of the form, the name of the table appears as a title, and the form icon appears as a placeholder for a logo.

3. Move the mouse pointer over the form, and click any label or text box control.

   In Layout view, you can adjust the controls on the form, so any control you click becomes selected, ready for manipulation.

4. On the **View Shortcuts** toolbar, click the **Form View** button. Then move the mouse pointer over the form, and click the **City** label.

In Form view, the Form Layout Tools contextual tabs are no longer displayed. Clicking a label doesn't select the label for manipulation; instead it selects the entry in the adjacent text box, ready for editing.

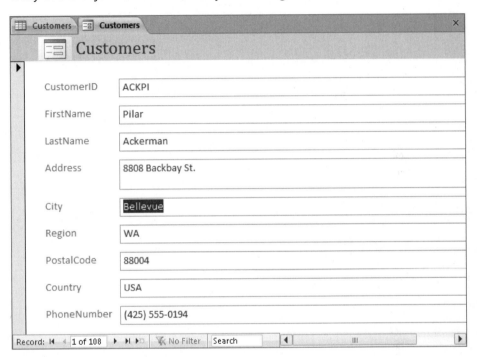

The first record, displayed in Form view.

5. In the record navigation bar at the bottom of the form, click the **Next Record** button.

Access displays the second record in the table.

6. Use the record navigation bar to display a few more records.

> **Tip** You can easily compare the information shown in the form to that in the table by alternately clicking the Customers table tab and the Customers form tab to switch back and forth between their pages.

7. At the right end of the record navigation bar, click the **New (Blank) Record** button.

Access displays a blank Customers form, ready for you to enter information for a new customer.

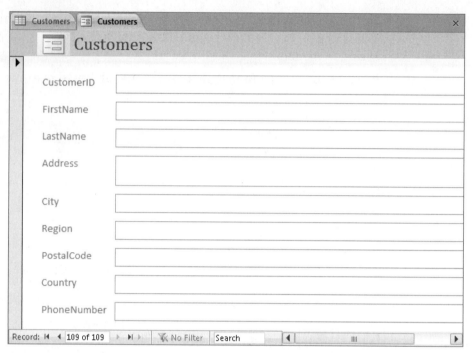

The record navigation bar shows that this will be record number 109.

8. Click the **CustomerID** label.

   The text box to the right now contains the cursor.

9. Type **ASHCH**, and press Tab.

   When you start typing, the icon that indicates a record is receiving data (two dots and a pencil) appears in the bar to the left. When you press Tab or Enter, the cursor moves to the next text box.

10. Type the following information, pressing the Tab key to move to the next text box.

FirstName	Chris
LastName	Ashton
Address	89 Cedar Way
City	Redmond
Region	WA
PostalCode	88052
Country	USA
PhoneNumber	(425) 555-0191

11. When you finish entering the phone number, press Enter.

Because you just typed the last field value in the record, Access displays another blank record. The record navigation bar now shows that this will be the 110th record in the table.

12. Type the following information, pressing the Tab key to move from text box to text box.

CustomerID	**BERJO**
FirstName	**Jo**
LastName	**Berry**
Address	**407 Sunny Way**
City	**Kirkland**
Region	**WA**
PostalCode	88053
Country	USA
PhoneNumber	**(425) 555-0187**

13. When you finish entering the phone number, press Enter. Then in the record navigation bar, click the **Previous Record** button.

Access cancels the new record and displays the record you just created.

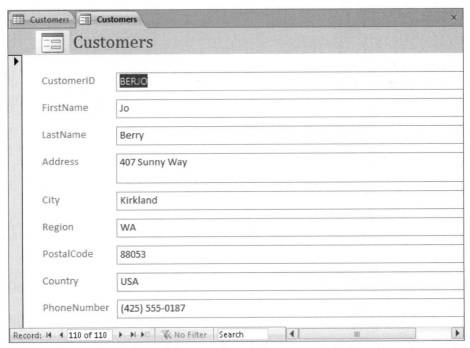

The information you entered for record number 110.

14. Click the **Customers** table tab, and on the record navigation bar, click the **Last Record** button.

The two records you entered in the form do not appear at the bottom of the table, and the record navigator bar indicates that there are only 108 records in the table.

Refresh All ▾

15. On the **Home** tab, in the **Records** group, click the **Refresh All** button.

Access synchronizes the form data input with the table, updates the record navigator bar to show 110 records, and displays the top of the table.

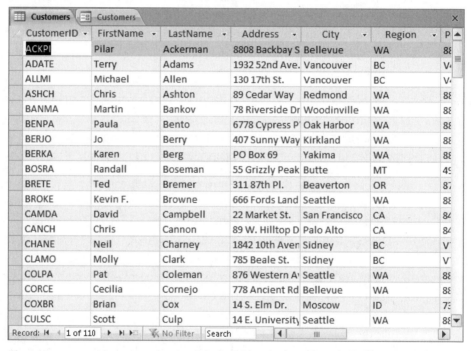

Customers		Customers				
CustomerID ▾	FirstName ▾	LastName ▾	Address ▾	City ▾	Region ▾	P ▲
ACKPI	Pilar	Ackerman	8808 Backbay S	Bellevue	WA	8ξ
ADATE	Terry	Adams	1932 52nd Ave.	Vancouver	BC	V
ALLMI	Michael	Allen	130 17th St.	Vancouver	BC	V
ASHCH	Chris	Ashton	89 Cedar Way	Redmond	WA	8ξ
BANMA	Martin	Bankov	78 Riverside Dr	Woodinville	WA	8ξ
BENPA	Paula	Bento	6778 Cypress P	Oak Harbor	WA	8ξ
BERJO	Jo	Berry	407 Sunny Way	Kirkland	WA	8ξ
BERKA	Karen	Berg	PO Box 69	Yakima	WA	8ξ
BOSRA	Randall	Boseman	55 Grizzly Peak	Butte	MT	4ξ
BRETE	Ted	Bremer	311 87th Pl.	Beaverton	OR	8
BROKE	Kevin F.	Browne	666 Fords Land	Seattle	WA	8ξ
CAMDA	David	Campbell	22 Market St.	San Francisco	CA	8
CANCH	Chris	Cannon	89 W. Hilltop D	Palo Alto	CA	8
CHANE	Neil	Charney	1842 10th Aven	Sidney	BC	V
CLAMO	Molly	Clark	785 Beale St.	Sidney	BC	V
COLPA	Pat	Coleman	876 Western A	Seattle	WA	8ξ
CORCE	Cecilia	Cornejo	778 Ancient Rd	Bellevue	WA	8ξ
COXBR	Brian	Cox	14 S. Elm Dr.	Moscow	ID	7
CULSC	Scott	Culp	14 E. University	Seattle	WA	8ξ ▾

Record: I◄ ◄ 1 of 110 ► ►I ►▦   No Filter   Search   ◄   IIII   ►

The two new records now appear in alphabetical order based on their CustomerID field values.

16. Close the **Customers** table.

17. On the Quick Access Toolbar, click the **Save** button. Then in the **Save As** dialog box, click **OK** to accept *Customers* as the form name.

Access saves the form. The Forms group appears on the Navigation bar, listing Customers as the only form in the database.

CLEAN UP Close the form. Retain the GardenCompany03 database for use in later exercises.

Changing the Look of Forms

y using the Form tool, as you did in the previous exercise, the ı the table on which it is based. Each field is represented on trol and its associated label control. The form is linked, or ıch text box is bound to its corresponding field. The table is ıd the field is called the *control source*.

ıave properties that determine how they behave and look. properties from the table on which it is based. For example, form reflects the corresponding field name in the source ço reflects the field name, unless the field has been assigned ːh case it reflects the caption. The width of each text box is ːe property in the table.

ıd to its table, the properties of the form are not bound to · you have created the form, you can change the properties ıdently of those in the table. You might want to change these orm's appearance—for example, you can change the font, or, and border.

ɔ change the look of a form is to change the theme applied ; a combination of colors and fonts that controls the look of of a form, it controls the color and text of the header at the t of the labels and text boxes. By default, the Office theme is sed on the Blank Database template and their objects, but you can easily change the theme by clicking the Themes button in the Themes group on the Design contextual tab, and then making a selection from the Themes gallery. While the gallery is displayed, you can point to a theme to display a live preview of how the active database object will look with that theme's colors and fonts applied.

If you like the colors of one theme and the fonts of another, you can mix and match theme elements. First apply the theme that most closely resembles the look you want, and then in the Themes group, change the colors by clicking the Colors button or the fonts by clicking the Fonts button.

Tip If you create a combination of colors and fonts that you would like to be able to use with other databases, you can save the combination as a new theme by clicking Save Current Theme at the bottom of the Themes gallery.

If you like most of the formatting of a theme but you want to fine-tune some elements, you can do so in Layout view. In this view, you can see the records from the table to which the form is bound, so when you make adjustments, you can see the impact on the data. (Changes to the data can be made only in Form view.) You might also want to add your organization's logo or a small graphic that represents the form's contents.

In this exercise, you'll change the form properties that control its colors and text attributes. You'll also add a logo to the form.

SET UP You need the GardenCompany03 database you worked with in the preceding exercise and the Logo graphic located in your Chapter03 practice file folder to complete this exercise. Open the GardenCompany03 database, and then follow the steps.

1. In the **Navigation** pane, under **Forms**, right-click **Customers**, and then click **Layout View**.

   The Customers form opens in Layout view.

2. On the **Design** contextual tab, in the **Themes** group, click the **Themes** button.

   The Themes gallery appears.

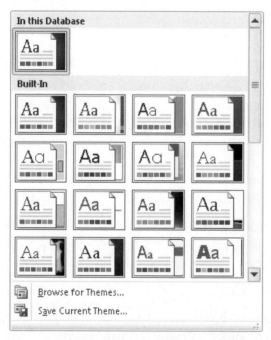

Each thumbnail represents a theme. By default, the Office theme is applied to this database.

3. Point to each thumbnail in turn, pausing to see its name in the ScreenTip that appears and the live preview of the form header and text.

4. Click the **Austin** thumbnail to apply that theme.

5. On the **Design** tab, in the **Header/Footer** group, click the **Logo** button.

6. With the contents of your **Chapter03** practice file folder displayed in the **Insert Picture** dialog box, double-click the **Logo** picture.

The logo replaces the form icon to the left of the title in the form header.

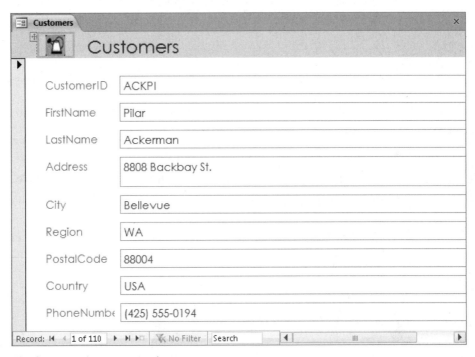

The form now has a custom logo.

Now let's experiment with individual properties.

7. On the **Customers** form, click the **CustomerID** label (not its text box).

The label is surrounded by a thick orange border.

11

8. On the **Format** contextual tab, in the **Font** group, click the **Font Size** arrow, and then in the list, click **8**.

The label text is now significantly smaller.

Property Sheet

9. Click the **CustomerID** text box (not its label), and then on the **Design** contextual tab, in the **Tools** group, click the **Property Sheet** button.

Keyboard Shortcut Press Alt+Enter to display the Property Sheet.

See Also For more information about keyboard shortcuts, see "Keyboard Shortcuts" at the end of this book.

The Property Sheet for this form opens and displays the properties for the object whose name appears in the text box at the top of the pane. Above the box, the type of object is identified. The properties are organized below the box on four pages: Format, Data, Event, and Other. You can display all the properties on one page by clicking the All tab.

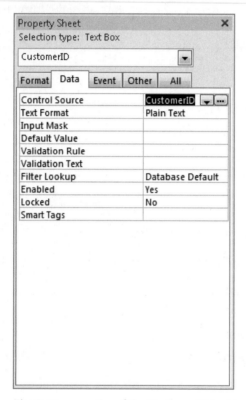

The Data properties of the CustomerID text box control.

Tip Don't change the properties on the Data page until you know more about controls and their sources.

10. In the **Property Sheet**, click the **Format** tab.

All the commands available in the Font group on the Format tab of the ribbon (plus a few more) are available on this page of the Property Sheet.

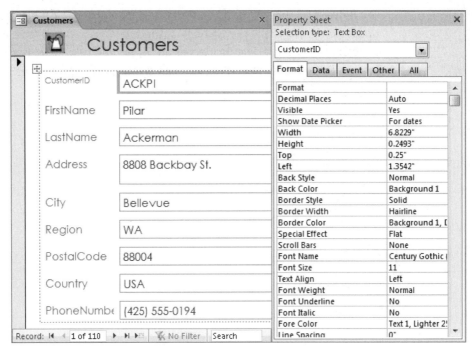

The Format properties for the CustomerID text box control.

11. On the **Format** page, click **Font Size**, click the arrow to the right of the adjacent property, and in the list, click **8**.

12. Set the **Font Weight** property to **Bold**.

    On the form, the entry in the CustomerID text box reflects your changes.

    Tip Sometimes the Property Sheet might obscure your view of the controls on the form. You can change the width of the Property Sheet or of any task pane by dragging its left border to the left or right. You can undock the Property Sheet from the edge of the window and move it elsewhere by dragging its title bar. Double-click the title bar to dock it again.

13. At the right end of the box at the top of the **Property Sheet**, click the arrow, and then in the object list, click **Label3**.

    The FirstName label is now selected. You can display the properties of any object on the form, including the form itself, by clicking the object you want in the object list.

14. Repeat step 11 to change the font size of the **FirstName** label to **8** points.

You have now made changes to three controls on this form.

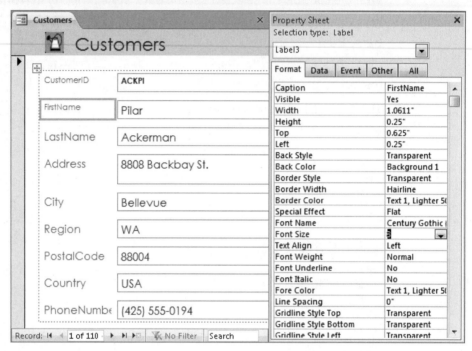

You have applied character formatting to the CustomerID label and text box control, and to the FirstName label.

These different ways of selecting a control and changing its properties provide some flexibility and convenience, but it would be a tedious way to make changes to several controls in a form. The next two steps provide a faster method.

15. In the upper-left corner of the dotted frame surrounding all the controls on the form, click the **Select All** button.

All the controls within the dotted frame are now surrounded by thick orange borders to indicate that they are selected. In the Property Sheet, the selection type is *Multiple selection*, and the box below is blank. Only the Format settings that are the same for all the selected controls are displayed. Because the changes you made in the previous steps are not shared by all the selected controls, the Font Size and Font Weight settings are now blank.

16. Repeat steps 11 and 12 to set the **Font Size** and **Font Weight** properties of the selected controls to **8** and **Bold**.

17. With the controls still selected, set the **Back Style** property to **Normal**.

    Although you can't see any change, the background of the labels is no longer transparent.

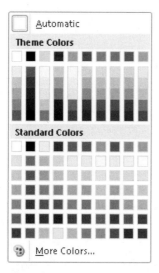

18. Click the **Back Color** property, and then click the **Ellipsis** button at the right end of the property.

    This Ellipsis button has different names and serves different purposes for different properties. In this case, clicking the Ellipsis button displays a color palette.

    The colors in this palette reflect the color scheme that is part of the Austin theme.

19. Under **Theme Colors** in the palette, click the third box (**Light Green, Background 2**).

    The background of all the controls changes to light green.

    Tip If the Back Color palette doesn't include a color you want to use, click More Colors at the bottom of the gallery, select a color on the Standard or Custom page of the Colors dialog box, and then click OK to set the color and add it to the list of recent colors at the bottom of the gallery.

20. Set the **Special Effect** property to **Shadowed**, and the **Border Color** property to the fifth box under **Theme Colors** in the color palette (**Green, Accent 1**).

21. In the form, click away from the selected controls to release the selection.

    You can now see the results.

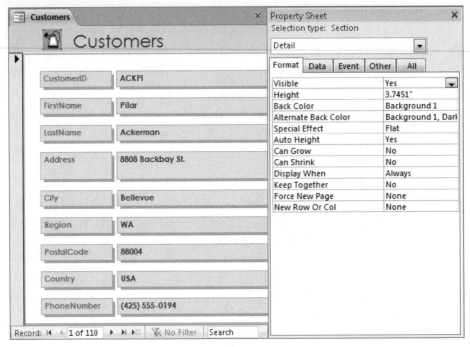

Applying a color and shadow to the labels and text boxes makes them stand out.

22. In the form, click the **FirstName** label. Then in the **Property Sheet**, click the **Caption** property, change **FirstName**: to **First Name**, and press Enter.

23. Repeat step 22 to change **LastName** to **Last Name** and **PhoneNumber** to **Phone**.

    Tip Changing the Caption property of the form does not affect the Caption property of the table.

24. On the Quick Access Toolbar, click the **Save** button to save the design of the **Customers** form, and then close it.

    The Property Sheet attached to the form also closes.

 CLEAN UP Retain the GardenCompany03 database for use in the last exercise.

Changing the Arrangement of Forms

Forms generated with the Form tool are functional, not fancy. By default, they are arranged in the Stacked layout, which arranges all the label controls in a single column on the left and all their corresponding text box controls in a single column to their right. All the boxes of each type are the same size, and in the boxes, the text is left-aligned.

If it suits the needs of your data better to display records in a tabular layout much like that of a table in Datasheet view, you can click Tabular in the Table group on the Arrange contextual tab.

See Also For more information about layouts, see the sidebar "Layouts" in Chapter 9, "Create Custom Reports."

If the default layout doesn't suit your needs or preferences, you can customize it. Most of the rearranging you are likely to want to do can be accomplished in Layout view, where you can see the impact on the underlying data. If you want to make more extensive changes to the layout of a non-Web database, you can switch to Design view.

See Also For information about customizing forms in Design view, see Chapter 7, "Create Custom Forms."

In Layout view, you can do the following to improve the form's layout and make it attractive and easy to use:

- Add and delete a variety of controls
- Change the size, color, and effects of controls
- Move controls
- Change text alignment
- Change control margins

Tip The order in which you make changes can have an impact on the results. If you don't see the expected results, click the Undo button on the Quick Access Toolbar to reverse your previous action, or click the Undo arrow, and click an action in the list to reverse more than one action.

In this exercise, you'll size, align, and rearrange the label and text box controls in a form.

SET UP You need the GardenCompany03 database you worked with in the preceding exercise to complete this exercise. Open the GardenCompany03 database, and then follow the steps.

1. In the **Navigation** pane, under **Forms**, right-click **Customers**, and click **Layout View**.

   Because the Property Sheet was open when you last closed the form, it opens with the form.

2. Click the **CustomerID** label (not its text box), and on the **Arrange** contextual tab, in the **Rows & Columns** group, click the **Select Column** button.

   Tip You can also point above the selected control, and when the pointer changes to a single downward-pointing arrow, click to select the column of controls.

3. With all the labels selected, on the **Format** page of the **Property Sheet**, set the **Text Align** property to **Right**.

   All the labels are right-aligned in their boxes. The Property Sheet indicates that by default, the Width property of the labels is 1.0611".

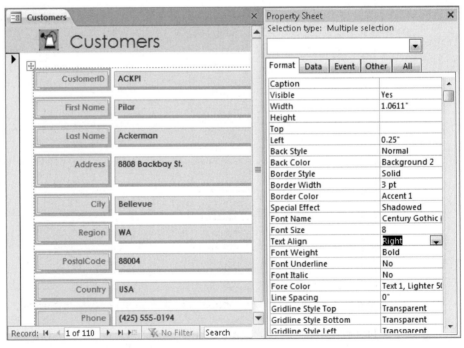

You can efficiently adjust the alignment of multiple controls by changing the Text Align property in the Property Sheet.

4. Point to the right border of the **CustomerID** label, and when the pointer changes to a two-headed horizontal arrow, drag to the left until **CustomerID** just fits in its box.

5. In the **Property Sheet**, adjust the **Width** property to **0.8"**, and press Enter.

   Tip It is often easier to adjust the size of controls visually and then fine-tune them in the Property Sheet than it is to guess what property settings might work.

6. Select the **CustomerID** text box (not its label), and change its **Width** property to **1.5"**.

   Tip Throughout this book, we refer to measurements in inches. If your computer is set to display measurements in centimeters, substitute the equivalent metric measurement. As long as you are entering the default units, you don't have to specify the unit type.

   The width of all the text box controls is adjusted, not just that of the CustomerID text box.

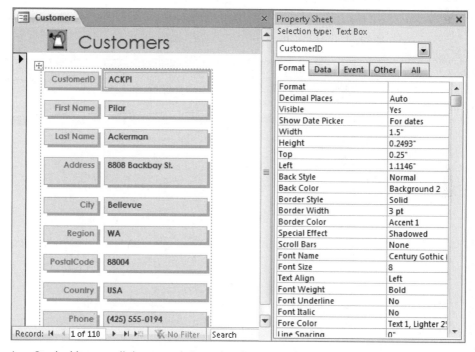

In a Stacked layout, all the controls in each column are the same width.

Notice that the controls are different heights. We'll fix that next.

7. Above the upper-left corner of the dotted border that surrounds all the controls, click the **Select All** button to select all the controls within the border. Then in the **Property Sheet**, set the **Height** property to **0.25"**.

8. On the **Arrange** contextual tab, in the **Position** group, click the **Control Margins** button, and then click **Narrow**.

   Now all the controls are the same height and width and have the same interior margins.

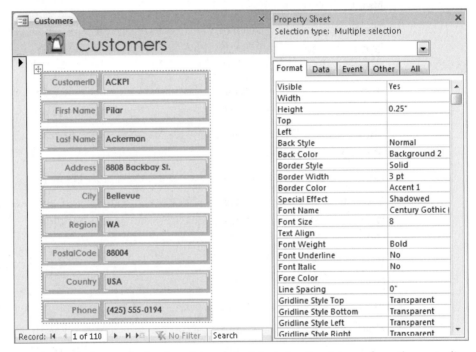

You can control not only the size of the controls but also the distance from the control's border to its text.

9. Click the **Phone** label (not its text box), and on the **Arrange** contextual tab, in the **Rows & Columns** group, click the **Select Row** button.

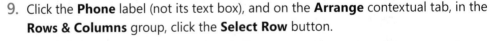

   Tip You can also point to the left of the selected control, and when the pointer changes to a single right-pointing arrow, click to select the row of controls.

10. Point anywhere in the selection, and drag upward, releasing the mouse button when the insertion line sits below the **Last Name** label or text box.

     The Phone label and text box move to their new location. As you can see, it is easy to move controls within the structure of the Stacked layout. But suppose you want to rearrange the form so that some controls are side by side instead of stacked.

11. Point to the selected label and text box, and try to drag it to the right of the **Last Name** controls above.

     The controls will not move out of their columns. They are confined by the Stacked layout applied to the form. To make more extensive layout adjustments, you need to remove the layout from the form.

12. Above the upper-left corner of the dotted border, click the **Select All** button. Then right-click the selection, click **Layout**, and click **Remove Layout**.

     The dotted border disappears, and the form is no longer constrained by the Stacked layout.

13. Click the **Last Name** label, and then press the Delete key.

14. Click the **LastName** text box, point to the **A** in *Ackerman*, and when the pointer is shaped like a four-headed arrow, drag up and to the right until the pointer sits slightly to the right of the **FirstName** text box.

     When you release the mouse button, the control snaps to an invisible grid that helps maintain consistent spacing on the form.

15. In the **Property Sheet**, adjust the **Left** property to **2.7"**.

16. Hold down the Shift key, and click the two adjacent controls to add them to the selection. Then top-align the controls by setting the **Top** property to **0.6"**.

17. Click the **First Name** label, and change the label's **Caption** property to Name.

18. Rearrange the remaining controls in logical groupings on the form, and then close the **Property Sheet**.

     We adjusted the position of the phone controls and then grouped and sized the address controls.

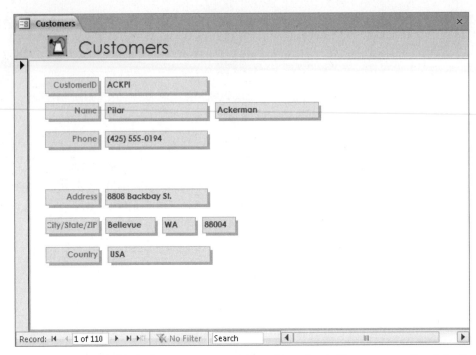

In Layout view, this kind of arrangement can be achieved only if you remove the default layout, which constrains the controls in columns.

> **Tip** If you rearrange controls or add new controls to a form and then find that pressing Tab jumps around erratically instead of sequentially from one control to the next, you can change the tab order. When working in Layout view, you click the Other tab in the Property Sheet and set the Tab Index property for each control in the tab order you want. When working in Design view, you click the Tab Order button in the Tools group on the Design tab to display the Tab Order dialog box, where you can drag fields into the correct order. For more information about working with forms in Design view, see Chapter 7, "Create Custom Forms."

19. Close the **Customers** form, clicking **Yes** when prompted to save its layout.

CLEAN UP Close the GardenCompany03 database.

Key Points

- The quickest way to create a form that includes all the fields from one table is by using the Form tool. You can then use the form to view and enter records.

- A form that is based on a table is bound to that form. The table is called the *record source*.

- By default, the form displays one text box control and its associated label control for each field in the table.

- Each text box control is bound to its field, which is called the *control source*.

- Each control has several properties that you can change in Layout view or Design view to improve the look and layout of the form.

Chapter at a Glance

Sort information in
tables, **page 102**

Filter information
in tables, **page 107**

Filter information by
using forms, **page 111**

Locate information that matches
multiple criteria, **page 115**

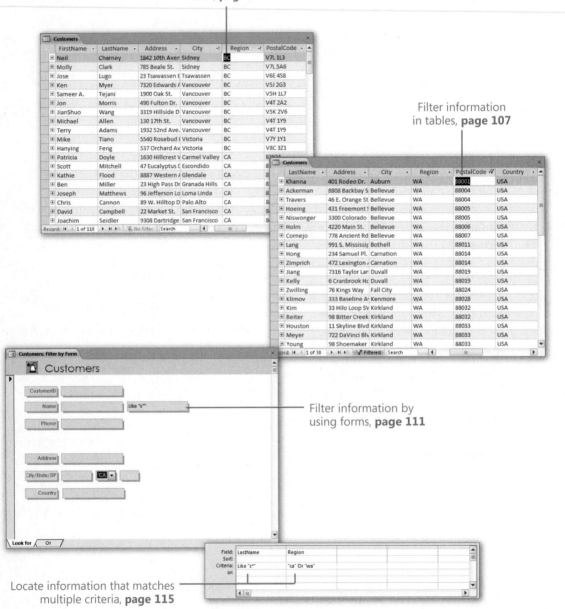

4 Display Data

In this chapter, you will learn how to

✔ Sort information in tables.

✔ Filter information in tables.

✔ Filter information by using forms.

✔ Locate information that matches multiple criteria.

A database is a repository for information. It might contain only a few records or thousands of records, stored in one table or multiple tables. No matter how much information a database contains, it is useful only if you can locate the information you need when you need it. In a small database, you can find information simply by scrolling through a table until you find what you are looking for. But as a database grows in size and complexity, locating and analyzing information becomes more difficult.

Microsoft Access 2010 provides a variety of tools you can use to organize the display of information stored in a database. For example, you can organize all the records in a table by quickly sorting it based on any field or combination of fields. You can also filter the table so that information containing a combination of characters is displayed or excluded from the display.

In this chapter, you'll first sort information in a table based on one and two columns. Then you'll explore three ways to filter tables and forms to display only the records that meet specific criteria.

Practice Files Before you can complete the exercises in this chapter, you need to copy the book's practice files to your computer. The practice file you'll use to complete the exercises in this chapter is in the Chapter04 practice file folder. A complete list of practice files is provided in "Using the Practice Files" at the beginning of this book.

Sorting Information in Tables

You can sort the information stored in a table based on the values in one or more fields, in either ascending or descending order. For example, you could sort customer information alphabetically by last name and then by first name. This would result in the order found in telephone books.

Last Name	First Name
Smith	Brian
Smith	Denise
Smith	Jeff
Taylor	Daniel
Taylor	Maurice

Sorting a table groups all entries of one type together, which can be useful. For example, to qualify for a discount on postage, you might want to group customer records by postal code before printing mailing labels.

Access can sort by more than one field, but it always sorts sequentially from left to right. You can sort by the first field, and if the second field you want to sort by is to the right of the first, you can then add the next field to the sort. If you want to sort by more than one field in one operation, the fields must be adjacent, and they must be arranged in the order in which you want to sort them.

See Also For information about moving fields, see "Manipulating Table Columns and Rows" in Chapter 2, "Create Databases and Simple Tables."

Tip You can sort records while viewing them in a form. Click the field on which you want to base the sort, and then click the Sort command you want. You can't sort by multiple fields at the same time in Form view, but you can sort by one field and then the next to achieve the same results.

In this exercise, you'll sort records first by one field, and then by multiple fields.

SET UP You need the GardenCompany04_start database located in your Chapter04 practice file folder to complete this exercise. Open the GardenCompany04_start database, and save it as *GardenCompany04*. Then follow the steps.

1. With **All Access Objects** displayed in the **Navigation** pane, under **Tables**, double-click **Customers**.

   The Customers table opens in Datasheet view.

2. Click the arrow to the right of the **Region** field name.

   A list of sorting and filtering options appears.

The list at the bottom includes check boxes for every unique value in the field.

3. Click **Sort A to Z**.

Access rearranges the records in alphabetical order by region.

FirstName	LastName	Address	City	Region	PostalCode
Jose	Lugo	23 Tsawassen E	Tsawassen	BC	V6E 4S8
Neil	Charney	1842 10th Aven	Sidney	BC	V7L 1L3
Mike	Tiano	5540 Rosebud I	Victoria	BC	V7Y 1Y1
Molly	Clark	785 Beale St.	Sidney	BC	V7L 5A6
JianShuo	Wang	3319 Hillside D	Vancouver	BC	V5K 2V6
Sameer A.	Tejani	1900 Oak St.	Vancouver	BC	V5H 1L7
Jon	Morris	490 Fulton Dr.	Vancouver	BC	V4T 2A2
Ken	Myer	7320 Edwards A	Vancouver	BC	V5J 2G3
Michael	Allen	130 17th St.	Vancouver	BC	V4T 1Y9
Hanying	Feng	537 Orchard Av	Victoria	BC	V8C 3Z1
Terry	Adams	1932 52nd Ave.	Vancouver	BC	V4T 1Y9
Kathie	Flood	8887 Western A	Glendale	CA	81203
David	Simpson	45 Park St.	San Jose	CA	85123
Scott	Mitchell	47 Eucalyptus D	Escondido	CA	82029
Patrick	Sands	98 N. Hyde St.	San Francisco	CA	84140
Joachim	Seidler	9308 Dartridge	San Francisco	CA	84167
Carole	Poland	10 Pepper Dr.	San Jose	CA	85111
David	Campbell	22 Market St.	San Francisco	CA	84112
Patricia	Doyle	1630 Hillcrest V	Carmel Valley	CA	83924

Record: 1 of 110   No Filter   Search

The upward-pointing arrow at the right end of the Region field name indicates that the table is sorted in ascending order on this field.

4. To reverse the sort order by using a different method, on the **Home** tab, in the **Sort & Filter** group, click the **Descending** button.

   The sort order reverses. The records for customers living in Washington (WA) are now at the top of the list, and the arrow at the right end of the field name is pointing downward.

   In both sorts, the region was sorted alphabetically, but the City field was left in a seemingly random order. Suppose you want to see the records arranged by city within each region. You can do this by sorting the City field and then sorting the Region field.

5. Click the arrow to the right of the **City** field name, and then click **Sort A to Z**.

   Access sorts the records alphabetically by city.

6. To finish the process, right-click anywhere in the **Region** column, and then click **Sort A to Z**.

   The two fields are now sorted so that the cities are listed in ascending order within each region.

FirstName	LastName	Address	City	Region	PostalCode
⊞ Neil	Charney	1842 10th Aven	Sidney	BC	V7L 1L3
⊞ Molly	Clark	785 Beale St.	Sidney	BC	V7L 5A6
⊞ Jose	Lugo	23 Tsawassen E	Tsawassen	BC	V6E 4S8
⊞ Ken	Myer	7320 Edwards A	Vancouver	BC	V5J 2G3
⊞ Sameer A.	Tejani	1900 Oak St.	Vancouver	BC	V5H 1L7
⊞ Jon	Morris	490 Fulton Dr.	Vancouver	BC	V4T 2A2
⊞ JianShuo	Wang	3319 Hillside D	Vancouver	BC	V5K 2V6
⊞ Michael	Allen	130 17th St.	Vancouver	BC	V4T 1Y9
⊞ Terry	Adams	1932 52nd Ave.	Vancouver	BC	V4T 1Y9
⊞ Mike	Tiano	5540 Rosebud I	Victoria	BC	V7Y 1Y1
⊞ Hanying	Feng	537 Orchard Av	Victoria	BC	V8C 3Z1
⊞ Patricia	Doyle	1630 Hillcrest V	Carmel Valley	CA	83924
⊞ Scott	Mitchell	47 Eucalyptus E	Escondido	CA	82029
⊞ Kathie	Flood	8887 Western A	Glendale	CA	81203
⊞ Ben	Miller	23 High Pass Dr	Granada Hills	CA	81344
⊞ Joseph	Matthews	96 Jefferson Lo	Loma Linda	CA	82350
⊞ Chris	Cannon	89 W. Hilltop D	Palo Alto	CA	84306
⊞ David	Campbell	22 Market St.	San Francisco	CA	84112
⊞ Joachim	Seidler	9308 Dartridge	San Francisco	CA	84167

Record: 1 of 110   No Filter   Search

Both the City and Region field names have upward-pointing arrows.

7. On the **Home** tab, in the **Sort & Filter** group, click the **Remove Sort** button to clear the sort from both fields.

The table reverts to the previously saved sort order. Now let's sort both columns at the same time.

8. Click the **City** field name, hold down the Shift key, and click the **Region** field name. Then in the **Sort & Filter** group, click the **Ascending** button.

Because the City field is to the left of the Region field, Access cannot achieve the result you want.

The City sort is overriding the Region sort.

9. Clear the sort, and then click away from the **City** and **Region** fields to clear the selection.

10. Click the **Region** field name, and drag the field name to the left of the **City** field name, releasing the mouse button when a heavy black line appears between the **Address** and **City** field names.

11. With the **Region** field selected, hold down the Shift key, and click the **City** field name to include that field in the selection.

12. In the **Sort & Filter** group, click the **Ascending** button.

Access arranges the records with the regions in ascending order and the cities in ascending order within each region.

13. Experiment with various ways of sorting the records to display different results. Then close the **Customers** table, clicking **No** when prompted to save the table layout.

 CLEAN UP Retain the GardenCompany04 database for use in later exercises.

How Access Sorts

The concept of sorting seems quite intuitive, but sometimes the way Access sorts numbers might seem puzzling. In Access, numbers can be treated as either text or numerals. Because of the spaces, hyphens, and punctuation typically used in street addresses, postal codes, and telephone numbers, the data type of these fields is usually Text, and the numbers are sorted the same way as all other text. In contrast, numbers in a field assigned the Number or Currency data type are sorted as numerals.

When Access sorts text, it sorts first on the first character in the selected field in every record, then on the next character, then on the next, and so on—until it runs out of characters. When Access sorts numbers, it treats the contents of each field as a single value, and sorts the records based on that value. This tactic can result in seemingly strange sort orders. For example, sorting the list in the first column of the following table as text produces the list in the second column. Sorting the same list as numerals produces the list in the third column.

Original	Sort as text	Sort as numerals
1	1	1
1234	11	3
23	12	4
3	1234	11
11	22	12
22	23	22
12	3	23
4	4	1234

If a field with the Text data type contains numbers, you can sort the field numerically by padding the numbers with leading zeros so that all entries are the same length. For example, 001, 011, and 101 are sorted correctly even if the numbers are defined as text.

Filtering Information in Tables

Sorting the information in a table organizes it in a logical manner, but you still have the entire table to deal with. For locating only the records containing (or not containing) specific information, filtering is more effective than sorting. For example, you could quickly create a filter to locate only customers who live in Seattle, only items that were purchased on January 13, or only orders that were not shipped by standard mail. When you filter a table, Access doesn't remove the records that don't match the filter; it simply hides them.

The Filter commands are available in the Sort & Filter group on the Home tab, on the menu displayed when you click the arrow at the right end of a field name, and on the shortcut menu displayed when you right-click anywhere in a field's column. However, not all Filter commands are available in all of these places.

To filter information by multiple criteria, you can apply additional filters to the results of the first one.

Tip You can filter records while displaying them in a form by using the same commands as you do to filter records in a table.

In this exercise, you'll filter records by using a single criterion and then by using multiple criteria.

SET UP You need the GardenCompany04 database you worked with in the preceding exercise to complete this exercise. Open the GardenCompany04 database, and then follow the steps.

1. In the **Navigation** pane, under **Tables**, double-click **Customers** to open the **Customers** table in Datasheet view.

2. In the **City** field, click any instance of **Vancouver**.

3. On the **Home** tab, in the **Sort & Filter** group, click the **Selection** button, and then in the list, click **Equals "Vancouver"**.

   Access displays a small filter icon shaped like a funnel at the right end of the City field name to indicate that the table is filtered by that field. The status bar at the bottom of the table has changed from *1 of 110* to *1 of 6* because only six records have the value Vancouver in the City field. Also on the status bar, the Filter status has changed to Filtered.

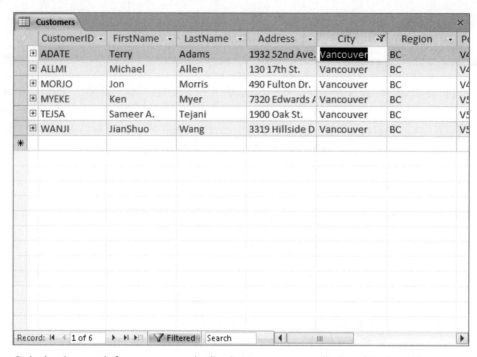

Customers						
CustomerID ▾	FirstName ▾	LastName ▾	Address ▾	City ▿	Region ▾	P(
⊞ ADATE	Terry	Adams	1932 52nd Ave.	Vancouver	BC	V4
⊞ ALLMI	Michael	Allen	130 17th St.	Vancouver	BC	V4
⊞ MORJO	Jon	Morris	490 Fulton Dr.	Vancouver	BC	V4
⊞ MYEKE	Ken	Myer	7320 Edwards A	Vancouver	BC	V5
⊞ TEJSA	Sameer A.	Tejani	1900 Oak St.	Vancouver	BC	V5
⊞ WANJI	JianShuo	Wang	3319 Hillside D	Vancouver	BC	V5

Record: ◄ ◄ 1 of 6 ► ►I ►⊞ ▼ Filtered Search

Only the six records for customers who live in Vancouver are displayed in the table.

Filter

Tip In the list displayed when you click the arrow to the right of a field name (or the Filter button in the Sort & Filter group) are check boxes for all the unique entries in the active field. Clearing the Select All check box clears all the boxes, and you can then select the check boxes of any values you want to be displayed in the filtered table.

In the Sort & Filter group on the Home tab, the Toggle Filter button is now active. You can use this button to quickly turn the applied filter on and off.

4. In the **Sort & Filter** group, click the **Toggle Filter** button.

   Access displays all the records. If you click the Toggle Filter button again, the filter will be reapplied.

   Now let's display a list of all customers with postal codes starting with 880.

5. Click the arrow to the right of the **PostalCode** field name, and point to **Text Filters** in the list.

A list of criteria appears.

You can specify criteria for the text you want to find.

Tip The sort and filter options displayed when you click the arrow to the right of a field name (or when you click the Filter button in the Sort & Filter group) are determined by the data type of the field. The PostalCode field is a Text field to allow for ZIP+4 codes. If you display the sort and filter list for a field that is assigned the Number data type, the sort and filter list includes Number Filters instead of Text Filters, and different options are available.

6. In the list, click **Begins With**.

   The Custom Filter dialog box opens.

The name of the text box is customized with the field name and the filer you chose.

7. In the **PostalCode begins with** box, type **880**. Then click **OK**.

   Access filters the table and displays only the records that match your criteria.

Only the 30 records for customers who live in postal codes starting with 880 are displayed in the table.

8. In the **Sort & Filter** group, click the **Toggle Filter** button to remove the filter and display all the records.

   Now let's display only the records of the customers who live outside of the United States.

9. In the **Country** field, right-click any instance of **USA**, and then click **Does Not Equal "USA"**.

Find

   Tip In this case, it is easy to right-click the text you want to base this filter on. If the text is buried in a large table, you can quickly locate it by clicking the Find button in the Find group on the Home tab, entering the term you want in the Find What box in the Find And Replace dialog box, and then clicking Find Next.

   Access displays the records of all the customers from countries other than the United States (in this case, only Canada).

10. Remove the filter, and close the **Customers** table, clicking **No** when prompted to save your changes.

11. Open the **Orders** table in Datasheet view.

12. In the **EmployeeID** field, right-click **7**, and then click **Equals 7**.

    Twenty records are displayed in the filtered table.

13. In the **OrderDate** field, right-click **2/1/2010**, and then click **On or After 2/1/2010**.

    Tip To see a list of the available options for date filters, right-click any cell in the OrderDate field, and then point to Date Filters.

    You now have a list of the orders customers placed with the selected employee on or after the specified date. You could continue to refine the list by filtering on another field, or you could sort the results by a field.

14. Close the **Orders** table, clicking **No** when prompted to save the table layout.

 **CLEAN UP** Retain the GardenCompany04 database for use in later exercises.

Filtering Information by Using Forms

When you want to filter a table based on the information in several fields, the quickest method is to use the Filter By Form command, which is available from the Advanced Filter Options list in the Sort & Filter group on the Home tab. When you choose this command with a table displayed, Access displays a filtering form that resembles a datasheet. Each of the cells in the form has an associated list of all the unique values in that field in the underlying table.

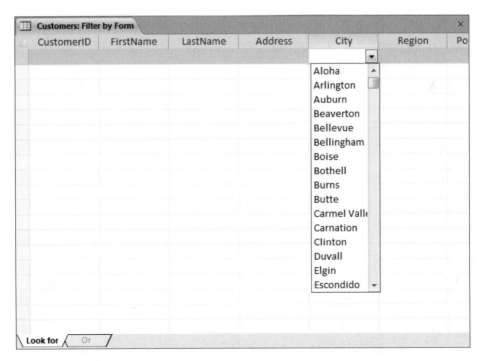

Using the Filter By Form command with a table.

For each field, you can select a value from the list or type a value. When you have finished defining the values you want to see, you click the Toggle Filter button to display only the records that match your selected criteria.

Using Filter By Form on a table that has only a few fields, such as the one shown above, is easy. But using it on a table that has a few dozen fields can be cumbersome, and it is often simpler to find information in the form version of the table. When you choose the Filter By Form command with a form displayed, Access filters the form the same way it filters a table.

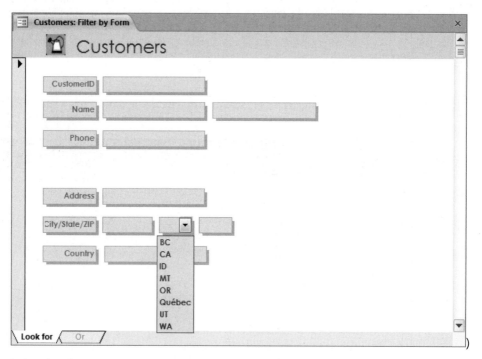

Using the Filter By Form command with a form.

After you have applied the filter, you move between the matched records by clicking the buttons on the record navigation bar at the bottom of the form page.

In this exercise, you'll filter a form by using the Filter By Form command.

 SET UP You need the GardenCompany04 database you worked with in the preceding exercise to complete this exercise. Open the GardenCompany04 database, and then follow the steps.

1. In the **Navigation** pane, under **Forms**, double-click **Customers**.

   The Customers form opens in Form view.

2. On the **Home** tab, in the **Sort & Filter** group, click the **Advanced Filter Options** button, and then in the list, click **Filter By Form**.

   The Customers form is replaced by its Filter By Form version, which has two pages: Look For and Or. Instead of displaying the information for one record from the table, the form now has a blank box for each field.

3. Click the second text box to the right of the **Name** label (the box that normally displays the customer's last name), type **s***, and then press Enter.

   The asterisk is a wildcard that stands for any character or string of characters. Access converts your entry to *Like "s*"*, which is the proper format, called the *syntax*, for this type of criterion.

   See Also For information about wildcards, see the sidebar "Wildcards" following this topic.

4. In the **Sort & Filter** group, click the **Toggle Filter** button.

   Access displays the first record that has a LastName value starting with *S*.

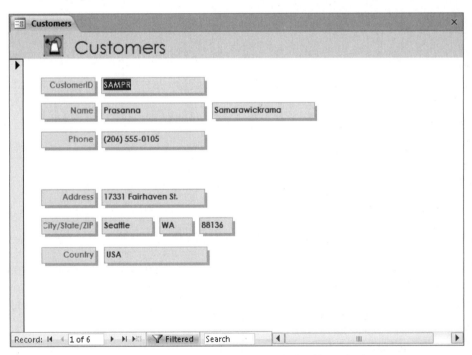

The record navigation bar shows that six records match the filter criterion.

5. Click the **Advanced Filter Options** button and then click **Filter By Form** to redisplay the filter form.

   Your filter criterion is still displayed in the form.

> **Tip** No matter what method you use to enter filter criteria, the criteria are saved as a form property and are available until they are replaced by other criteria.

6. Click the second box to the right of the **City/State/ZIP** label (the box that normally displays the state or region), click the arrow that appears, and then in the list, click **CA**.

   You are instructing Access to find and display records that have both a Region value of CA *and* LastName values starting with *S*.

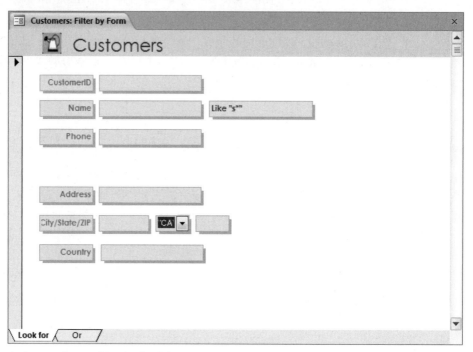

Only records matching both of the criteria will be displayed.

7. Click the **Toggle Filter** button.

   Access displays the first of three records that meet the filtering criteria.

8. Switch back to the filter form, and at the bottom of the form page, click the **Or** tab.

   The criteria you entered on the Look For page are still there, but on this page, all the fields are blank so that you can enter alternatives for the same fields.

   > **Tip** When you display the Or page, a second Or tab appears so that you can include a third criterion for the same field if you want.

9. Type **s*** in the second **Name** box, and click **WA** in the list for the second **City/State/ZIP** box.

   You are instructing Access to find and display records that have either a Region value of CA *and* LastName values starting with *S*, *or* a Region value of WA *and* LastName values starting with *S*.

10. Click the **Toggle Filter** button.

11. Use the record navigation bar to view the six records in the filtered **Customers** form.

12. Click the **Toggle Filter** button to remove the filter. Then close the form.

 CLEAN UP Retain the GardenCompany04 database for use in the last exercise.

Wildcards

If you want to filter a table to display records containing certain information but you aren't sure of all the characters, or if you want your filter to match variations of a base set of characters, you can include wildcard characters in your filter criteria. The most common wildcards are:

- ***** The asterisk represents any number of characters. For example, filtering the LastName field on *Co** returns records containing *Colman* and *Conroy*.

- **?** The question mark represents any single alphabetic character. For example, filtering the FirstName field on *er??* returns records containing *Eric* and *Erma*.

- **#** The number sign represents any single numeric character. For example, filtering the ID field on *1##* returns any ID from *100* through *199*.

Tip Access supports several other wildcards. For more information, search for *wildcards* in Access Help.

When searching for information in a Text field, you can also use the Contains text filter to locate records containing words or character strings.

Locating Information That Matches Multiple Criteria

As long as your filter criteria are fairly simple, filtering is a quick and easy way to narrow down the amount of information displayed in a table or to locate information that matches what you are looking for. But suppose you need to locate something more complex, such as all the orders shipped to Midwestern states between specific dates by either of two shippers. When you need to search a single table for records that meet multiple criteria, or when the criteria involve complex expressions, you can use the Advanced Filter/Sort command, available from the Advanced Filter Options list.

Choosing the Advanced Filter/Sort command displays a design grid where you enter filtering criteria. As you'll see, filters with multiple criteria are actually simple queries.

See Also For information about queries, see Chapter 8, "Create Queries."

In this exercise, you'll filter a table to display the data for customers located in two states. Then you'll experiment with the design grid to better understand its filtering capabilities.

 SET UP You need the GardenCompany04 database you worked with in the preceding exercise to complete this exercise. Open the GardenCompany04 database, and then follow the steps.

1. In the **Navigation** pane, under **Tables**, double-click **Customers** to open the **Customers** table in Datasheet view.

 2. On the **Home** tab, in the **Sort & Filter** group, click the **Advanced Filter Options** button, and then in the list, click **Advanced Filter/Sort**.

The CustomersFilter1 page opens, displaying the Query Designer with the Customers field list in the top pane and the design grid in the bottom pane.

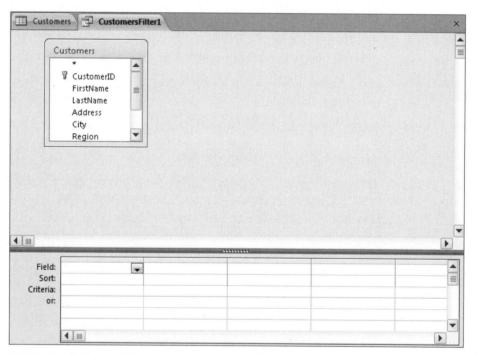

Clicking the Advanced Filter/Sort button displays the Query Designer.

3. In the **Customers** field list, double-click **LastName** to copy it to the **Field** row of the first column of the grid.

4. In the **Criteria** row of the **LastName** field, type s*, and then press Enter.

Because you have used the * wildcard, Access changes the criterion to *Like "s*"*.

5. In the **Customers** field list, double-click **Region** to copy it to the **Field** row of the next available column of the grid.

6. In the **Criteria** row of the **Region** field, type **ca or wa**, and then press Enter.

Tip If you want to find the records for customers who live in California or Oregon, you cannot type *ca or or*, because Access treats *or* as a reserved word. You must type *ca or "or"* in the Criteria row. Anytime you want to enter a criterion that will be interpreted as an instruction rather than a string of characters, enclose the characters in quotation marks to achieve the desired results.

Your entry changes to *"ca" Or "wa"*. The query will now filter the table to display the records for only those customers with last names beginning with the letter *S* who live in California or Washington.

The grid with two criteria.

7. In the **Sort & Filter** group, click the **Toggle Filter** button to display only records that match the criteria.

Access switches to the Customers table page and displays the filter results.

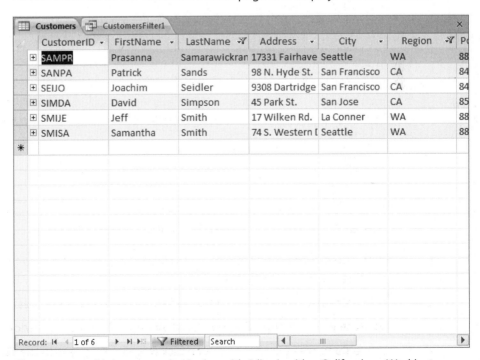

Six customers with last names beginning with S live in either California or Washington.

8. Click the **CustomersFilter1** tab to switch to the filter page.

9. In the **or** row of the **LastName** field, type **b***, and then press Enter.

   We want to filter the table to display only the records for customers with last names beginning with the letter *S* or *B* who live in California or Washington.

Field:	LastName	Region				
Sort:						
Criteria:	Like "s*"	"ca" Or "wa"				
or:	Like "b*"					

The design grid with three criteria.

10. In the **Sort & Filter** group, click the **Toggle Filter** button to apply the filter.

    On the Customers table page, the result includes records for all customers with last names that begin with *S* or *B*, but some of the *B* names live in Montana and Oregon.

11. Click the **CustomersFilter1** tab to switch to the filter page, and look carefully at the design grid.

    The filter first works with the two criteria in the Criteria row and searches for customers with names beginning with *S* who live in California or Washington. Then it works with the criteria in the Or row and searches for customers with names beginning with *B*, regardless of where they live. To get the results we want, we need to repeat the criterion from the Region field in the Or row.

12. In the **or** row of the **Region** field, type **ca or wa**, and then press Enter.

13. Apply the filter.

    Access switches to the Customers table page and displays only the records for customers with last names beginning with S or B who are located in California or Washington.

14. Close the **Customers** table, clicking **Yes** when prompted to save changes to the design of the table.

 CLEAN UP Close the GardenCompany04 database.

Saving Filters as Queries

If a filter takes more than a few minutes to set up and you are likely to want to use it again, you might want to save it as a query. Then you can run the query to display the filtered results at any time.

To save a filter as a query:

1. On the Home tab, in the Sort & Filter group, click the Advanced Filter Options button and then click Save As Query.

2. In the Save As Query dialog box, assign the query an appropriate name, and then click OK.

See Also For information about queries, see Chapter 8, "Create Queries."

Key Points

- You can sort a table in either ascending or descending order, based on the values in any field (or combination of fields).

- You can filter a table so that information containing a combination of characters is displayed (or excluded from the display).

- You can apply another filter to the results of the previous one to further refine your search.

- The Filter By Form command filters a table or form based on the information in several fields.

- You can use the Advanced Filter/Sort command to search a single table for records that meet multiple criteria.

Chapter at a Glance

Create reports by
using a wizard, **page 122**

Modify report design,
page 129

Preview and print
reports, **page 136**

5 Create Simple Reports

In this chapter, you will learn how to

✔ Create reports by using a wizard.

✔ Modify report design.

✔ Preview and print reports.

Like forms, reports give people easy access to the information stored in a database. However, there are several differences between forms and reports, including the following:

● Forms are used to enter, view, and edit information. Reports are used only to view information.

● Forms are usually displayed on-screen. Reports can be previewed on the screen, but they are usually printed.

● Forms generally provide a detailed look at records and are usually for the people who actually work with the database. Reports are often used to group and summarize data, and are often for people who don't work with the database but who use the information stored in the database for other business tasks.

Reports usually present summaries of larger bodies of information. For example, your database might hold detailed information about thousands of orders. If you want to edit those orders or enter new ones, you can do so directly in the table or through a form. If you want to summarize those orders to illustrate the rate of growth of the company's sales, you generate a report.

Like a book report or an annual report of a company's activities, a report created in Microsoft Access 2010 is typically used to summarize and organize information to express a particular point of view to a specific audience. When you are designing a report, it is important to consider the point you are trying to make, the intended audience, and the level of information they will need.

In this chapter, you'll create a report by using a wizard. After modifying the layout and content of the report, you'll see how it will look when printed.

> **Practice Files** Before you can complete the exercises in this chapter, you need to copy the book's practice files to your computer. The practice file you'll use to complete the exercises in this chapter is in the Chapter05 practice file folder. A complete list of practice files is provided in "Using the Practice Files" at the beginning of this book.

Creating Reports by Using a Wizard

You can divide the content of an Access report into two general categories: information derived from records in one or more tables, and everything else. The *everything else* category includes the title, page headers and footers, introductory and explanatory text, and any logos and other graphics.

Just as you can create a form that includes all the fields in a table by using the Form tool, you can create a report that includes all the fields by using the Report tool, which is located in the Reports group on the Create tab. But such a report is merely a prettier version of the table, and it does not summarize the data in any meaningful way. You are more likely to want to create a report based on only some of the fields, and that is a job for the Report wizard.

Tip In addition to basing a report on a table, you can base it on the datasheet created when you run a query. For information about queries, see Chapter 8, "Create Queries."

The Report wizard leads you through a series of questions and then creates a report based on your answers. So the first step in creating a report is to consider the end result you want and what information you need to include in the report to achieve that result. After you provide that information, the wizard creates a simple report layout and adds a text box control and its associated label for each field you specify.

For example, you might want to use a Products table as the basis for a report that groups products by category. When you give the grouping instruction to the wizard, it first sorts the table based on the category, and then sorts the products in each category. In the space at the top of each group (called the group *header*), the wizard inserts the name of the category.

In this exercise, you'll use the Report wizard to create a simple report that displays an alphabetical list of products.

Canaryville Branch

642 W. 43rd Street, Chicago, IL 60609 ~ 312-747-0644

Thu	Fri	Sat
		1 Saturday's Kids Craft (Kids & Families) 11am-12pm
6 Computer Help 10:00-4:00pm Open Exploration Time (Ages 0-6) 10am-2pm Story Time & Craft (Ages 0-6) 11am-12pm	**7** Open Exploration Time (Ages 0-6) 10am-2pm Lil' Kids ArtSmart (Ages 1-6) 11am-12pm	**8**
13 Computer Help 10:00-4:00pm Open Exploration Time (Ages 0-6) 10am-2pm **Choose Kind Story Time & Elmer the Elephant Craft (Ages 0-6) 11am-12pm**	**14** Open Exploration Time (Ages 0-6) 10am-2pm	**15** Saturday's Kids Autumn Craft (Kids & Families) 11am-12pm
20 Computer Help 10:00-4:00pm Open Exploration Time (Ages 0-6) 10am-2pm Story Time & Craft (Ages 0-6) 11am-12pm	**21** Open Exploration Time (Ages 0-6) 10am-2pm	**22**
27 Computer Help 10:00-4:00pm Open Exploration Time (Ages 0-6) 10am-2pm **Read for the Record Story Time & Craft (Ages 0-6) 11am-12pm**	**28** Open Exploration Time (Ages 0-6) 10am-2pm	**29** Saturday's Kids: Spooky Spider Craft (Kids & Families) 11am-12pm

Chicago Public Library
Canaryville Branch

642 W. 43rd Street, Chgo, IL 60609
Phone: 312-747-0644

<u>Branch Hours:</u>
Mon & Wed   12-8 pm
Tues & Thurs 10-6 pm
Fri & Sat   9-5 pm

PROGRAMS FOR KIDS & FAMILIES

Open Exploration Time (Kids & Families)
Did you know Early Childhood research strongly
supports that free play is extremely important in a
child's intellectual and physical development? Every
Tuesday, Thursday and Friday we'll have blocks, Legos,
puzzles, puppets and other activities allowing families
time to read, discover and create together!

Story Time & Craft (Ages 0-6)
Join Ms. Jocelyn for stories, songs and a craft.
Come early or stay after for Open Exploration Time.

Lil' Kids ArtSmart (ages 1-6)
Ms. Shelley will have a fun, creative age-appropriate
art activity to engage your little one and build
creativity and motor skills. Older siblings welcome.

Fun & Games (All Ages)
Bored afterschool? Stop in to read, play a game,
color, make art or get on the computer with friends.

Saturday's Kids Craft (Kids & Families)
Returning books and picking up movies for the
weekend? Drop-in for a fun do-it-yourself craft.

Homework Help at the Library!

*See our certified teacher in the library for
homework help. No appointment necessary.*

Wednesdays 3:30-6:30 pm

PROGRAMS FOR TEENS

YOUmedia digital labs are a
following nearby locations:
Hall, Chinatown, Lozano, W
and Harold Washington Libr

PROGRAMS FOR ADULT

Computer Help (All Ages)
Our Cyber Navigator is available
Thursdays to assist with printing,
applications and other computer

Digital Learn Chicago Session
A few times a month we will offe
our Cyber Navigator to set up a *D*
account which allows you to take
12-22 minute online computer cla
available for each class you comp
personal headphones to participat

Adult Book Discussion (Ages 1
Join us for our active book club fo
of this year's One Book, One Chica
a staff member for a copy of the b

One Book, One
Book Discussion

*Animal, Vegetable, Mirac
A Year of Food Life* by
Barbara Kingsolver

Wednesday, October 26th
6:30-7:30 pm

*The author and her family vow
to only buy food raised in their
hood, grown themselves, or liv
Part memoir, part journalistic
<u>Animal, Vegetable, Miracle</u> is a
narrative opening your eyes to th
You are what you eat.*

October

able at the
k of the Yards,
son Regional
Center.

t Tuesdays and
ail, resumes, job
ated inquiries.

ges18+)
ecial sessions with
al Learn Chicago
multitude of free
s. Certificates are
e. *Please bring your

)
lively discussion
book. Please see
k.

Celebrate Diversity

On behalf of the Chicago Public Library and the Polish American Heritage Month Committee, we invite you to celebrate the achievements in the field of visual arts by artists of Polish descent. The Canaryville Branch will be exhibiting the art work of artist, Robin Dluzen, in our entry display case.

Robin Dluzen is a Chicago-based artist and art critic whose artwork has been featured in venues throughout the country. The former Editor-in-Chief of Chicago Art Magazine, Dluzen now writes regularly for Art Ltd Magazine, Visual Art Source and other publications. Dluzen received an MFA in Painting and Drawing from the School of the Art Institute of Chicago.

October is "Choose Kind Chicago" Month! Inspired by RJ Pacacio's Wonder, Choose Kind Chicago is a project that promotes acceptance and understanding of others. Please come in and share kind thoughts to create a paper "Kindness Chain" at our branch throughout the month of October.

Choose Kind Story Time & Elmer the Elephant Craft

Thursday, October 13th
11:00 am-12:00 pm

Chicago

:

e:

ed for one year
own neighbor-
e without it.
investigation,
enthralling
e old truth:

Need help on the computers?

Visit our Cyber Navigator! Stop in or call to make a one-on-one appointment.

Tuesdays: 10-4pm
Thursdays: 10-4pm

Sun	Mon	Tue	Wed

October

2 *Closed*	3 Fun & Games (All Ages) 3-6pm Afterschool Craft (All Ages) 4-5pm	4 Computer Help 10:00-4:00pm Open Exploration Time (Ages 0-6) 10am-2pm	5 Teacher in the Libra Homework Help 3:30--6:30pm
9 *Closed*	10 Fun & Games (All Ages) 3-6pm	11 Computer Help 10:00-4:00pm Open Exploration Time (Ages 0-6) 10am-2pm Digital Learn Session (Ages 18+) 2:00-3:00 pm	12 Teacher in the Libra Homework Help 3:30--6:30pm
16 *Closed*	17 Fun & Games (All Ages) 3-6pm Afterschool Craft (All Ages) 4-5pm	18 Computer Help 10:00-4:00pm Open Exploration Time (Ages 0-6) 10am-2pm	19 Teacher in the Libra Homework Help 3:30--6:30pm
23 *Closed*	24 Fun & Games (All Ages) 3-6pm	25 Computer Help 10:00-4:00pm Open Exploration Time (Ages 0-6) 10am-2pm Digital Learn Session (Ages 18+) 2:00-3:00 p..	26 Teacher in the Libra Homework Help 3:30--6:30pm **One Book. One Chi Adult Book Discuss** (Ages 18+) 6:30-7
30	31 Trick or Treat Bookmark Craft (Age 2-14) 3-6pm	Happy Halloween	

SET UP You need the GardenCompany05_start database located in your Chapter05 practice file folder to complete this exercise. Open the GardenCompany05_start database, and save it as *GardenCompany05*. Then follow the steps.

1. With **All Access Objects** displayed in the **Navigation** pane, under **Tables**, click (don't double-click) **Categories**.

2. On the **Create** tab, in the **Reports** group, click the **Report** button.

Access creates a report based on all the fields in the Categories table, displays the report in Layout view, and adds four Report Layout Tools contextual tabs to the ribbon.

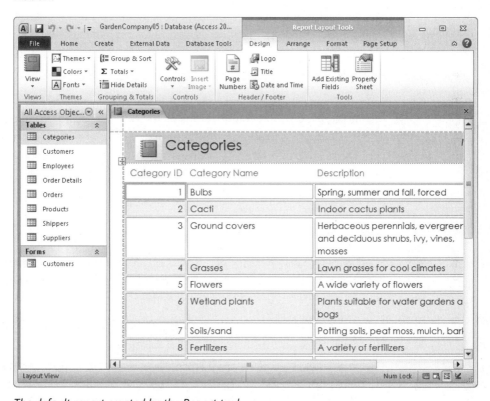

The default report created by the Report tool.

Troubleshooting The appearance of buttons and groups on the ribbon changes depending on the width of the program window. For information about changing the appearance of the ribbon to match our screen images, see "Modifying the Display of the Ribbon" at the beginning of this book.

3. This is not the report we want, so close the **Categories** report, clicking **No** when prompted to save it.

4. On the **Create** tab, in the **Reports** group, click the **Report Wizard** button.

   The Report wizard starts. Because the Categories table is still selected in the Navigation pane, that table is specified in the Tables/Queries box and its fields are listed in the Available Fields box.

5. Display the **Tables/Queries** list, and then click **Table: Products**.

   The Available Fields box now lists the fields in the Products table.

The first page of the Report wizard with the correct table selected.

6. In the **Available Fields** list, double-click **ProductName**, **QuantityPerUnit**, and **UnitsInStock** to move them to the **Selected Fields** box.

   Tip Fields appear in a report in the order in which they appear in the Selected Fields list. You can save yourself the effort of rearranging the fields in the report by entering them in the desired order in the wizard.

7. At the bottom of the page, click **Next**.

   The wizard asks whether you want to group the records. When you group by a field, the report inserts a group header at the top of each group of records that have the same value in that field.

8. In the field list on the left, double-click **ProductName**.

   In the preview pane on the right, the wizard moves ProductName into the group header area to show that records will be grouped by this field.

9. In the lower-left corner of the page, click **Grouping Options**.

   The Grouping Intervals dialog box opens.

You can refine the grouping specification in this dialog box.

10. Display the **Grouping intervals** list, click **1st Letter**, and then click **OK**.

    The group header now indicates the grouping interval you have assigned to the grouping field.

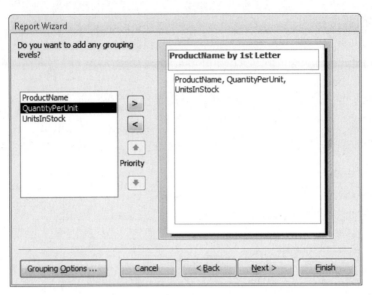

The types of grouping intervals available vary depending on the data type of the field by which you are grouping records.

11. Click **Next**.

The wizard asks how you want to sort and summarize the records.

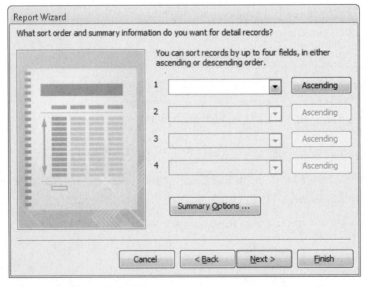

You can sort by up to four fields, each in ascending or descending order.

Tip For any field that contains numeric information, you can click Summary Options near the bottom of the wizard page to display the Summary Options dialog box, where you can instruct Access to insert a group footer in the report and to display the sum, average, minimum, or maximum value for the field. The only numeric field in this report is UnitsInStock, and it is not appropriate to summarize that field.

12. Click the arrow to the right of the **1** box to display a list of fields, and click **ProductName**. Then click **Next**.

   The wizard asks which of three layouts and which orientation you want for this report.

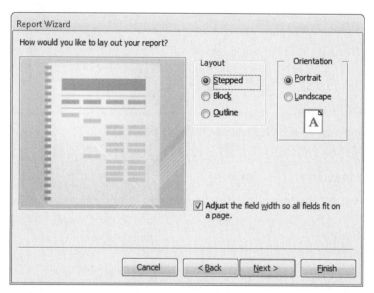

The preview on the left shows the effect of the options on the right.

13. In the **Layout** area, click each option in turn to see a preview in the report thumbnail to the left.

14. When you have finished exploring, click **Outline**.

15. With **Portrait** selected in the **Orientation** area and the **Adjust the field width so all fields fit on a page** check box selected, click **Next**.

   The wizard prompts you to supply a title for the report.

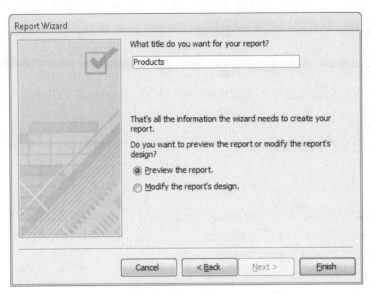

For ease of use, you should make the title more specific.

16. In the title box, type **Alphabetical List of Products**, and then with **Preview the report** selected, click **Finish**.

    Access creates the report and displays it in Print Preview.

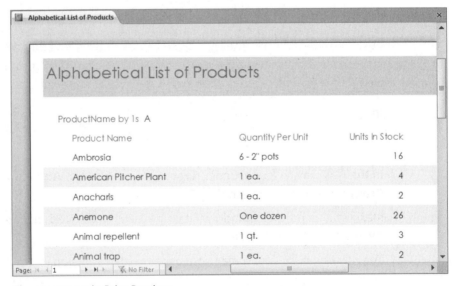

The new report in Print Preview.

17. Page through the nine-page report, noticing how it is arranged. Then close it.

 CLEAN UP Retain the GardenCompany05 database for use in later exercises.

Modifying Report Design

You can use the Report wizard to get a quick start on a report, but you will frequently want to modify the report to get the result you need. As with forms, the report consists of text box controls that are bound to the corresponding fields in the underlying table and their associated labels. You can add labels, text boxes, images, and other controls, and you can format them, either by using commands on the ribbon or by setting their properties in the report's Property Sheet.

Tip Property Sheets for reports work the same way as those for forms. For information, see "Changing the Look of Forms" in Chapter 3, "Create Simple Forms."

You can adjust the layout and content of reports in either Layout view or Design view. For simple adjustments, it is easier to work in Layout view, where you can see the layout with live data, making the process more intuitive.

See Also For information about creating and modifying reports in Design view, see Chapter 9, "Create Custom Reports."

Tip Automatic error checking identifies common errors in forms and reports and gives you a chance to fix them. For example, Access informs you if a report is wider than the page it will be printed on. Error checking is turned on by default. If you want to turn it off, display the Backstage view, and click Options to open the Access Options dialog box. In the left pane, click Object Designers, clear the error-checking check boxes at the bottom of the page, and then click OK.

In this exercise, you'll modify the layout of a report. You'll then apply a theme, change some of the colors, and dress up the text with character formatting. You will also apply a simple rule that formats values differently if they meet a specific criterion.

 SET UP You need the GardenCompany05 database you worked with in the preceding exercise to complete this exercise. Open the GardenCompany05 database, and then follow the steps.

1. In the **Navigation** pane, under **Reports**, right-click the **Alphabetical List of Products** report, and then click **Print Preview**.

2. Maximize the program window if it isn't already maximized, and then point to the previewed report page.

   The pointer changes to a magnifying glass with a plus sign in it.

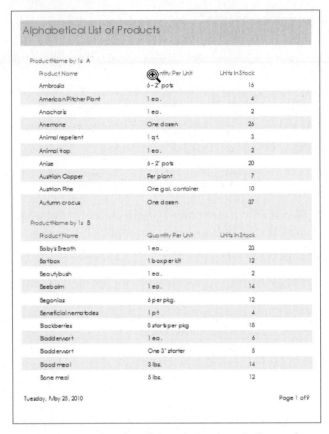

In Print Preview, the magnifying glass pointer indicates that you can zoom in on the page.

3. Click the previewed page once to zoom in.

   Tip You can also zoom in and out by dragging the Zoom slider in the lower-right corner of the program window. The current zoom level appears to the left of the slider.

   Notice that the report has the following design problems:

   ○ Extraneous text

   ○ Spacey arrangement

   ○ Uninviting formatting

   To fix these problems, we need to switch to Layout view.

4. On the **View Shortcuts** toolbar, click the **Layout View** button.

   Access adds four Report Layout Tools contextual tabs to the ribbon. First let's work with the group header controls.

5. On the **Design** contextual tab, in the **Grouping & Totals** group, click the **Hide Details** button.

   The controls that are bound to fields in the Products table are hidden so that you can concentrate on the group header controls.

6. Below the title, click **ProductName by 1s**, and press the Delete key.

   The label is removed from all the group headers.

7. Click the control containing **A**, and drag it to the left edge of the header.

   When you release the mouse button, all the corresponding controls move to the corresponding location in their own group headers.

   Keyboard Shortcut Hold down the Alt key and press the Arrow keys to move the selected control in small increments. When the shadow box is positioned where you want it, click away from the control.

   See Also For more information about keyboard shortcuts, see "Keyboard Shortcuts" at the end of this book.

8. Point to the right border of the selected **A** control, and when the pointer changes to a double-headed arrow, drag to the left until the control is just big enough to hold its contents.

   Again, all the corresponding controls assume the new size.

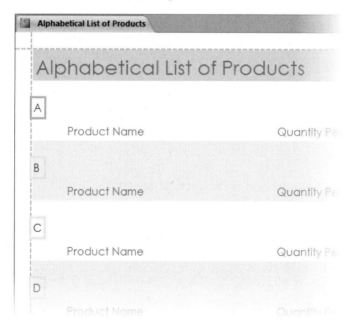

It is easier to work with the controls in the group header when the report details are hidden.

9. With the **A** control still selected, hold down the Shift key, and in turn, click the **Product Name**, **Quantity Per Unit**, and **Units In Stock** label controls to add them to the selection.

10. On the **Design** tab, in the **Tools** group, click the **Property Sheet** button.

   The Property Sheet opens.

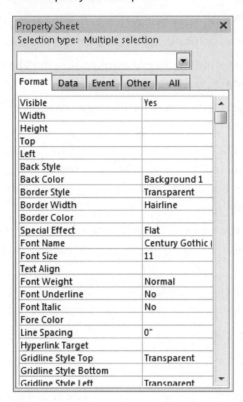

Because more than one control is selected, the Selection Type of this Property Sheet is Multiple Selection.

11. On the **Format** page of the **Property Sheet**, in the **Top** property box, type **0.25″**, and press Enter. Then close the **Property Sheet**.

   In the group header, the letter control and label controls are now aligned 0.25 inch from the top of the header, and the height of the header has decreased because less space is needed to accommodate the controls.

Now let's see how the group header looks with its data.

12. In the **Grouping & Totals** group, click the **Hide Details** button to turn it off and display the data from the table.

The numbers in the Units In Stock column are right-aligned. Let's center them.

13. Click the first text box control under the **Units In Stock** label, and on the **Format** contextual tab, in the **Font** group, click the **Center** button.

Now we'll add some color and format the text.

14. On the **Design** contextual tab, in the **Themes** group, click the **Themes** button, and in the gallery, click the **Austin** thumbnail.

Although nothing much appears to change, the report takes on the color scheme and font scheme assigned to the selected theme.

15. Inside the shaded area of the report header, but away from the title, click a blank area. On the **Format** contextual tab, in the **Control Formatting** group, click the **Shape Fill** button. Then under **Theme Colors** in the palette, click the third box (**Light Green, Background 2**).

Notice that by default, a row color has been applied to alternate group headers and that this coloring confuses rather than clarifies the report structure. Let's turn off this alternate row color.

16. Click outside the dotted border to the left of the first group header. In the **Background** group, click the **Alternate Row Color** arrow, and at the bottom of the palette, click **No Color**.

17. In the **Control Formatting** group, click the **Shape Fill** button, and in the palette, click a light brown color.

The entire group header is shaded except the alphabet controls (A, B, C, and so on) that you moved earlier. If you wanted to shade them as well, you could select one of them and repeat step 17 to apply the light brown fill.

18. Click outside the dotted border to the left of the first row of data in the report, and remove the alternate row color of the data rows. Then click the white space above the report header to see the result.

Only the backgrounds of the report header and group headers are now colored.

Alphabetical List of Products

A	Product Name	Quantity Per Unit	Units Ir
	Ambrosia	6 - 2" pots	1
	American Pitcher Plant	1 ea.	4
	Anacharis	1 ea.	2
	Anemone	One dozen	2
	Animal repellent	1 qt.	3
	Animal trap	1 ea.	2
	Anise	6 - 2" pots	2
	Austrian Copper	Per plant	7
	Austrian Pine	One gal. container	1

Removing the alternate row color makes the structure of this report more obvious.

Tip Above the first object and below the last object of a report in Layout view are the only places you can click that don't select at least one object on the report.

19. Click any control, and then in the **Selection** group, click the **Select All** button.

    Keyboard Shortcut Press Ctrl+A to select all the controls.

20. In the **Font** group, click the **Font Size** arrow, and then click **9**.

    Tip It is usually most efficient to change the character formatting of all the controls and then adjust the ones you want to be different.

21. Click the report's title control, and then use the commands in the **Font** group to make the text 24 points, bold, and dark green.

22. Select the controls in the group header, and make them bold and dark green.

23. Scroll down the report, noticing that a few of the values in the **Units In Stock** column are 0.

    We want these values to stand out in the report to remind buyers that it is time to order more of these products.

24. Click any control in the **Units In Stock** column. Then in the **Control Formatting** group, click the **Conditional Formatting** button.

    The Conditional Formatting Rules Manager dialog box opens.

25. Click **New Rule**.

The New Formatting Rule dialog box opens.

You can create rules that compare the current field value to a specific value or to other values in the same field.

26. With **Check values in the current record or use an expression** selected as the rule type, in the **Format only cells where the** area, click the arrow for the second box, and click **less than**. Then in the third box, type **1**.

27. In the bottom area, click the **Bold** button, and change the **Font color** setting to red. Then click **OK**.

In the Conditional Formatting Rules Manager dialog box, the rule is listed in the Rule column with the formatting that will be applied to values that meet the rule's criteria in the Format column.

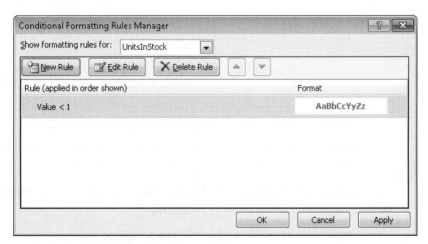

Values that are less than 1 will be bold and red.

28. Click **OK**. Then scroll down the report again, noticing that all the 0 values are now bold and red.

29. Close the report, clicking **Yes** to save your changes to its design.

 CLEAN UP Retain the GardenCompany05 database for use in the last exercise.

Previewing and Printing Reports

Using Print Preview to preview Access reports is very similar to using this view in other Microsoft Office 2010 programs. If you preview your reports carefully, you won't have any major surprises when you print them.

When previewing reports, you will want to pay special attention to how the pages break. In a grouped report, you can control whether group headings are allowed to appear at the bottom of a page with no data and whether groups are allowed to break across pages.

You can make changes to the setup of your report pages from the Page Setup contextual tab in Layout view or from the tab displayed when you switch to Print Preview. For example, you can specify the following:

- Paper size
- Margins
- Orientation
- Number of columns
- Whether Access should print the report's structural elements or only its data

You can also click the Page Setup button to display the Page Setup dialog box, where you can change all these settings in one place, as well as make additional refinements.

When you are ready to print, you click the Print button on the Print Preview tab of the ribbon to display the Print dialog box. You can also display the Print page of the Backstage view and then print one copy of the report with the default print settings by clicking the Quick Print button.

In this exercise, you'll preview a report, and you'll specify that groups should not break across pages. Then you'll explore the available page setup and printing options.

 **SET UP** You need the GardenCompany05 database you worked with in the preceding exercise to complete this exercise. Open the GardenCompany05 database, and then follow the steps.

1. In the **Navigation** pane, right click the **Alphabetical List of Products** report, and then click **Print Preview.**

Only the Print Preview tab appears on the ribbon.

2. On the page navigation bar at the bottom of the window, click the **Next Page** button repeatedly to view each page of this report.

    Because of the changes you made to the report in the previous exercise, the report is now six pages. Several of the groups start on one page and continue on the next page. For readability, let's fix this layout problem.

The group at the top of this page is a continuation of one that started on the previous page.

3. Switch to Layout view, and then on the **Design** tab, in the **Grouping & Totals** group, click the **Group & Sort** button.

    The Group, Sort, And Total pane opens at the bottom of the report page.

You can use this pane to quickly add grouping and sorting levels and set related properties.

4. In the **Group, Sort, and Total** pane, in the **Group on ProductName** bar, click **More**.

Access displays additional options.

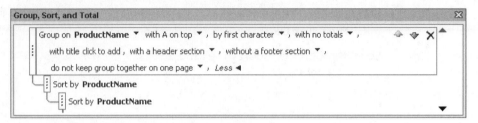

These are the current grouping settings.

5. Click the **do not keep group together on one page** arrow, and in the list, click **keep whole group together on one page**. Then close the **Group, Sort, and Total** pane by clicking the **Group & Sort** button again.

6. Switch to Print Preview, and page through the report.

   Now none of the groups is broken across pages. However, the report would look better with wider top, left, and right margins.

7. On the **Print Preview** tab, in the **Page Layout** group, click the **Page Setup** button.

   The Page Setup dialog box opens.

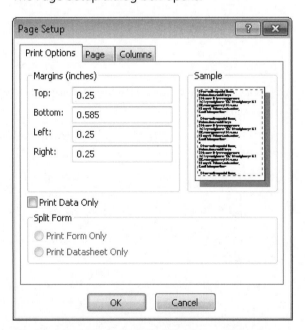

The Print Options page of the Page Setup dialog box.

8. Click the **Page** tab, and verify that the paper size is **Letter**.

9. Return to the **Print Options** page, and change the **Top**, **Left**, and **Right** margins to **0.75**. Then click **OK**.

10. Scroll through the report to see the results.

    Although all the data in the report fits on the page, the page number in the footer is set too far to the right and is producing extra pages.

11. Switch to Layout view, scroll down to the bottom of the report, and then scroll to the right until you can see the page number.

12. Click the page number control, and move and resize it so that it aligns approximately with the **Units In Stock** column heading.

13. Switch to Print Preview, and page through the report.

    The report now fits neatly on seven pages.

14. If you want, print the report by using the same techniques you would use to print any database object.

15. Close the report, clicking **Yes** to save your changes.

 **CLEAN UP** Close the GardenCompany05 database.

Key Points

-   When designing a report, consider the point you are trying to make, the intended audience, and the level of detail needed.

-   You can create a report that displays only some of the fields in a table by using the Report wizard. The report can be sorted and grouped to summarize the data in a table in a meaningful way.

-   You can refine a report in Layout view by manipulating its controls and setting its properties. You can also format the controls to structure and highlight data.

-   In Print Preview, you can see how the report will look when printed and make adjustments before you print.

Part 2

Relational Database Techniques

Chapter at a Glance

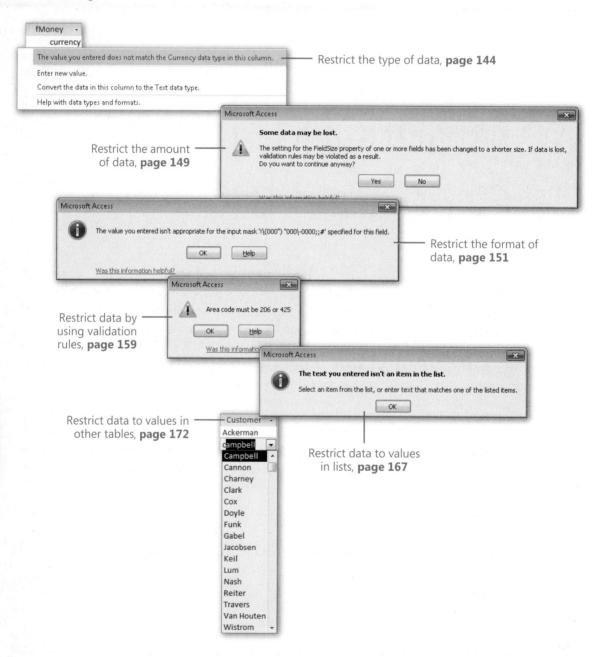

Restrict the type of data, **page 144**

Restrict the amount of data, **page 149**

Restrict the format of data, **page 151**

Restrict data by using validation rules, **page 159**

Restrict data to values in other tables, **page 172**

Restrict data to values in lists, **page 167**

6 Maintain Data Integrity

In this chapter, you will learn how to

✔ Restrict the type of data.

✔ Restrict the amount of data.

✔ Restrict the format of data.

✔ Restrict data by using validation rules.

✔ Restrict data to values in lists.

✔ Restrict data to values in other tables.

Depending on how organized you are, you might compare a database to a cardboard box or to a file cabinet, into which you toss items such as bills, receipts, statements, and a variety of other paperwork for later retrieval. The box or file cabinet does not restrict what items you can place in it (unless they are simply too big to physically fit) or impose any order on the items. It is up to you to decide what you store there and to organize it so that you can find it the next time you need it.

When you create a database by using Microsoft Access 2010, you can set properties that restrict what data can be entered and you can impose a structure on the data to help you keep the database organized and useful. For example, you can prevent employees from entering text in a Price field, and you can require a simple "yes" or "no" answer in a Signature Required field.

In this chapter, you'll restrict the type, amount, and format of data allowed in a field. You'll create validation rules that accept only data that meets specific criteria. You'll also use lookup lists and lookup fields to limit the possible values allowed in a field.

> **Practice Files** Before you can complete the exercises in this chapter, you need to copy the book's practice files to your computer. The practice file you'll use to complete the exercises in this chapter is in the Chapter06 practice file folder. A complete list of practice files is provided in "Using the Practice Files" at the beginning of this book.

Restricting the Type of Data

You learned in Chapter 2, "Create Databases and Simple Tables," that a field's data type restricts entries in that field to a specific type of data. For example, if the data type is set to Number and you try to enter text, Access refuses the entry and displays a warning.

When setting the data type of a field in a table in Design view, you can choose from the following types:

- **Text** Use for text fields that require up to 255 alphanumeric characters.

- **Memo** Use for text fields that require up to 65,535 alphanumeric characters.

- **Number** Use for numeric values. The size of the entry is controlled by the Field Size property.

  See Also For information about the possible Field Size settings for Number fields, see "Restricting the Amount of Data" later in this chapter.

- **Date/Time** Use for dates from January 2, 100 through December 31, 9999. Dates and times can be expressed in a variety of formats.

- **Currency** Use for decimal values with up to 15 digits to the left of the decimal point and up to 4 digits to the right.

- **AutoNumber** Use when you want Access to assign a unique number to each new record. If you delete a record, its AutoNumber value is not reused, and remaining records are not updated.

- **Yes/No** Use for fields that can have only two possible mutually exclusive values, such as True or False.

  Tip In the database world, the Yes/No data type is more commonly called *Boolean*, in honor of George Boole, an early mathematician and logistician.

- **OLE Object** Use to hold a graphic or other object. The object can be linked or embedded.

- **Hyperlink** Use to hold a clickable path to a folder on your hard disk, a network location, or a Web site.

- **Attachment** Use to attach a file to a record in the same way that you might attach a file to an e-mail message.

Tip The Attachment data type can be assigned to a field only when the field is first created. You can't assign the Attachment type to an existing field, nor can you change an Attachment field to another data type. For information about the Attachment data type, search for *Attach files and graphics to the records in your database* in Access Help.

● **Calculated** Use to hold the results of a calculation based on other fields in the same table.

See Also For information about Lookup Wizard (the last option in the list displayed when you click the Data Type arrow in Design view), see "Restricting Data to Values in Lists" later in this chapter.

When adding a field in Datasheet view, you can choose what seems to be an additional data type:

● **Rich Text** Use for text fields that require up to 65,535 alphanumeric characters with character formatting.

This is actually the Memo data type with the Text Format property set to Rich Text instead of Plain Text.

You can also click the More Fields button in the Add & Delete group on the Fields contextual tab to display a gallery of data types with predefined properties that produce fields with common data type refinements.

In this exercise, you'll use various methods to add fields of the most common data types to a table. Then you'll enter data to test the data type restrictions.

SET UP You need the GardenCompany06_start database located in your Chapter06 practice file folder to complete this exercise. Open the GardenCompany06_start database, and save it as *GardenCompany06*. Then follow the steps.

Table

1. On the **Create** tab, in the **Tables** group, click the **Table** button.

   Access opens a new blank table. As is normal with new tables, Access has automatically generated an ID field that has been assigned the AutoNumber data type.

Text

2. On the **Fields** contextual tab, in the **Add & Delete** group, click the **Text** button. Then change the selected field name to **fText**.

   If you use the name of a data type as the name of a field, Access warns you that the name might cause problems. We will identify all the fields in this table by their data type, preceded by the letter *f*.

3. Display the **Click to Add** list, click **Currency**, and then change the field name to **fMoney**.

4. In the **Add & Delete** group, click the **More Fields** button.

A gallery of data types, some with refinements, appears.

Clicking an option in the list sets the data type and any predefined property settings.

5. In the gallery, under **Number**, click **Standard**. Then change the field name to **fNumber**.

6. Display the **More Fields** gallery, click **Medium Date** under **Date and Time**, and change the field name to **fDate**. Then display the gallery again, click **Check Box** under **Yes/No**, and name the field **fBoolean**.

The table now has six fields.

Clicking the check box in the fBoolean field will indicate a Yes or True entry.

7. Save the table with the name **FieldTest**, and then switch to Design view.

   Keyboard Shortcut Press Ctrl+S to display the Save As dialog box.

   See Also For more information about keyboard shortcuts, see "Keyboard Shortcuts" at the end of this book.

8. In turn, click each field in the list at the top of the design page, noticing the setting in the **Data Type** column and the property settings in the **Field Properties** area.

   Only the properties that you can set for each type of field are displayed. For the fNumber, fMoney, and fDate fields, the Format property reflects the choice you made when creating the field.

9. Switch back to Datasheet view. Then in the **fText** cell, type **This entry is 32 characters long**.

10. In the **fMoney** field, type the word **currency**, and press Tab.

    Access tells you that it cannot accept the unexpected type of data.

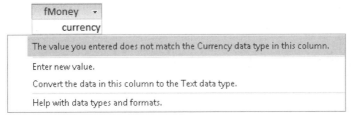

Options for correcting the erroneous entry.

11. In the list, click **Enter new value**. Then type **–45.3456**, and press Tab.

    Access stores the number the way you entered it but displays ($45.35), the default format for negative currency numbers.

    Tip Access uses the region and language settings in Windows Control Panel to determine the display format for date, time, currency, and other numbers. So although the numbers won't change, your currency symbol might be different; for example, Access might display the pound, peso, or euro symbol. If you want the symbol to remain the same no matter what the region and language settings, you can create a custom format to ensure that currency values always display a specific symbol. For information about custom formats, see the sidebar "Creating Custom Formats" later in this chapter.

12. In the **fNumber** cell, type **Five hundred**, and then press Tab.

    Again, Access tells you that it cannot accept this type of entry in this field.

13. In the list of options, click **Enter new value**, type **500**, and press Tab.

14. In the **fDate** cell, type **123456**, and press Tab. When Access prompts for the correct type of entry, click **Enter new value**, click the **Calendar** button to the right of the field, and click **Today** to insert today's date. Then press Tab.

    All Date/Time fields come with an associated interactive calendar. Using the Calendar button to insert a date works well if the date you want is close to the current date. (You can click the arrows at either end of the title bar to display the previous or next month.) However, for distant dates such as birthdates, it is easier to ignore the Calendar button and type the date. Access accepts almost any entry that can be recognized as a date and displays it in the format you specified when you created the field.

    Tip If you enter a month and day but no year in a date field, Access assumes the date is in the current year. If you enter a month, day, and two-digit year from 00 through 29, Access assumes the year is 2000 through 2029. If you enter a two-digit year that is greater than 29, Access assumes you mean 1930 through 1999.

15. In the **fBoolean** field, try to enter **abc** and **123**. Then click several times anywhere in the field to toggle the check box between the checked and not checked states, finishing with the field in the checked state.

    This field won't accept anything you type; you can only switch between two predefined values.

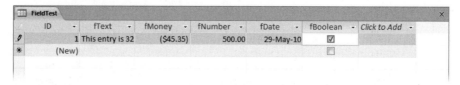

The table, with the correct type of data in each field.

Tip The stored value of a Yes/No field is always either 1 (Yes) or 0 (No). On the General page of the Field Properties area in Design view, you can set the Format property of the field to interpret the stored value as True/False, Yes/No, or On/Off. On the Lookup page, you can set the field to display as a check box, text box, or combo box. (In a combo box, you can select from a list or type an entry.)

 CLEAN UP Save the FieldTest table, and then close it. Retain the GardenCompany06 database for use in later exercises.

Restricting the Amount of Data

In Chapter 2, "Create Databases and Simple Tables," you changed the Field Size property of several Text fields. You entered the new sizes by making adjustments to the Field Size setting in the Properties group on the Fields tab and to the Field Size property in the Field Properties area in Design view. As you saw, changing the size of a Text field is a simple matter of estimating the largest number of characters you will need to type in the field, up to 255.

Like the Text data type, the AutoNumber and Number data types have an associated Field Size property that restricts the number of digits that can be entered in the field. Of the two, the Field Size property of the Number data type is the most complex. You can set Number fields to any of the settings shown in the following table.

Setting	Description
Byte	Whole numbers from 0 to 255
Integer	Whole numbers from −32,768 to 32,767
Long Integer	Whole numbers from −2,147,483,648 to 2,147,483,647 (the default)
Single	Negative numbers from −3.402823E38 to −1.401298E−45 and positive numbers from 1.401298E−45 to 3.402823E38
Double	Negative numbers from −1.79769313486231E308 to −4.94065645841247E−324 and positive numbers from 1.79769313486231E308 to 4.94065645841247E−324
Replication ID	Randomly generated numbers that are 16 bytes long
Decimal	Numbers from -10^28 -1 through 10^28 -1

The Field Size property of AutoNumber fields can be set to either Long Integer (the default) or Replication ID.

By setting the Field Size property to the setting that allows the largest valid entry, you prevent the entry of invalid values. Access rejects any value that is below or above the size limits of the field when you try to move out of the field.

See Also For more information about data restrictions, search for *Introduction to data types and field properties* in Access Help.

In this exercise, you'll change the Field Size property for two fields to see the impact on data already in the table and on new data that you enter.

SET UP You need the GardenCompany06 database you worked with in the preceding exercise to complete this exercise. Open the GardenCompany06 database, and display the FieldTest table in Datasheet view. Then follow the steps.

1. Review the field values in the only record in the **FieldTest** table.

2. Switch to Design view, click anywhere in the **fText** row, and then in the **Field Properties** area, change the **Field Size** property from **255** to **18**.

   Access will now restrict the number of characters that can be entered in the fText field to 18.

3. Click any cell in the **fNumber** row, click anywhere in the **Field Size** property, click the arrow that appears, and then in the list, click **Byte**.

   Access will restrict the values that can be entered in the fNumber field to the range 0 through 255 (inclusive).

4. Switch to Datasheet view, clicking **Yes** when prompted to save the table.

   Access displays a warning that some data might be lost.

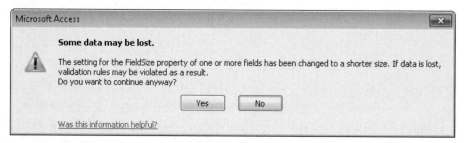

The table contains data that doesn't fit the new property settings.

5. Click **Yes** to acknowledge the risk, and click **Yes** again to accept the deletion of the contents of one field.

6. Double-click the right border of the **fText** field to widen the column to fit its entry.

   You can now see the impact of the field size changes on the fields.

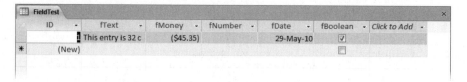

The fText value has been truncated, and the fNumber value has been deleted.

You entered 32 characters in the fText field, and it can now hold only 18. So 14 characters have been permanently deleted. You entered 500 in the fNumber field, and it can now hold only whole numbers from 0 through 255. So the value has been permanently deleted.

7. In the **fNumber** field, type **2.5**, and press Tab.

Access rounds the value you entered to the nearest whole number.

 **CLEAN UP** Close the FieldTest table, saving your changes. Retain the GardenCompany06 database for use in later exercises.

Restricting the Format of Data

Two properties control the format of information in database tables: the Format property and the Input Mask property. Both properties affect how information is displayed after it has been entered in a table, but the Input Mask property also serves an important function during data entry. As its name implies, an input mask allows anyone entering new records to see at a glance the format required and how long the entry should be.

See Also For information about the Format property, see the sidebar "Creating Custom Formats" later in this chapter.

You can use the Input Mask property to control how data is entered in Text, Number, Date/Time, and Currency fields. For Text and Date/Time fields, an Input Mask wizard is available to help you apply several common, predefined masks. For Number and Currency fields, you have to know how to create a mask from scratch.

The Input Mask property has three sections, separated by semicolons. For example, the following mask is for a telephone number:

!\(000") "000\-0000;1;#

The first section contains characters that are used as placeholders for the information to be typed, as well as characters such as parentheses and hyphens. Together, all these characters control the appearance of the entry. The following table explains the purpose of the most common input mask characters.

Character	Description
0	Required digit (0 through 9).
9	Optional digit or space.
#	Optional digit or space; blank positions are converted to spaces; plus and minus signs are allowed.
L	Required letter (A through Z).
?	Optional letter (A through Z).
A	Required letter or digit.
a	Optional letter or digit.
&	Required character (any kind) or a space.
C	Optional character (any kind) or a space.
<	All characters that follow are converted to lowercase.
>	All characters that follow are converted to uppercase.
!	Characters typed into the mask fill it from left to right. You can include the exclamation point anywhere in the input mask.
\	Character that follows is displayed as a literal character.
"any text"	Characters enclosed in double quotation marks are treated as literal characters.
Password	Creates a password entry box. Any character typed in the box is stored as the character but displayed as an asterisk (*).

Any characters not included in this list are displayed the way you type them and are known as *literal characters*. If you want to use one of the special characters in this list as a literal character, precede it with the \ (backslash) character.

The second and third sections of the input mask are optional. Including a 1 in the second section (or leaving it blank) tells Access to store only the characters entered; including a 0 tells it to store both the characters entered and the literal characters. Entering a character in the third section causes Access to display that character as the placeholder for each of the characters to be typed; leaving it blank causes Access to display an underscore as the placeholder.

The input mask *!\(000") "000\-0000;1;#* creates this display in a field in either a table or a form:

(###) ###-####

In this example, the 0s in the first part of the mask restrict the entry to 10 digits—no more and no less. The database user does not enter the literal characters—the parentheses, space, and hyphen. The 1 in the second part tells Access not to store the literal characters; it should store only the 10 digits. The # sign in the third part tells Access to use that character as the placeholder for the required 10 digits.

Tip An input mask can contain text as well as placeholders for the data to be entered. For example, if you type *The number is* in front of the telephone number input mask, the default entry for the field is *The number is (###) ###-####*. The numbers you type still replace the # placeholders, not the text. The Field Size property does not apply to the literal characters in the mask, so if this property is set to 15, the entry will not be truncated even though the number of displayed characters (including spaces) is 28.

In this exercise, you'll use the Input Mask wizard to apply a predefined input mask for a telephone number to a Text field. Then you'll modify the input mask to display the telephone number in a slightly different way. Finally, in another field you'll create a custom mask that displays a text entry with an initial capital letter, no matter how it is actually typed.

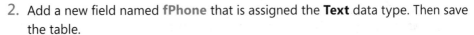

SET UP You need the GardenCompany06 database you worked with in the preceding exercise to complete this exercise. Open the GardenCompany06 database, and display the FieldTest table in Design view. Then follow the steps.

1. Click the row selector for the **fText** field, and on the **Design** contextual tab, in the **Tools** group, click the **Insert Rows** button.

2. Add a new field named **fPhone** that is assigned the **Text** data type. Then save the table.

3. With the **fPhone** field still selected, in the **Field Properties** area, click anywhere in the **Input Mask** property.

4. Click the **Ellipsis** button to the right of the property, and save the table when prompted.

    The Input Mask wizard displays its first page.

You can click the Try It box to see how the mask will look and then type a number to see how the mask behaves.

5. With **Phone Number** selected in the **Input Mask** list, click **Next**.

   The second page of the wizard is displayed.

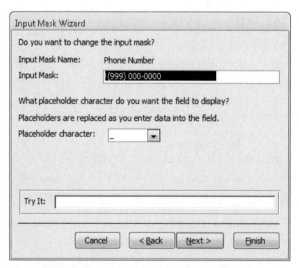

You can change the structure of the input mask and the placeholder character that will indicate what to type.

The barely visible exclamation point at the left end of the mask causes Access to fill the mask from left to right with whatever is typed. The parentheses and hyphen are characters that Access will insert in the specified places. The nines represent optional digits, and the zeros represent required digits. This allows you to enter a telephone number either with or without an area code.

Tip Because Access fills the mask from left to right, you would have to press the Right Arrow key to move the insertion point past the first three placeholders to enter a telephone number without an area code.

6. Change **999** to **000** to require an area code. Then display the **Placeholder character** list, click **#**, and click **Next**.

On the third page of the wizard, you specify whether you want to store the symbols with the data. (The symbols take up space, meaning that your database will be larger.)

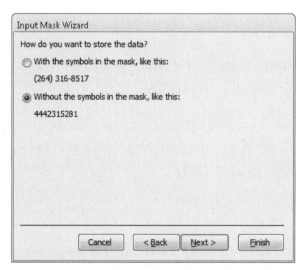

If you store the symbols, they will always be included when the data is displayed in tables, forms, and reports.

7. Accept the default selection—to store the data without the symbols—by clicking **Finish**.

(Clicking Next simply displays a page announcing that the wizard has all the information it needs to create the mask.) Access closes the wizard.

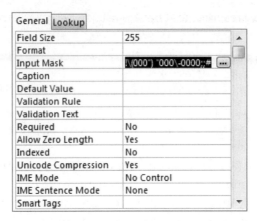

The edited mask is inserted into the Input Mask property.

8. Press Enter to accept the mask.

   Access changes the format of the mask to *!\(000") "000\-0000;;#*. Notice the two semicolons that separate the mask into its three sections. Because you told Access to store data without the symbols, nothing is displayed in the second section of the mask. Notice also that Access added double quotation marks to ensure that the closing parenthesis and following space are treated as literal characters.

9. Save the table, and then switch to Datasheet view.

10. Click the **ID** field in the first record, and press the Tab key to move to the **fPhone** field. Then type a series of numbers to see how the mask works.

    Access formats the first 10 numbers you enter as a telephone number. If you type more than 10, Access ignores the additional digits. If you type fewer than 10 and then press Tab or Enter, Access warns that your entry doesn't match the input mask.

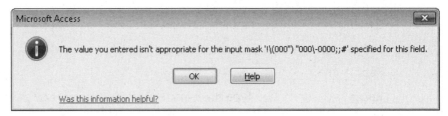

The input mask requires 10, and only 10, digits.

   Now let's see how an input mask can be used to control the display of data entries.

11. Switch to Design view, and click anywhere in the **fText** field.

12. In the **Field Properties** area, click the **Input Mask** property, type the following, and then press Enter:

    >L<???????????????? (16 question marks)

    Tip When you press Enter, the Property Update Options button appears. Clicking this button displays a list of options. In this case, the only options are to apply the input mask everywhere fText is used (which is called *propagating the property*), and to display Access Help to find out more about this task. This button disappears when you edit any other property or change to a different field, so you can ignore it.

    The greater than symbol (>) forces all following text to be uppercase. The *L* requires a letter. The less than symbol (<) forces all following text to be lowercase. Each question mark allows any letter or no letter. The total number of characters (17) is one fewer than the maximum number allowed in the field by this field's Field Size property.

General	Lookup
Field Size	18
Format	
Input Mask	>L<????????????????
Caption	
Default Value	
Validation Rule	
Validation Text	
Required	No
Allow Zero Length	Yes
Indexed	No
Unicode Compression	Yes
IME Mode	No Control
IME Sentence Mode	None
Smart Tags	

The Field Size setting must be greater than the maximum number of characters allowed by the mask.

13. Save your changes to the table, and switch back to Datasheet view.

14. Delete the current entry in the **fText** field, type **smith**, and press Tab.

15. Replace the entry with **SMITH**, and then **McDonald**.

    Regardless of how you type the name, only its first letter is capitalized.

    Tip You can create custom input masks and have the Input Mask wizard store them for future use. On the wizard's first page, click Edit List, and in the record navigation bar of the Customize Input Mask Wizard dialog box, click the New Record button. Then enter the information for the custom mask, and click Close.

 CLEAN UP Close the FieldTest table. Retain the GardenCompany06 database for use in later exercises.

Creating Custom Formats

You can construct custom Format properties to control the display of Text fields in much the same way you construct input masks. The following table describes the characters that are available.

Character	Description
@	Required character (can be blank).
&	Optional character.
!	Characters typed into the placeholder string fill it from left to right. You can include the exclamation point anywhere in the string.
<	All characters that follow are converted to lowercase.
>	All characters that follow are converted to uppercase.
*	Character that follows becomes a fill character.
\	Character that follows is displayed as a literal character.
"any text"	Characters enclosed in double quotation marks are treated as literal characters.
[color]	Applies a color to all characters in a section of the format. Can be black, blue, cyan, magenta, red, yellow, or white.

Tip Blank spaces; plus (+), minus (-), and financial symbols ($, £, ¥); and parentheses are recognized as literal characters without double quotation marks.

To build a custom format:

1. With the table open in Design view, select the field you want to apply the custom format to.

2. In the Field Properties pane, in the Format box, type the format.

3. Switch to Datasheet view, saving the table.

Any existing data will be displayed according to the format. New data you enter will conform to the format when you leave the field. As an example, consider the following format:

@".com";"no link"[red]

This format specifies two customizations separated by a semicolon. The part before the semicolon specifies what Access should do if characters are entered—in this case, append .com; and the part after the semicolon specifies what Access should do if the field is empty—in this case, display *no link* in red.

Restricting Data by Using Validation Rules

A validation rule precisely defines the information that will be accepted in one or several fields in a record. You might use a validation rule in a field containing the date an employee was hired to prevent a date in the future from being entered. Or if you deliver orders to only certain local areas, you could use a validation rule on the postal code field to refuse entries from other areas. You can create validation rules for all data types except AutoNumber, OLE Object, and Attachment.

You can create validation rules for individual fields or for entire records:

- **Field validation** At this level, Access uses the validation rule to test an entry when you attempt to leave the field.

- **Record validation** At this level, Access uses the rule to test the contents of more than one field when you attempt to leave the record.

If a field or record doesn't satisfy the rule, Access rejects the entry and displays a message explaining why.

You create a validation rule by building an expression. In Access jargon, the term *expression* is synonymous with *formula*. It is a combination of operators, constants, functions, and identifiers that evaluates to a single value. Access builds a formula in the format $a=b+c$, where a is the result and $=b+c$ is the expression.

Tip In addition to using expressions as validation rules, you can use them to assign properties to tables or forms, to determine values in fields or reports, to define a set of conditions that a record must meet to be included in the result of a query, and so on. For information about queries, see Chapter 8, "Create Queries."

The expression you use in a validation rule combines multiple criteria to define a set of conditions that a value in a field must meet in order to be a valid entry for that field. Multiple criteria are combined using logical, comparison, and arithmetic operators. Different types of expressions use different operators. The following are the most common operators:

- Logical operators
  - **And** This operator selects records that meet all the specified criteria.
  - **Or** This operator selects records that meet at least one of the criteria.
  - **Not** This operator selects records that don't match the criteria.
- Comparison operators
  - < Less than
  - > Greater than
  - = Equal to

You can combine these basic operators to form the following:

- ○ **<=** Less than or equal to
- ○ **>=** Greater than or equal to
- ○ **<>** Not equal to

The Like operator is sometimes grouped with the comparison operators and is used to test whether or not text matches a pattern.

- ● Arithmetic operators
  - ○ **+** Add
  - ○ **-** Subtract
  - ○ ***** Multiply
  - ○ **/** Divide

A related operator, & (a text form of +) is used to concatenate (combine) two text strings.

You can type validation rules in the Validation Rule property box by hand, or you can use a tool called the *Expression Builder* to create them. The Expression Builder isn't a wizard; it doesn't lead you through the process of building an expression. It provides a hierarchical list of the most common elements that you can include in an expression and an expression box to build the expression in. You open the Expression Builder dialog box by clicking the Validation button in the Field Validation group on the Fields contextual tab, and then clicking either Field Validation Rule or Record Validation Rule. In the dialog box, you can either select functions, operators, and other elements from the list to copy them into the expression box, or you can type the expression in the expression box.

To explain a validation rule to users, you can create a message that appears if someone tries to enter an invalid value in a field. A well-crafted message tells users what data is expected in the field and what format it should be entered in. For example, the message *Please enter a whole number between 1 and 99* is more useful than *Invalid entry*.

In this exercise, you'll create and test a field validation rule and a record validation rule.

SET UP You need the GardenCompany06 database you worked with in the preceding exercise to complete this exercise. Open the GardenCompany06 database, and display the FieldTest table in Datasheet view. Then follow the steps.

1. Click the **fPhone** field value, and replace the current entry with **6785550101**, allowing the mask to format the entry for you.

2. Click anywhere in the **fPhone** field, and on the **Fields** contextual tab, in the **Field Validation** group, click the **Validation** button.

A list of options appears.

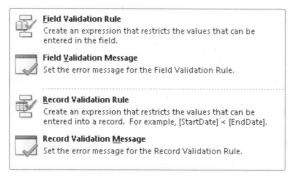

The Validation options.

3. Click **Field Validation Rule**.

The Expression Builder dialog box opens.

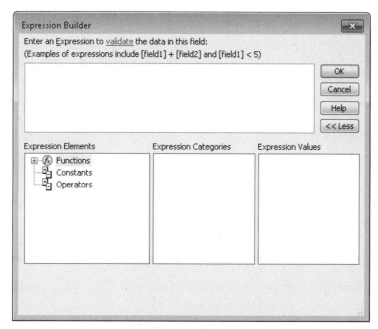

You build your expression in the box at the top of the dialog box.

Let's specify that only phone numbers in the 206 or 425 area codes can be accepted in the fPhone field.

4. In the **Expression Elements** list, click **Operators**; in the **Expression Categories** list, click **Comparison**; and in the **Expression Values** list, double-click **Like**.

The Like comparison operator is transferred to the expression box.

5. In the expression box, type **"206*"** (including the quotation marks and the asterisk). Then type a space.

   Troubleshooting Be sure to include the asterisk after 206. This wildcard tells Access to allow any number of characters after the area code. It is necessary because the fPhone field contains the phone number as well as the area code. For information about wildcards, see the sidebar "Wildcards" in Chapter 4, "Display Data."

6. In the **Expression Categories** list, click **Logical**, and in the **Expression Values** list, double-click **Or**.

   The Or logical operator is transferred to the expression box.

7. In the **Expression Categories** list, click **Comparison**, and in the **Expression Values** list, double-click **Like**.

   The Expression Builder inserts <<Expr>> before the Like operator as a placeholder for any other expressions you might add. You can ignore this for now.

8. In the expression box, type **"425*"** (including the quotation marks and the asterisk).

9. Double-click **<<Expr>>**, and press the Delete key. Then delete the extra space before **Like**.

   The expression now requires that the fPhone field include either of two area codes.

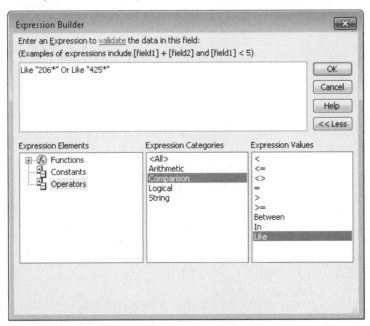

If you want to simply type an expression in the expression box, you can click Less to hide the hierarchical boxes.

10. Click **OK** to close the **Expression Builder** dialog box.

    Access warns that existing data violates the new validation rule, because the fPhone field contains a phone number that is not in either of the required area codes.

11. Click **Yes** to close the message box and keep the rule.

12. On the **Fields** contextual tab, in the **Field Validation** group, click the **Validation** button, and then click **Field Validation Message**.

    The Enter Validation Message dialog box opens.

You can enter a guiding message here.

13. In the box, type **Area code must be 206 or 425**, and then click **OK**.

    Access will display this message if someone attempts to enter a phone number with an invalid area code.

14. Save the table, and then switch to Design view.

    In the Field Properties area, the Validation Rule property and Validation text property are set to the new rule and message.

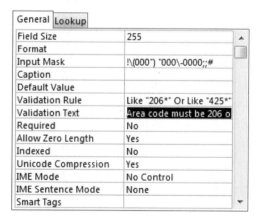

If you prefer, you can enter the rule and message directly in their property boxes.

15. Switch back to Datasheet view, click anywhere in the **fPhone** entry, and then press the Home key to place the cursor at the beginning of the field.

    Tip To select an entire field, point to the left end of the field, and when the pointer changes to a thick cross, click the mouse button.

16. Type **3605550109**, and then press Tab.

    Access displays an alert box.

    Access warns that the area code must be either 206 or 425.

    Tip You will see the Was This Information Helpful link only if you have enrolled in the Microsoft Customer Experience Improvement Program. Clicking the link displays a dialog box where you can give your opinion about the usefulness of the validation text.

17. Click **OK** to close the alert box, type a new phone number with one of the allowed area codes, and press Tab.

    Now let's create a record validation rule that compares one date with another to verify that it is later.

18. Scroll to the right, and click the **Click to Add** field. Then create a **Date/Time** field with the **Medium Date** format, and name the field **fDate2**.

19. On the **Fields** contextual tab, in the **Field Validation** group, click the **Validation** button, and then click **Record Validation Rule**.

    The Expression Builder dialog box opens. In the Expression Elements list, the FieldTest table is selected, and its fields are displayed in the expression Categories list.

20. In the **Expression Categories** list, double-click **fDate2** to insert it into the expression box. Then double-click **fDate**.

    The Expression Builder inserts <<Expr>> between fDate2 and fDate.

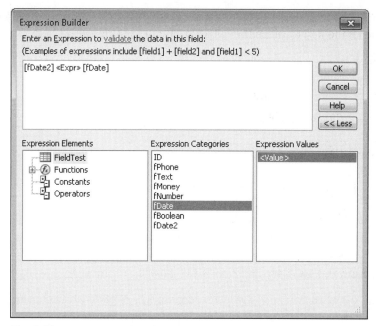

The field names are enclosed in square brackets to indicate that they are identifiers (that is, they identify the elements this expression will use in its evaluation).

21. In the expression box, double-click **<<Expr>>** to select it. Then in the **Expression Elements** list, click **Operators**; in the **Expression Categories** list, click **Comparison**; and in the **Expression Values** list, double-click **>**.

    The greater than sign replaces <<Expr>> in the expression.

22. Click **OK** to close the **Expression Builder** dialog box, and then click **Yes** to keep the new rule.

23. Create a record validation message that says **fDate2 must be later than fDate**.

24. Save the table. Then replace the entry in the **fDate** field with **11/22/22**.

 25. Click the **fDate2** field, click the **Calendar** button, and click today's date. Then click in the record below.

    Access displays an alert box containing the record validation text.

You cannot leave the record until you resolve this data error.

26. Click **OK**, change the value in **fDate2** to **12/22/22**, and then click in the record below.

 CLEAN UP Close the FieldTest table. Retain the GardenCompany06 database for use in later exercises.

Simple Validation Tests

The Field Validation group on the Fields contextual tab includes two commands that provide simple validation tests for fields without requiring you to build an expression:

- **Required** By default, the Required property is set to No. Selecting the Required check box in the Field Validation group sets this property to Yes, meaning that every record must have an entry in this field; it cannot be blank. (A blank field is called a *Null field*.)

- **Unique** By default, the Indexed property of all fields except AutoNumber fields is set to No. This property has two Yes options:

  - **Yes (Duplicates OK)** This option is set if you select the Indexed check box in the Field Validation group.

  - **Yes (No Duplicates)** This option is set if you select the Unique check box. (It is set by default for AutoNumber fields.)

  In both Yes cases, Access creates an index of the data in the field and its location, similar to the index in a book. The index speeds up data searching, because Access can look up the location of the data in the index instead of searching the actual database.

In terms of validation, selecting the Required check box will cause Access to verify that there is an entry in the field before it will accept the record. Selecting the Unique check box will cause Access to verify that no other record has the same value in the field before it will accept the field entry.

Tip For Text, Memo, and Hyperlink fields, the Required property can be refined by the Allow Zero Length property. When this property is set to Yes (the default), you can enter an empty string (two quotation marks with nothing between them) and the field will not be considered blank. In other words, a required field can be empty but not Null. The differentiation between Null and empty might seem silly, but it becomes important if someone uses programming code to work with the database, because some commands produce different results for Null fields than they do for empty fields.

Restricting Data to Values in Lists

It is interesting how many different ways people can come up with to enter the same items of information in a database. Asked to enter the name of their home state, for example, residents of the state of Washington will type *Washington*, *Wash*, or *WA*, plus various typographical errors and misspellings.

Minor inconsistencies in the way data is entered might not be really important to someone who later reads the information and makes decisions. For example, *Arizona* and *AZ* refer to the same state. But a computer is very literal, and if you tell it to create a list so that you can send catalogs to everyone living in *AZ*, the computer won't include anyone whose state is listed in the database as *Arizona*.

You can limit the options for entering information in a database in several ways:

- If one entry is more likely than any other, you can set the Default Value property of the field to that entry. Users can then press Tab to skip over that field, leaving the default entry intact. Even if users enter something else, the format of the default entry might guide them when choosing their entry's format.

- For only two options, you can use a Yes/No field represented by a check box. A check in the box indicates one choice, and no check indicates the other choice.

- For a short list of choices that won't change often, you can use a combo box. Clicking the arrow at the right end of the combo box displays the list of choices, which you provide as a lookup list. Depending on the properties associated with the combo box, database users might be able to type something else or they might be able to add entries to the lookup list displayed in the future. Although you can create a lookup list by hand, it is a lot easier to use the Lookup wizard.

Tip Access comes with three Quick Start lookup lists that are commonly used in businesses: Payment Type, Priority, and Status. You can efficiently add one of these ready-made lookup lists to a table by clicking the More Fields button in the Add & Delete group on the Fields contextual tab, and then clicking the field you want.

In this exercise, you'll use the Lookup wizard to create a list of states and provinces from which users can choose.

SET UP You need the GardenCompany06 database you worked with in the preceding exercise to complete this exercise. Open the GardenCompany06 database, and display the FieldTest table in Datasheet view. Then follow the steps.

1. At the right end of the table, click the **Click to Add** field. On the **Fields** contextual tab, in the **Add & Delete** group, click the **More Fields** button, and then click **Lookup & Relationship**.

The Lookup wizard starts.

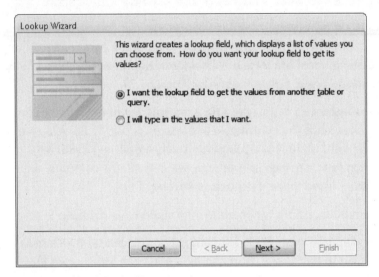

The first page of the Lookup wizard.

If a field has a lot of potential entries, or if they will change often, you can link them to a table. (You might have to create a table expressly for this purpose.) If a field has only a few possible entries that won't change, typing the list directly in the wizard is easier.

See Also For information about creating lookup fields based on another table, see "Restricting Data to Values in Other Tables" later in this chapter.

2. Click **I will type in the values that I want**, and then click **Next**.

3. Leave the number of columns set to **1**, and click in the first cell in the **Col1** column.

4. Enter the following state and province abbreviations, pressing Tab (not Enter) after each one to move to a new row.

   BC
   CA
   ID
   MT
   OR
   WA

5. Click **Next**.

   The wizard needs a little more information before it can create the field.

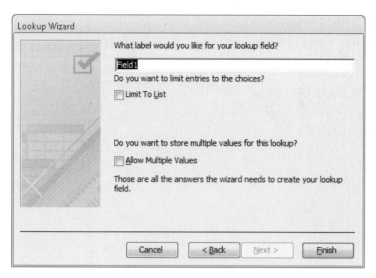

You assign a name to the new field on this page.

See Also For information about creating fields that can hold multiple values, see the sidebar "Multivalued Fields" later in this chapter.

6. Type **fLookup** as the name of the field, and select the **Limit To List** check box. Then click **Finish**.

7. Save the table, and switch to Design view.

8. Click anywhere in the **fLookup** field, and then in the **Field Properties** area, click the **Lookup** tab.

The Lookup page shows the properties that control the lookup list.

General	Lookup
Display Control	Combo Box
Row Source Type	Value List
Row Source	"BC";"CA";"ID";"MT";"OR";"W/
Bound Column	1
Column Count	1
Column Heads	No
Column Widths	1"
List Rows	16
List Width	1"
Limit To List	Yes
Allow Multiple Values	No
Allow Value List Edits	Yes
List Items Edit Form	
Show Only Row Source V	No

You can see the list you typed in the Row Source property.

9. In the **Field Properties** area, click the **General** tab. Then click anywhere in the **Default Value** property, type **WA**, and press Enter.

10. Switch to Datasheet view, clicking **Yes** to save your changes to the table.

    The entry *WA* appears in the fLookup field of the new record.

11. Click in the **fLookup** field of the first record, and then click the arrow at the right end of the field.

    The list of possible entries for this field appears.

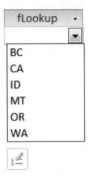

The list reflects the entries you typed on the wizard's second page.

Tip Clicking the button that appears below the options list opens the Edit List Items dialog box. If you don't want users to be able to edit the list, you can disable this property, as we do later in this exercise.

12. Click **MT** to enter the abbreviation for Montana in the field.

13. With **MT** selected, type **b**.

    Access completes the entry by displaying C.

14. Click the record below.

    Access converts *bC* to *BC*.

15. Select **BC**, type **Utah**, and press Tab. Then when Access tells you that the entry isn't in the list and asks whether you want to edit the list, click **Yes**.

16. When the **Edit List Items** dialog box opens, click **Cancel**, and then click **BC** in the list.

17. Switch to Design view, and click the **Lookup** tab.

    The Limit To List property on the Lookup page for the fLookup field is set to Yes, but the Allow Value List Edits property is also set to Yes, meaning that users can change the list.

18. Click the **Allow Value List Edits** property, click the arrow that appears, and then click **No**.

19. Save the table, return to Datasheet view, type **Utah** in the **fLookup** field, and then press Tab.

Access informs you that the text you entered is not in the list.

Access will not accept your entry.

20. Click **OK** to close the message box. Then click **BC** in the list, and press Tab.

 CLEAN UP Close the FieldTest table. Retain the GardenCompany06 database for use in the last exercise.

Multicolumn Lookup Lists

If you want people to be able to select a friendly name from a list but you want the database to store a more compact name or number, you can create a two-column lookup list that associates the two types of entries.

To set up a multicolumn lookup list:

1. Create a new lookup field, and indicate on the first page of the Lookup wizard that you want to type the values.

2. On the second page, change the Number Of Columns setting to 2, and then enter the data you want Access to store in Col1 and the friendly name in Col2.

3. Assign a name to the field, select the Limit To List check box if appropriate, and click Finish.

Clicking the field's arrow will then display a two-column list from which the user can select an entry. The stored value will be displayed in the field.

To display only the friendly name in the list and in the table:

1. Switch to Design view.

2. In the Field Properties area, on the Lookup tab, change the Column Widths property from 1";1" to 0;1".

3. Save the table.

Restricting Data to Values in Other Tables

In "Creating Relationships Between Tables" in Chapter 2, "Create Databases and Simple Tables," you learned how to link tables in such a way that a user could not enter a customer ID that did not exist in the Customers table or an employee ID that did not exist in the Employees table. These relationships are critical to ensuring that any specific item of data is stored in the database only once. But relationships also provide a powerful means to improve the accuracy of the database's data.

If you ask a dozen sales clerks to enter the name of a specific customer, product, and shipper in an invoice, it is unlikely that all of them will type the same thing. In cases like this, in which the number of correct choices is limited (to actual customer, actual product, and actual shipper), providing the means to choose the correct information from a list derived from the Customers table, the Products table, and the Shippers table will improve your database's accuracy and consistency.

One of the key concerns when looking up information in another table is the efficiency of the process. Looking up an employee in an Employees table with nine records is not very difficult. Looking up a customer in a Customers table with 200 records, however, could be quite tedious. If you use an intuitive CustomerID instead of relying on an auto-generated number as the primary key of the Customers table, database users can type the CustomerID and then verify it in the list. For example, using the first three letters of a customer's last name plus the first two of his or her first name will almost certainly result in unique CustomerID values. These values will not only serve as the primary key for the Customers table but will be easy for users to intuit when working in other tables linked to the Customers table.

In this exercise, you'll use the Lookup wizard to create a list of possible values for a field from the entries in a field in a related table. You'll also change the primary key in a table to facilitate the lookup process.

SET UP You need the GardenCompany06 database you worked with in the preceding exercise to complete this exercise. Open the GardenCompany06 database, and then follow the steps.

Relationships

1. On the **Database Tools** tab, in the **Relationships** group, click the **Relationships** button.

The Relationships page shows that in this database, there is a relationship between the Customers and Orders tables and between the Employees and Orders tables. You want to create Customer and Employee lookup fields in the Orders table, so you first need to delete the existing relationships.

2. Right-click the diagonal part of the line between the **Customers** and **Orders** tables, and click **Delete**, clicking **Yes** to confirm the deletion. Repeat this step for the line between the **Employees** and **Orders** tables. Then close the **Relationships** page, clicking **Yes** to save the change.

   Tip If you want to remove a table's box from the Relationships page, you can right-click the box and click Hide Table. If you want to remove all the boxes, you can click the Clear Layout button in the Tools group on the Design contextual tab.

3. Open the **Orders** table, and drag across the **CustomerID** and **EmployeeID** field names to select those fields. On the **Fields** contextual tab, in the **Add & Delete** group, click the **Delete** button. Then click **Yes** to permanently delete the fields and **Yes** to delete their indexes.

   Now we'll add a new Employee lookup field.

4. At the right end of the table, click the **Click to Add** field. On the **Fields** contextual tab, in the **Add & Delete** group, click the **More Fields** button, and then click **Lookup & Relationship**.

   The Lookup wizard starts and displays its first page.

5. With **I want the lookup field to get the values from another table or query** selected, click **Next**.

   The Lookup wizard asks you to identify the table on which the lookup field will be based.

6. Click **Table: Employees** in the list, and click **Next**.

7. On the next page, in the **Available Fields** list, double-click **EmployeeID**, then **FirstName**, and then **LastName** to transfer those fields to the **Selected Fields** list. Then click **Next**.

8. On the next page, click the arrow for the first sort box, click **LastName** in the list, and then click **Next**.

   The wizard displays the lookup list with the EmployeeID field (the key column) hidden.

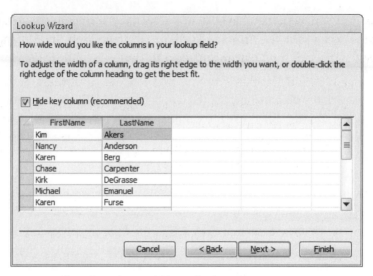

You can adjust the column widths to fit the values.

9. Click **Next**. On the wizard's last page, type **Employee** as the name of the field, and select the **Enable Data Integrity** check box. Then click **Finish**.

10. Click in the **Employee** field of the first record, and then click the arrow at the right end of the field.

    The list of possible entries for this field appears.

The list is in alphabetical order by last name.

11. Click **Nancy Anderson** to enter the name *Nancy* as the salesperson for this order.

    Now let's work with the Customers table. First we want to change the primary key for this table.

Primary
Key

12. Open the **Customers** table in Design view. On the **Design** contextual tab, in the **Tools** group, click the **Primary Key** button to turn it off. Then change the **Data Type** setting for the **CustomerID** field to **Text**.

13. Change the **Field Size** property to **5**, and enter an **Input Mask** property of **>LLLLL;;.**

    This input mask will force Access to display the CustomerID in capital (uppercase) letters, no matter how it is entered.

14. Click the **CustomerID** field in the **Field Name** column, and in the **Tools** group, click the **Primary Key** button. Then save the table.

15. Switch to Datasheet view. For each customer, assign a **CustomerID** that consists of the first three letters of the last name and the first two letters of the first name.

    Even if you type the ID in all lowercase letters, Access displays them in uppercase.

16. Sort the table in ascending order on the **CustomerID** field, and then close it, clicking **Yes** to save your changes.

17. In the **Orders** table, use the Lookup wizard to create a new lookup field based on the **CustomerID**, **FirstName**, and **LastName** fields of the **Customers** table. Sort the lookup list on **LastName**, and then click **Next**.

18. On the page that asks you to adjust the width of the columns in the lookup field, point to the right border of the **FirstName** field name, and when the pointer changes to a double-headed arrow, drag all the way to the left to hide that column. Click **Next**.

19. Name the field **Customer**, and enforce referential integrity. Then click **Finish**.

    Now try entering an order for Pilar Ackerman.

20. In the **Customer** field of the first record, type **ack**.

    Ackerman is the only LastName value beginning with those letters, so Access completes the entry for you.

21. Click the field in the record below.

    Access enters the name *Ackerman* as it appears in the Customers table.

22. In the active record, type **c**.

    Access enters *campbell*, the first LastName value beginning with *c* in the Customers table. This is not the customer we want.

23. Click the arrow at the right end of the field.

    Access displays the list with Campbell highlighted.

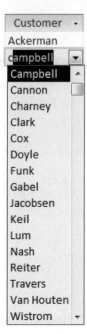

Because Access has scrolled the list, it is easy to select the name you want.

24. Click **Cox**, and press Tab. Then close the **Orders** table.

25. On the **Database Tools** tab, in the **Relationships** group, click the **Relationships** button.

The Lookup wizard automatically created one-to-many relationships between the Customers and Orders tables and between the Employees and Orders tables.

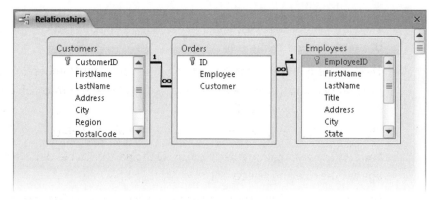

Access created these relationships to support the lookup fields in the Orders table.

 CLEAN UP Close the GardenCompany06 database.

Multivalued Fields

Usually you will be able to build database tables in which each field holds only one value. However, sometimes you might need to store more than one value in a single field. For example, in a Projects table, you might need to store multiple employee names in a Team field.

To set up a multivalued field that restricts values to those in a table:

1. Create a new lookup field, and indicate on the first page of the Lookup wizard that you want to look up the values in a table.

2. On the second page, select a table from the list.

3. On the third page, select the fields you want to include.

4. On the fourth page, indicate any sorting.

5. On the fifth page, make any necessary adjustments to the column width.

6. On the last page of the wizard, type a name for the field, indicate whether to enforce referential integrity, and select the Allow Multiple Values check box.

When the table is open in Datasheet view, clicking the field's arrow displays a list from which users can choose entries by selecting their check boxes. Clicking OK then displays the selected values in the field.

Key Points

- The Data Type setting restricts the data that can be entered into an Access database to a specific type.

- The Field Size property for the Text, Number, and AutoNumber data types restricts the number of characters allowed in a Text field or the number of digits allowed in a Number or AutoNumber field.

- The Input Mask property controls the format in which data can be entered.

- You can use a validation rule to precisely define acceptable data. Access tests entries against the rule and rejects any that don't comply.

- For fields with a fixed set of possible entries, a lookup list ensures consistent data entry.

- If it is important that values in one table match values in another, you can create a lookup field based on that table to keep entries accurate.

Chapter at a Glance

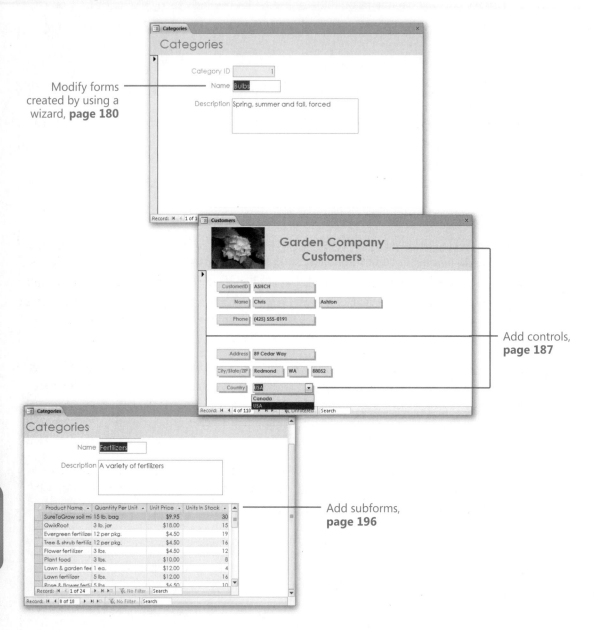

Modify forms created by using a wizard, **page 180**

Add controls, **page 187**

Add subforms, **page 196**

7 Create Custom Forms

In this chapter, you will learn how to

- ✔ Modify forms created by using a wizard.
- ✔ Add controls.
- ✔ Add subforms.
- ✔ Use e-mail forms to collect data.

Every form has three basic sections: Form Header, Detail, and Form Footer. When you use the Form tool or a wizard to create a form, a logo placeholder and a title is added to the Form Header section, a set of text box and label controls for each field in the underlying table is added to the Detail section, and the Form Footer section is left blank. You can customize any form by adding controls to its sections and by rearranging controls to make the form easy to work with.

Ease of data entry is the major consideration when designing a form, because the easier this process is, the less likely people are to make mistakes. One of the ways to eliminate mistakes is to have Microsoft Access 2010 enter data automatically based on existing entries. Another is to make it possible to enter data in more than one table at a time by using subforms.

In this chapter, you'll control a form's function and appearance by inserting controls and modifying the form and control properties. You'll present information from multiple tables in one form by using subforms. You'll also learn how to collect data through e-mail survey forms.

Tip This chapter builds on the discussion of forms in Chapter 3, "Create Simple Forms."

> **Practice Files** Before you can complete the exercises in this chapter, you need to copy the book's practice files to your computer. The practice files you'll use to complete the exercises in this chapter are in the Chapter07 practice file folder. A complete list of practice files is provided in "Using the Practice Files" at the beginning of this book.

Modifying Forms Created by Using a Wizard

When a form is intended as the primary method of entering new records, it usually includes all the fields from the underlying table. As you saw in Chapter 3, "Create Simple Forms," the quickest way to create a form that includes all the fields from one table is to use the Form tool. Another method, which provides more control over the creation of the form, is to use a wizard. In either case, you can easily customize the form after it is created.

In Chapter 3, we showed you how to work with forms in Layout view. Because you can see the data in the underlying table or tables in this view, it is easy to gauge the effects of moving and sizing the controls and their labels. You can display the Property Sheet and adjust properties to fine-tune form elements, and you can make most of the adjustments you are likely to want in the custom form.

When you want more control over the layout of a form, you can work in Design view. In this view, you see the structure of the form laid out on a design grid, but you don't see the data from the underlying table or tables.

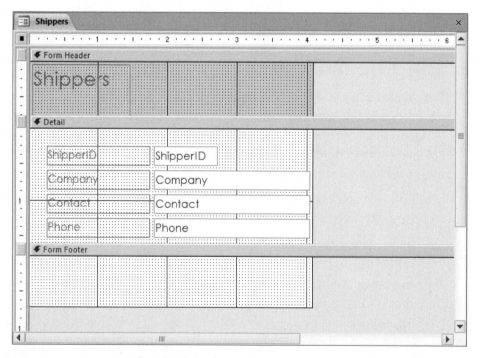

In Design View, Access displays horizontal and vertical rulers and a grid to help you position controls and labels.

Tip You cannot work with forms in a Web database in Design view; you must use Layout view.

The design grid is divided into three sections:

- **Form Header** This section contains information to be displayed at the top of the form, such as a title.

- **Detail** This section contains a text box control and an associated label control for each of the fields you selected for inclusion in the form.

- **Form Footer** This section can contain information to be displayed at the bottom of the form. By default, this section is blank, so it is closed.

In Design view, you can work with the form in the following ways:

- Adjust the size of sections.

- Apply a theme.

- Change the size of controls.

- Arrange controls logically to facilitate data entry.

- Adjust the properties of form elements in the Property Sheet.

- Add fields from the Field List, which you display by clicking the Add Existing Fields button in the Tools group on the Design contextual tab.

- Add controls to limit data entry choices or add functionality to a form.

  See Also For information about adding controls to forms, see "Adding Controls" later in this chapter.

In this exercise, you'll use the Form wizard to create a form that displays a list of product categories. You'll then modify the form in Design view by formatting its title, making a control inaccessible to users, changing a label, and adding and resizing a control for a new field.

 SET UP You need the GardenCompany07_start database located in your Chapter07 practice file folder to complete this exercise. Open the GardenCompany07_start database, and save it as *GardenCompany07*. Then follow the steps.

1. In the **Navigation** pane, click **Customers**. Then on the **Create** tab, in the **Forms** group, click the **Form Wizard** button.

   The Form wizard starts.

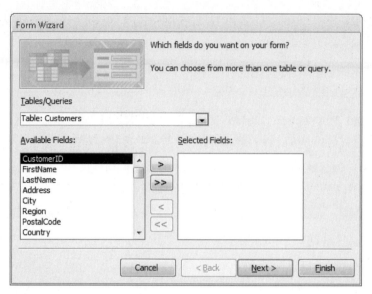

If a table is selected in the Navigation pane when you click the button, that table's information populates the wizard's first page.

2. Display the **Tables/Queries** list, and click **Table: Categories**. In the **Available Fields** list, double-click **CategoryID** to move it to the **Selected Fields** list, and double-click **CategoryName**. Then click **Next**.

   On the wizard's second page, you choose a layout for the new form. The preview area on the left shows how the form will look with the selected option applied.

3. With **Columnar** selected, click **Next**.

   On the wizard's last page, Access suggests the table's name as the title of the form.

4. With **Open the form to view or enter information** selected, click **Finish**.

   The new Categories form opens.

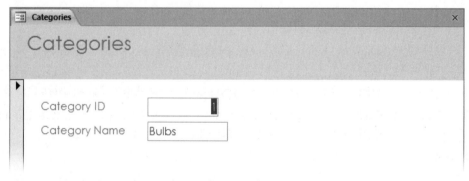

The new form displays the first record in the Categories table.

5. Scroll through a few records by using the controls on the record navigation bar at the bottom of the form.

Let's make a few changes in Design view.

6. On the **View Shortcuts** toolbar, click the **Design View** button.

Access displays the design grid for the Categories form.

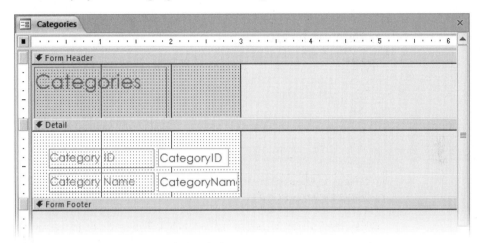

The design grid for the Categories form.

7. On the **Design** contextual tab, in the **Themes** group, click the **Themes** button. Then in the gallery that appears, click the **Austin** thumbnail.

You might notice only a subtle change in the font used for the control text. But behind the scenes, Access also makes the color scheme of the Austin theme available to the form.

8. Click the **Form Header** section bar to select that section. Then on the **Format** contextual tab, in the **Control Formatting** group, click the **Shape Fill** button. Under **Theme Colors** in the palette that appears, click the third box (**Light Green, Background 2**).

9. Point to the bottom of the **Form Header** section (just above the Detail section bar), and when the pointer changes to a two-headed arrow, drag downward to enlarge the section until you can see the entire **Categories** title control.

10. Click the **Categories** title control. On the **Arrange** contextual tab, in the **Sizing & Ordering** group, click the **Size/Space** button.

A list of sizing and spacing options appears.

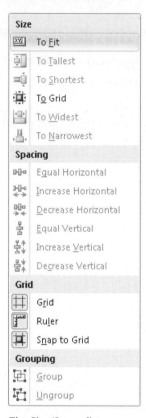

The Size/Space list.

11. Under **Size** in the list, click **To Fit**.

12. Point to the bottom of the **Form Header** section, and drag upward until the section is just tall enough to contain the title control.

13. In the **Detail** section, click the **CategoryID** text box control, and on the **Design** contextual tab, in the **Tools** group, click the **Property Sheet** button.

Property Sheet

Keyboard Shortcut Press F4 to open the Property Sheet.

See Also For more information about keyboard shortcuts, see "Keyboard Shortcuts" at the end of this book.

14. In the **Property Sheet**, click the **Data** tab. Click the **Enabled** property, click its arrow, and click **No**. Then close the **Property Sheet**.

Disabling the CategoryID text box control changes its text and background to gray, indicating that users can no longer change this value.

15. Click the **Category Name** label, double-click **Category**, and then delete it and the following space.

    Now let's add the category description from the Categories table to this form.

16. Point to the bottom of the **Detail** section, and drag downward until the section is about 2.5 inches tall. Then point to the right edge of the section and drag to the right until the section is about 5 inches wide.

17. On the **Design** tab, in the **Tools** group, click the **Add Existing Fields** button.

    Keyboard Shortcut Press Alt+F8 to open the Field List.

    The Field List opens.

You can click Show All Tables to display the fields from other tables in the database.

18. In the **Field List**, click **Description**, drag the field below the **Category Name** text box control in the **Detail** section, and then close the **Field List**.

19. Point to the border of the **Description** text box control, and drag the control so that its left edge is aligned with the **Category Name** control above and its top edge sits at the **1** inch mark on the vertical ruler.

    Tip If you point to the border of a text box control and drag it to a new location, the associated label moves with it. Similarly, if you point to the border of a label control and drag, the associated text box control moves as well. If you want to move either control independently of the other, you need to drag the large gray square in the control's upper-left corner.

20. Click the **Description** label control, and drag the large handle in the upper-left corner to the left until the control is aligned with the labels above. Then widen the control to match the other controls.

21. Hold down the Shift key, and click the **Name** and **CategoryID** labels to add their controls to the selection. Then on the **Format** contextual tab, in the **Font** group, click the **Align Text Right** button.

22. Make the **Detail** section just tall enough to contain its controls.

The form now occupies the smallest possible amount of space.

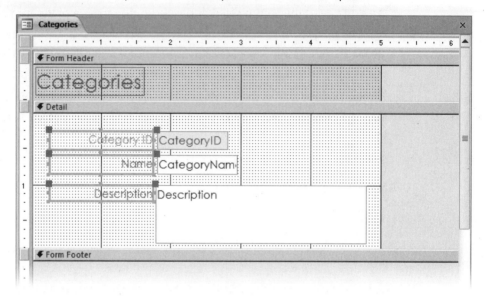

You have added a text box control and its associated label control.

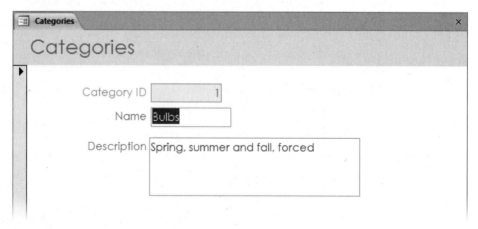

23. On the **View Shortcuts** toolbar, click the **Form View** button.

You can now see the results of your changes.

The labels and their controls now look neater on the form.

24. Scroll through a few category records. Try to edit entries in the **CategoryID** field to confirm that you can't.

    We don't need the record selector bar down the left side of this form, so let's return to Design view and turn it off.

25. Switch to Design view, click the form selector (the box in the upper-left corner at the junction of the horizontal and vertical rulers), and then display the **Property Sheet** for the form.

26. On the **Format** page of the **Property Sheet**, change the **Record Selectors** property to **No**. Then close the **Property Sheet**.

27. Switch to Form view to verify that the form no longer has a record selector.

 **CLEAN UP** Close the Categories form, saving your changes. Retain the GardenCompany07 database for use in later exercises.

Adding Controls

Although text box and label controls are the most common controls found in forms, you can also enhance your forms with many other types of controls. For example, you can add groups of option buttons, check boxes, and list boxes to present people with choices instead of having them type entries in text boxes.

When a form is displayed in Layout view or Design view, the available controls are located in the Controls gallery on the Design contextual tab. There are three categories of controls:

● **Bound** A control that is linked to a field in a table or the datasheet created by a query. These controls include:

  ○ Text boxes and labels

  ○ Option groups, combo boxes, and list boxes

  ○ Charts

  ○ Subforms/Subreports

- **Unbound** A control that is not bound to any underlying data. These controls include:

  - Buttons and toggle buttons
  - Tabs and page breaks
  - Hyperlinks and Web Browser controls
  - Lines
  - Images

- **Calculated** A control that displays the results of an expression.

Tip If you create a form for a table with many fields, or if you add many controls to a form, you can organize the controls on pages by using the Page Break control, or on tabbed pages by using the Tab control.

In this exercise, you'll insert a picture into the Form Header of a form and replace the default title with a custom one. You'll also replace a text box control in the Detail section with a combo box control.

SET UP You need the GardenCompany07 database you worked with in the preceding exercise and the Hydrangeas graphic located in your Chapter07 practice file folder to complete this exercise. Open the GardenCompany07 database, open the Customers form in Design view, and then follow the steps.

1. In the **Customers** form, point to the bottom of the **Form Header** section, and when the pointer changes to a double-headed arrow, drag downward to increase the header size to about 1.5 inches.

2. In the **Form Header** section, select the logo control, hold down the Shift key, and select the label control. Then press the Delete key.

3. On the **Design** contextual tab, in the **Controls** group, click the **Insert Image** button, and then click **Browse**.

   Tip If the Hydrangeas image already appears in the Image gallery displayed when you click the Insert Image button, you can simply click the image instead of browsing to it.

4. In the **Insert Picture** dialog box, navigate to your **Chapter07** practice file folder. Then change the type of file from **Web-Ready Image Files** to **All Files**, and double-click **Hydrangeas**.

5. Point to the upper-left corner of the **Form Header** section, and drag diagonally to draw a box about 1 inch high and 1.5 inches wide.

The picture is inserted into the image control.

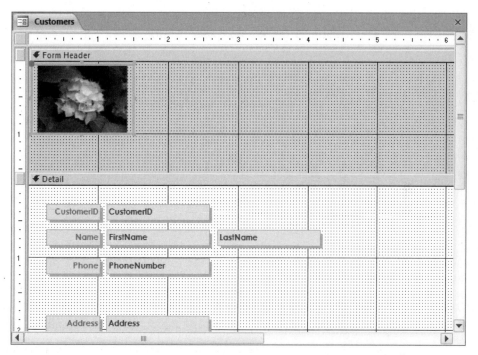

The Hydrangeas photograph has been inserted into the Form Header section.

Tip How an image fits into an image control is determined by the Size Mode property of the control. If the property is set to Clip and the control isn't large enough to display the entire image, the image is cropped. If the property is set to Stretch, you can enlarge the control to display the entire image. If the property is set to Zoom (the default), the image automatically resizes to fit the control.

6. In the **Controls** group, display the **Controls** gallery.

Depending on the size of your program window and your screen resolution, you might need to click the More button or the Controls button to display this gallery.

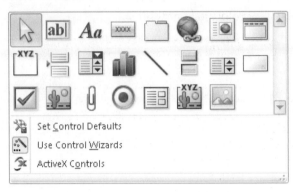

You can insert any control from this gallery.

7. In the gallery, click the **Label** button, and then to the right of the picture in the **Form Header** section, drag diagonally to draw a box about 2 inches wide and 0.5 inch tall.

   Access inserts a label control containing the cursor, ready for you to enter a title for the form.

8. In the active label control, type **Garden Company**. Then press Shift+Enter to insert a line break, and type **Customers**.

9. Click the **Form Header** section bar. On the **Format** contextual tab, in the **Control Formatting** group, click the **Shape Fill** button. Then under **Theme Colors** in the palette, click the third box (**Light Green, Background 2**).

10. Select the label text, and in the **Font** group, make the text 20 points, bold, and dark green. Then center the text.

11. If **Garden Company** wraps to two lines, drag the sizing handle in the middle of the right side of the label frame to the right until the text fits on one line. Then on the **Arrange** tab, in the **Sizing & Ordering** group, click the **Size/Space** button, and under **Size** in the **Size/Space** gallery, click **To Fit**.

    The label control now fits its text.

12. Reduce the height of the **Form Header** section so that it is just big enough to contain its controls.

The form now has a more prominent title.

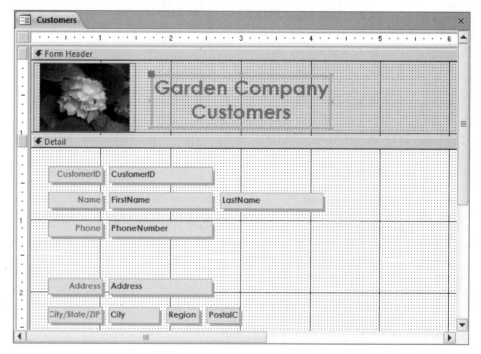

The completed Form Header section.

13. On the **Design** tab, display the **Controls** gallery, and verify that the **Use Control Wizards** button is not orange. If the button is orange (active), click it to deactivate it.

When the Control Wizards feature is turned off, you can add a control with all its default settings, without having to work through the associated wizard's pages.

14. Enlarge the **Detail** section to create at least an inch of space below the **Country** controls.

We want to create a combo box that displays a list of possible countries but that also allows users to type the country if it is not already in the list.

15. In the **Controls** gallery, click the **Combo Box** button. Then drag diagonally to draw a box below the **Country** text box control. Make it about 1.5 inches wide and about 0.25 inch tall.

When you release the mouse button, Access displays a combo box control and an associated label control.

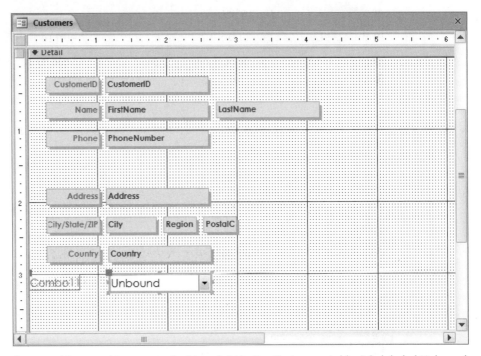

Because this control is not attached to a field in the Customers table, it is labeled Unbound.

Tip Access assigns a number to each control when it is created. Don't be concerned if the numbers associated with the controls you create are different from those in our graphics.

16. Click the **Country** text box control. On the **Format** contextual tab, in the **Font** group, click the **Format Painter** button, and then click the combo box control.

Access copies the formatting of the Country text box to the combo box control and its label.

17. Right-click the combo box, and then click **Properties** to open the **Property Sheet**.

Now let's create a simple query that extracts one example of every country in the Country field of the Customers table and displays the results as a list when users click the combo box arrow.

18. Click the **Data** tab of the **Property Sheet**. Then click the **Control Source** arrow, and in the list, click **Country**.

In the combo box control on the form, *Unbound* has been replaced by *Country*.

19. Verify that the **Row Source Type** property is set to **Table/Query**. Then in the **Row Source** box, type the following:

SELECT DISTINCT Customers.Country FROM Customers;

There is a period (but no space) between *Customers* and *Country*, and a semicolon at the end of the text.

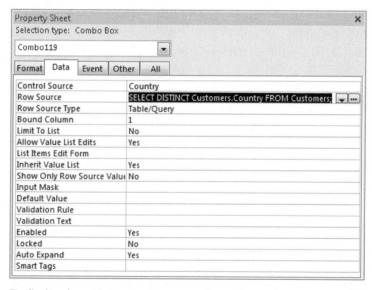

To display the entire query, you can widen the Property Sheet by dragging its left border to the left.

20. Click the combo box label control. Click the **Format** tab of the **Property Sheet**, and change the **Caption** property to *Country*.

21. Click the original **Country** text box control, and press Delete to delete the control and its associated label. Then move the new combo box and label into their places, resizing them as needed.

    Tip To ensure that new controls are aligned with existing controls, you can click an existing control and make a note of its Width, Height, Top, and Left properties. Then use whichever of those settings is relevant to fine-tune the new control.

22. Shrink the size of the **Detail** section until it is only as wide and as tall as it needs to be to hold its controls.

23. On the **Design** tab, in the **Controls** gallery, click the **Line** control, and drag a line across the width of the form to separate the name and phone number information from the address.

24. In the **Property Sheet**, set the **Height** property to **0** and the **Border Width** property to **2 pt**. Then close the **Property Sheet**.

    Tip Setting the height to 0 does not make the line invisible; it ensures that the line is straight.

25. With the line still selected, on the **Format** tab, in the **Control Formatting** group, click the **Shape Outline** button, and set the line color to dark green.

    Now let's make sure that no matter what size the program window is, the line always stretches across the width of the form.

26. On the **Arrange** tab, in the **Position** group, click the **Anchoring** button.

    The Anchoring gallery appears.

Top Left	Stretch Across Top	Top Right
Stretch Down	Stretch Down and Across	Stretch Down and Right
Bottom Left	Stretch Across Bottom	Bottom Right

You can anchor a control in four positions and make it stretch in five directions.

27. In the gallery, click the **Stretch Across Top** thumbnail.

28. Switch to Form view, and try making the program window various sizes.

    Even though the width of the form was only about 5 inches in Design view, the form header and the line always span the width of the window.

29. Scroll through a couple of records, and then click the **Country** combo box arrow.

    Access displays the country list.

Selecting possible entries is quick and easy with a combo box.

 CLEAN UP Close the Customers form, saving your changes. Retain the GardenCompany07 database for use in the last exercise.

Adding Subforms

As you saw in "Exploring Forms" in Chapter 1, "Explore an Access 2010 Database," if a one-to-many relationship exists between two tables, you can display information from both the "one" and the "many" sides of the relationship by using a main form and a subform. For example, the main form for related Customers and Orders tables might display information about a customer (the "one" side), and the subform might list all the orders that customer has placed (the "many" side).

Suppose you want to create a main form that includes all the fields of one table with a subform that includes all the fields of another table. As long as there is only one one-to-many relationship between the tables already defined on the Relationships page, the fastest way to create the form and its subform is by using the Form tool. Simply click the primary table in the Navigation pane, and then on the Create tab, in the Forms group, click the Form button. The Form tool creates and displays a form and subform, each containing all the fields of its source table.

If you want to create a main form and subform that include only some of the fields in their underlying tables, you can use the Form wizard. To do so:

1. On the Create tab, in the Forms group, click the Form Wizard button.

2. On the Form wizard's first page, in the Tables/Queries list, click the table on which you want to base the form.

3. In the Available Fields list, double-click the fields you want to include in the main form to move them to the Selected Fields list.

4. In the Tables/Queries list, click the table on which you want to base the subform.

5. In the Available Fields list, double-click the fields you want to include in the subform, and then click Next.

   Troubleshooting If the relationship between the selected tables has not been defined, Access displays a message. You can click OK to display the Relationships page, where you can define the relationship. You will then need to start the wizard again.

6. On the wizard's second page, with the primary table and Form With Subform(s) selected, click Next.

7. On the third page, select the layout you want, and then click Next.

8. On the last page, enter the titles you want for your forms, and with Open The Form To View Or Enter Information selected, click Finish.

   The wizard creates and opens the form and subform. You can then use normal techniques to modify the form created by the Form wizard to suit your needs.

If you have already created a main form and you now want to add a subform to it, you can add a Subform/Subreport control to the form.

In this exercise, you'll add a subform to an existing form in Design view, and you'll then modify its appearance in Layout view.

 SET UP You need the GardenCompany07 database you worked with in the preceding exercise to complete this exercise. Open the GardenCompany07 database, open the Categories form in Design view, and then follow the steps.

1. To give yourself space to work, expand the **Detail** section until it is about 3 inches tall.

 2. On the **Design** tab, in the **Controls** group, display the **Controls** gallery, and at the bottom of the gallery, click the **Use Control Wizards** button.

   You want this button to be active (orange).

 3. In the **Controls** gallery, click the **Subform/Subreport** button, and then drag a box below the **Description** label and text box controls in the lower portion of the **Detail** section.

   A white unbound control appears in the form, and the SubForm wizard starts.

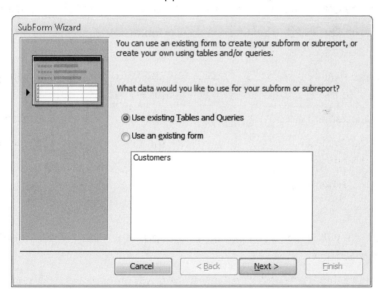

The first page of the SubForm wizard.

4. With **Use existing Tables and Queries** selected, click **Next**.

5. Display the **Tables/Queries** list, and click **Table: Products**.

6. In the **Available Fields** list, double-click the **ProductName**, **CategoryID**, **QuantityPerUnit**, **UnitPrice**, and **UnitsInStock** fields to add them to the **Selected Fields** list. Then click **Next**.

Because there is a relationship between the Products table and the Categories table that is based on the CategoryID field, the wizard selects Choose From A List and indicates the relationship it will use.

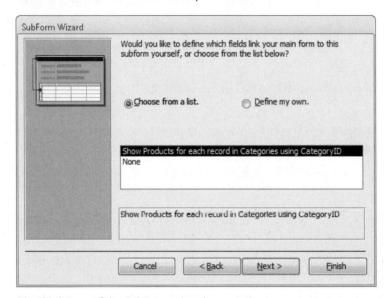

The third page of the SubForm wizard.

Tip If the wizard can't figure out which fields are related, it selects the Define My Own option and displays list boxes in which you can specify which fields should be related.

7. With **Choose from a list** selected, click **Next**, and then click **Finish** to accept the suggested name for the subform.

   Access embeds the Products subform in the Categories form. The subform control has its own Form Header, Detail, and Form Footer sections, and can be scrolled independently of the main form.

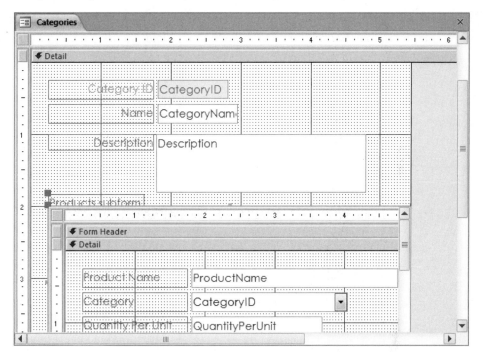

The name of the subform appears in a label control above the upper-left corner of the subform control.

8. Above the subform, click the **Products subform** label, and press the Delete key. Then switch to Form view.

In this view, the subform looks like a datasheet.

The subform has its own scroll bars and record navigation bar.

> **Tip** This main form and subform are ideal for checking which products are assigned to which categories and for looking up information about the products in a category. But if you want to create a form whose main purpose is data entry, you obviously need to include all the fields in which the database user will need to enter information.

9. Right-click the subform, point to **Subform**, and then click **Form**.

   In this view, the layout of the subform reflects its layout in Design view.

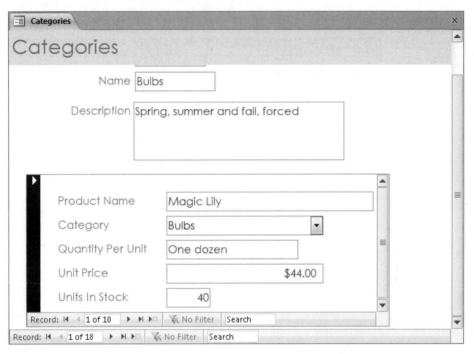

The form layout is not as useful as the datasheet layout.

10. Repeat step 9 to switch back to Datasheet view. Then, so that you can modify the layout of the subform, switch to Layout view.

11. Click any cell in the subform, and on the **Format** tab, in the **Font** group, click the **Font Size** arrow, and click **9**.

12. Point to the right border of the **Product Name** field name, and when the pointer changes to a two-headed arrow, double-click to adjust the column to its widest entry. Then repeat this step for all the other columns.

13. Widen the subform so that **Units in Stock** is visible, by dragging the subform's right border to the right.

You can now see all the fields of the subform.

Product Name ▾	Category ▾	Quantity Per Unit ▾	Unit Price ▾	Units In Stock ▾
Magic Lily	Bulbs	One dozen	$44.00	40
Autumn crocus	Bulbs	One dozen	$20.63	37
Anemone	Bulbs	One dozen	$30.80	26
Lily-of-the-Field	Bulbs	One dozen	$41.80	34
Siberian Iris	Bulbs	6 per pkg.	$14.25	30
Daffodil	Bulbs	6 per pkg.	$14.25	24
Peony	Bulbs	6 per pkg.	$21.95	20
Lilies	Bulbs	6 per pkg.	$11.55	18
Begonias	Bulbs	6 per pkg.	$20.85	12

Categories — Name: Bulbs — Description: Spring, summer and fall, forced

Record: ◄ ◄ 1 of 10 ► ►I ►▯   No Filter   Search

Record: ◄ ◄ 1 of 18 ► ►I ►▯   No Filter   Search

Adjusting field widths is often easier in Layout view, where you can see the underlying data from the table.

14. Switch to Form view, and scroll through several categories by using the record navigation bar for the main form.

    As each category appears at the top of the form, the products in that category are listed in the datasheet in the subform.

15. Click the **First Record** button to return to the first category (Bulbs). In the subform, click **Bulbs** in the **Category** column to the right of the first product (Magic Lily).

    The arrow at the right end of the box indicates that this is a combo box.

16. Click the arrow to display the list of categories, and then change the category to **Cacti**.

17. Click the **Next Record** navigation button to move to the **Cacti** category.

    Magic Lily is now included in this category.

18. Display the **Category** list for the **Magic Lily** record, and return it to the **Bulbs** category.

We need to prevent people from changing a product's category.

19. Switch to Design view, clicking **Yes** when prompted to save the form and the subform.

20. In the subform, click the **CategoryID** combo box control, and then press Delete.

The CategoryID combo box and its label no longer appear on the form.

21. Save the form, switch back to Layout view, and then adjust the width of the subform, allowing space for the scroll bar.

22. Switch to Form view, and scroll through the categories.

The results are shown here.

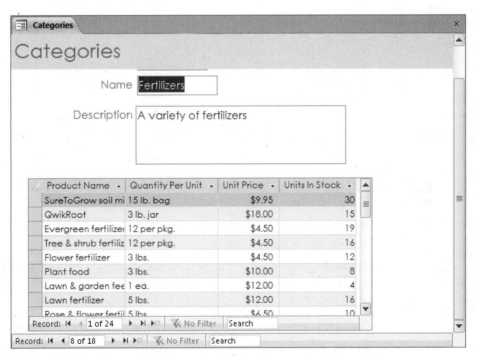

You can easily use this form to check the assignments of products to categories.

 CLEAN UP Close the Categories form, saving your changes. You don't need the GardenCompany07 database for the next topic, so you can close it.

Different Types of Forms

Most forms facilitate data entry—adding or editing records in one or more tables. However, some forms are more specialized than others, and some serve purposes other than data entry. Here is an overview of the types of forms you can create from the Forms group on the Create tab:

- **Blank form in Design view** Clicking the Form Design button displays a blank design grid where you can design a form from scratch.

- **Blank form in Layout view** Clicking the Blank Form button displays a blank canvas and opens the Field List, from which you can drag fields from the database tables onto the form.

- **Navigation** Clicking the Navigation button displays a gallery of predefined navigation form layouts. You must use a navigation form to provide access to the objects in a Web database, which has no Navigation pane. But navigation forms can be useful for any database.

  See Also For information about navigation forms, see "Creating Navigation Forms" in Chapter 11, "Make Databases User Friendly."

Clicking the More Forms button displays a gallery of additional types of forms:

- **Multiple Items** This form, sometimes called a *Continuous form*, allows you to see more than one record at a time on a single form page.

- **Datasheet** This form looks and behaves like a datasheet (table).

- **Split Form** This form provides two synchronized views of the same data, one in a form and the other in a datasheet. This greatly simplifies the process of finding and editing records.

- **Modal Dialog** This form looks and behaves like a dialog box. It has default OK and Cancel buttons. When it is active, nothing else can be done until it is closed.

- **PivotChart** This form displays interactive information in a chart.

- **PivotTable** This form displays an interactive table that uses whatever calculation methods you specify to summarize the data.

Using E-Mail Forms to Collect Data

If you use Microsoft Outlook, you can create survey forms that you can send to other people in e-mail messages. When people respond, you can have Access automatically add the responses to a database table. For example, you might use this capability to gather status reports or order information.

For this process to work, the survey form recipients must be using an e-mail program that supports e-mail messages formatted as HTML. These days, most mainstream e-mail programs support this format. If your organization uses Microsoft Outlook 2007 or Outlook 2010 and Microsoft Office InfoPath 2007 or later, you can also collect data via an InfoPath form.

See Also For information about additional options and refinements you can make to e-mail surveys, search for *Add the data collected through e-mails to your Access database* in Access Help.

The Collect Data Through E-mail Messages wizard guides you through the process of creating an e-mail survey form. You can create different types of surveys depending on the applications that are installed on your computer.

To collect data from an e-mail survey form:

1. Create a database table containing the fields you want to include in your survey form, and position the cursor in the first empty record.

2. On the External Data tab, in the Collect Data group, click the Create E-mail button. The wizard displays its first page.

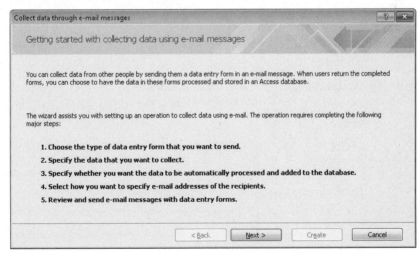

The wizard provides an overview of the process.

3. Follow the steps in the wizard to create the form, add and reorder the fields from the table, change field labels, specify the Outlook folder to which the survey results will be delivered, specify that Outlook should automatically add replies to the original Access database table, and specify the survey recipients.

4. Customize the subject and text of the e-mail message that will be created, and then on the Create The E-Mail Message page, click Create.

   If Outlook is not already running on your computer, the program starts and displays a generic message along with a form based on the selected table.

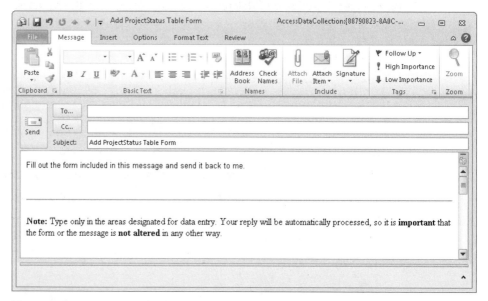

The e-mail message contains instructions to the recipients about what to do with the survey form.

Troubleshooting The appearance of buttons and groups on the ribbon changes depending on the width of the program window. For more information, see "Modifying the Display of the Ribbon" at the beginning of this book.

5. Make any necessary changes to the Subject line and message, enter the addresses of the survey recipients on the To line, and then send the message.

   Tip When sending a data collection e-mail message to more than one person, it is good e-mail etiquette to enter your own e-mail address on the To line and other people's addresses on the Bcc line. That way, if a message recipient clicks Reply All, his or her response will go only to you, rather than to all the original recipients.

Message recipients respond to the survey by replying to your message. Outlook delivers survey responses to the Access Data Collection Replies folder (which it creates the first time you need it). You can view individual survey responses and the status of the data collection process in this folder, and you can view the collected survey data in the original table.

To change the way Access processes message replies, display the table and then click the Manage Replies button in the Collect Data group. In the Manage Data Collection Messages dialog box, you can click Message Options to adjust the automatic processing options, specify the number of replies to be processed, and choose when to stop collecting data. You can also resend or delete the message containing the survey form.

Key Points

- Forms have three main sections: Form Header, Detail, and Form Footer. You can size them to suit the needs of the form.

- You can customize any section of your form's layout by adding and deleting labels, moving labels and text box controls, and adding graphics.

- After you define a relationship between tables, you can add subforms to your forms.

- You can create forms to send in Outlook e-mail and automatically update an Access database with the responses.

Chapter at a Glance

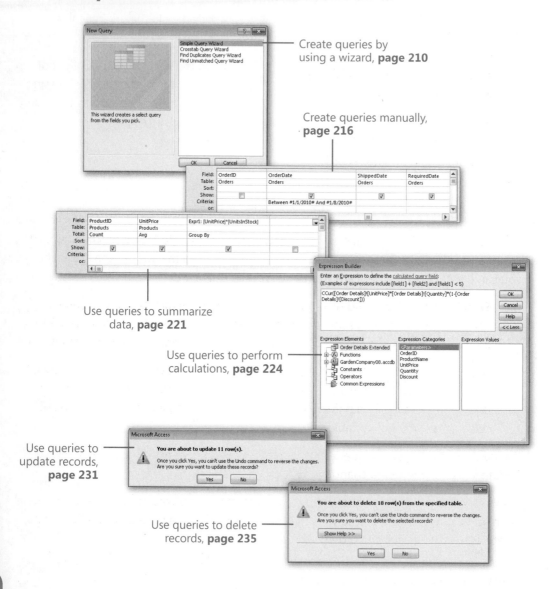

Create queries by
using a wizard, **page 210**

Create queries manually,
page 216

Use queries to summarize
data, **page 221**

Use queries to perform
calculations, **page 224**

Use queries to
update records,
page 231

Use queries to delete
records, **page 235**

8 Create Queries

In this chapter, you will learn how to

- ✔ Create queries by using a wizard.
- ✔ Create queries manually.
- ✔ Use queries to summarize data.
- ✔ Use queries to perform calculations.
- ✔ Use queries to update records.
- ✔ Use queries to delete records.

Microsoft Access 2010 provides a variety of tools you can use to locate specific items of information. In addition to sorting and filtering tables and forms, with a little more effort, you can create queries. There are two basic types of queries:

- **Select queries** These find records in the database that match the criteria you specify and then display those records in a datasheet, form, or report. You can use select queries to display specific fields from specific records from one or more tables.

- **Action queries** These find records in the database that match the criteria you specify and then do something with those records. You can use action queries to ensure the ongoing accuracy of a database; for example, by updating information or deleting selected records from a table.

You can save both types of queries and run the saved queries at any time to generate updated results when data changes.

In this chapter, you'll create queries to locate information that matches multiple criteria. Then you'll create queries to summarize data and perform calculations. Finally, you'll create an update query and a delete query.

> **Practice Files** Before you can complete the exercises in this chapter, you need to copy the book's practice files to your computer. The practice file you'll use to complete the exercises in this chapter is in the Chapter08 practice file folder. A complete list of practice files is provided in "Using the Practice Files" at the beginning of this book.

Creating Queries by Using a Wizard

In Chapter 4 "Display Data," you learned how to retrieve information from a database table by filtering it. These techniques are effective, but limited in the following ways:

- The Filter commands are not saved, or are saved only temporarily.
- The Filter commands are applied only to the table or form that is currently open.

If you want a filter to be permanently available, or if you want to filter more than one table or tables that are not open, you need to move beyond filters and into the realm of queries.

The most common type of query is the select query. The easiest way to set up a select query, especially when you are first learning about them, is to use a Query wizard. Four wizards are available:

- **Simple** This wizard sets up a query to retrieve data from one or more tables and displays the results in a datasheet. For example, you could use a simple query to extract the name and address of every customer who has ever placed an order.

- **Find Duplicates** This wizard sets up a query to locate records that have the same information in one or more fields that you specify. For example, you could use this type of query to extract the name and address of every customer who has placed more than one order.

- **Find Unmatched** This wizard sets up a query to locate records in one table that don't have related records in another table. For example, you could use this type of select query to locate people in the Customer table who have never placed an order.

- **Crosstab** This wizard sets up a query to calculate and restructure data for easier analysis. You can use a crosstab query to calculate a sum, average, count, or other type of total for data that is grouped by two types of information, one down the left side of the datasheet and one across the top. The cell at the junction of each row and column displays the results of the query's calculation.

The process of creating a simple select query by using the Query wizard is almost identical to that of creating a form by using the Form wizard. For a query to work effectively with multiple tables, Access must understand the relationships between the fields in those tables.

See Also For more information about creating relationships, see "Creating Relationships Between Tables" in Chapter 2, "Create Databases and Simple Tables."

Regardless of whether you create a query by using a wizard or manually, what you create is a statement describing the conditions that must be met for records to be matched in one or more tables. When you run the query, the matching records appear in a new datasheet.

In this exercise, you'll use the Simple Query wizard to create a query that combines information from two tables that are related through a common field. You'll then look at the underlying structure of the query, hide some fields, and sort the query results.

SET UP You need the GardenCompany08_start database located in your Chapter08 practice file folder to complete this exercise. Open the GardenCompany08_start database, and save it as *GardenCompany08*. Then follow the steps.

Query
Wizard

1. On the **Create** tab, in the **Queries** group, click the **Query Wizard** button.

   The New Query dialog box opens.

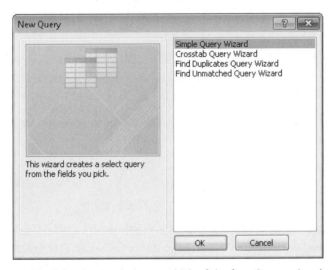

In this dialog box, you choose which of the four Query wizards you want to use.

2. With **Simple Query Wizard** selected in the list, click **OK**.

   The Simple Query wizard starts.

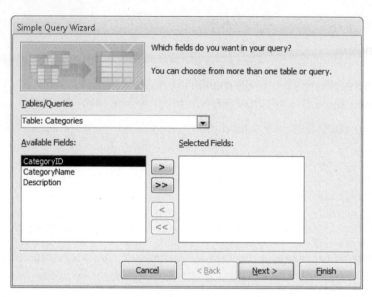

If no table is selected in the Navigation pane when you click the Query wizard button, the first table in the list is selected on the wizard's first page.

3. Display the **Tables/Queries** list, and click **Table: Customers**. Then click the **Move All** button to move all the fields from the **Available Fields** list to the **Selected Fields** list.

4. In the **Selected Fields** list, click the **PhoneNumber** field, and then click the **Remove** button.

   This is the quickest way to move all but one or two fields to the Selected Fields list, especially if a table has many fields.

5. Display the **Tables/Queries** list, and click **Table: Orders.**

6. In the **Available Fields** list, double-click the **OrderID**, **OrderDate**, **ShippedDate**, and **RequiredDate** fields to move them to the **Selected Fields** list. Then click **Next**.

   Tip If a relationship between the tables hasn't already been defined, you will be prompted to define it. You will then need to restart the wizard.

   On the wizard's second page, you specify whether you want to see detailed or summarized query results.

7. With **Detail** selected, click **Next**.

   See Also For information about summarizing data with a query, see "Using Queries to Summarize Data" later in this chapter.

8. On the wizard's last page, change the query title to **Customer Orders**. Then with **Open the query to view information** selected, click **Finish**.

   Access runs the query and displays the results in a datasheet.

9. Scroll the datasheet to the right.

   The requested order information is displayed to the right of each customer's information.

PostalCode ▾	Country ▾	OrderID ▾	OrderDate ▾	ShippedDate ▾	RequiredDat ▾
88004	USA	11080	1/5/2010	1/6/2010	
V4T 1Y9	Canada	11140	2/1/2010	2/2/2010	
V4T 1Y9	Canada	11149	2/2/2010	2/3/2010	2/7/2010
88052	USA	11092	1/16/2010	1/19/2010	
88072	USA	11094	1/22/2010	1/23/2010	
88277	USA	11093	1/19/2010	1/21/2010	
88053	USA	11110	1/24/2010	1/25/2010	
88902	USA	11139	1/31/2010	2/1/2010	
49707	USA	11103	1/23/2010	1/24/2010	1/28/2010
87008	USA	11105	1/23/2010	1/25/2010	
88121	USA	11081	1/6/2010	1/7/2010	
84112	USA	11125	1/29/2010	1/30/2010	2/3/2010
84306	USA	11129	1/30/2010	1/31/2010	
V7L 1L3	Canada	11153	2/3/2010	2/7/2010	
V7L 5A6	Canada	11151	2/3/2010	2/5/2010	
88119	USA	11152	2/3/2010	2/7/2010	
88007	USA	11096	1/22/2010	1/23/2010	
73844	USA	11084	1/12/2010	1/14/2010	
88115	USA	11131	1/30/2010	1/31/2010	

Record: ◄ ◄ 1 of 87 ► ►I ►※ ※ No Filter Search

The customers who have placed orders appear in the query results.

10. On the **View Shortcuts** toolbar, click the **Design View** button.

    Access displays the query in the Query Designer.

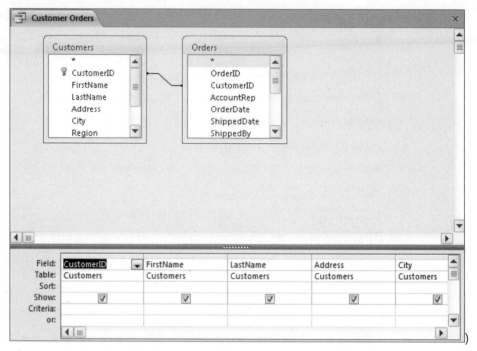

The Customer Orders query in the Query Designer.

In the top pane of the Query Designer, the Customers and Orders field lists are linked by a relationship based on the CustomerID field in both tables. In the bottom pane, the fields used in the query appear in the cells of the Field row, and each field's table is identified in the Table row. In the Show row, each field's check box is selected by default. If you want to use a field in a query—for example, to sort by, to set criteria for, or in a calculation—but don't want to see the field in the results datasheet, you can clear its Show check box in the design grid.

See Also For more information about the Query Designer, see the next section, "Creating Queries Manually."

11. In the **Show** row, clear the check boxes for **CustomerID**, **Address**, **Country**, and **OrderID**.

12. In the **Sort** row, click the **PostalCode** field, click the arrow that appears, and then click **Ascending**.

   When you run the query, the results in the datasheet will now be sorted on this field.

The modified Customer Orders query.

13. On the **Design** tab, in the **Results** group, click the **Run** button.

> **Tip** When a query is open, you can also simply switch to Datasheet view to run a query.

The datasheet shows the new results.

FirstName	LastName	City	Region	PostalCode	OrderDate	Sh
Luciana	Ramos	Helena	MT	49624	1/12/2010	
Randall	Boseman	Butte	MT	49707	1/23/2010	
Scott	Gode	Pocatello	ID	73204	1/30/2010	
Richard	Lum	Boise	ID	73704	2/2/2010	
Brian	Cox	Moscow	ID	73844	1/12/2010	
Parul	Manek	Provo	UT	74606	2/6/2010	
Kathie	Flood	Glendale	CA	81203	1/29/2010	
Ben	Miller	Granada Hills	CA	81344	2/7/2010	
Scott	Mitchell	Escondido	CA	82029	2/7/2010	
Patricia	Doyle	Carmel Valley	CA	83924	1/26/2010	
David	Campbell	San Francisco	CA	84112	1/29/2010	
Patrick	Sands	San Francisco	CA	84140	2/6/2010	
Chris	Cannon	Palo Alto	CA	84306	1/30/2010	
Ted	Bremer	Beaverton	OR	87008	1/23/2010	
Sydney	Higa	Portland	OR	87201	1/22/2010	
Andrew R.	Hill	Portland	OR	87210	1/29/2010	
Modesto	Estrada	Burns	OR	87710	1/14/2010	
Anne	Hellung-Larsen	Elgin	OR	87827	1/26/2010	
Karan	Khanna	Auburn	WA	88001	1/6/2010	

Record: 1 of 87   No Filter   Search

Four fields no longer appear in the datasheet, and the extracted records are sorted on the PostalCode field.

 CLEAN UP Close the Customer Orders query, saving your changes. Retain the GardenCompany08 database for use in later exercises.

Creating Queries Manually

The Query wizards guide you through the creation of the common queries, but you create less common queries manually in Design view, by using the Query Designer.

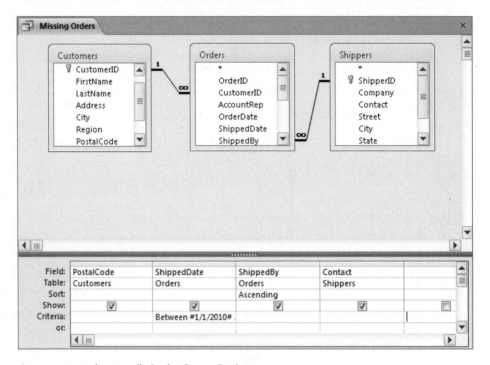

A query created manually in the Query Designer.

You are already somewhat familiar with the Query Designer, but let's review:

- In the Diagram pane at the top the Query Designer are field lists for the tables that can be included in the query.

- Lines connecting the field lists indicate that the tables are related by common fields.

- A table's primary key field is indicated in its field list by a key icon.

- The Field row of the Grid pane at the bottom of the Query Designer contains the names of the fields actually included in the query.

- The Table row shows which table each field belongs to.

- The Sort row indicates which field(s) the query results will be sorted on, if any.

- A selected check box in the Show row means that the field will be displayed in the results datasheet. (If the check box isn't selected, the field can be used in determining the query results, but it won't be displayed.)

- The Criteria row can contain criteria that determine which records will be displayed.

- The Or row sets up alternate criteria.

When you create a query manually, you add field lists for the tables you want to use to the Diagram pane of the Query Designer and then either double-click or drag fields from the lists to consecutive columns of the Grid pane. You then indicate which field to sort the matched records on and which field values to show in the results datasheet. But as with filters, the power of queries lies in the criteria you can set up in the Criteria and Or rows. This is where you can specify precisely which information you want to extract.

See Also For information about filters, see Chapter 4, "Display Data."

If you want to run an existing query with a variation of the same basic criteria, you can display the existing query in Design view, modify the criteria, and then rerun the query. However, it would be tedious to do this more than a couple of times. If you know you will often run variations of the same query, you can set it up as a parameter query. Parameter queries display a dialog box to prompt for the information to be used in the query. For example, suppose you know you are getting low on the stock of an item and you need to place an order for more of that product with the supplier. You might use a parameter query to request the name of a supplier so that you can identify other products you purchase from that supplier before placing the order. This type of query is particularly useful when used as the basis for a report that is run periodically.

In this exercise, you'll re-create the Customer Orders query by manually specifying criteria in the design grid. You'll add criteria to extract the records for specific dates, and then modify the query so that it requests the dates to extract at run time.

SET UP You need the GardenCompany08 database you worked with in the preceding exercise to complete this exercise. Open the GardenCompany08 database, and then follow the steps.

1. On the **Create** tab, in the **Queries** group, click the **Query Design** button.

    Access displays a blank query design grid and opens the Show Table dialog box.

The Tables page of the Show Table dialog box.

2. In the dialog box, double-click **Customers**, double-click **Orders**, and then click **Close**.

   Access adds a Query Tools Design contextual tab to the ribbon.

   Tip To add the field list for another table to an existing query, you can redisplay the Show Table dialog box at any time by clicking the Show Table button in the Query Setup group on the Design contextual tab. You can also drag the table from the Navigation pane to the Diagram pane of the Query Designer. To delete a table from a query, right-click the table's field list, and then click Remove Table.

3. Double-click the title of the **Customers** field list to select all the fields in the list. Then point to the selection, and drag down to the **Field** row of the first column in the grid.

   Access copies all the fields into consecutive columns and inserts Customers into the Table row of each column to indicate the source of the field.

   Tip The asterisk at the top of each field list represents all the fields in the table. Dragging the asterisk to a column in the Field row inserts a single field that represents all the fields, meaning that you cannot then manipulate the fields individually.

4. Scroll the grid to the right, and click in the **Field** row of the next blank column. Then in the **Orders** field list, in turn double-click the **OrderID**, **OrderDate**, **ShippedDate**, and **RequiredDate** fields.

   Access adds the fields from the Orders table to the next four columns.

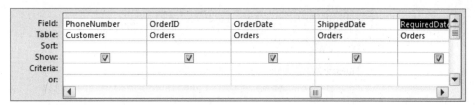

You have added fields from two tables to the design grid.

5. Point to the gray field selector above the **PhoneNumber** field, and when the pointer changes to a black down arrow, click to select the column. Then in the **Query Setup** group, click the **Delete Columns** button.

   Keyboard Shortcut Press Delete to delete the selected column.

   See Also For more information about keyboard shortcuts, see "Keyboard Shortcuts" at the end of this book.

6. In the **Show** row, clear the check boxes of the **OrderID**, **Country**, **Address**, and **CustomerID** fields.

7. In the **Sort** row, set the **PostalCode** field to **Ascending**.

   You have now manually recreated the Customer Orders query from the previous exercise.

Run

8. In the **Results** group, click the **Run** button. Check the datasheet to ensure that the query produces the correct results, and then switch back to Design view.

   Let's make this query return the records for a specific range of dates.

9. In the **Criteria** row of the **OrderDate** field, type the following, and then press Enter:

   Between 1/1/2010 And 1/8/2010

   Tip When you type the *A* of *And*, Access displays a list of operators you might be intending to type. You can click an option in the list to save yourself a few keystrokes. In this case, ignore the list, and it will disappear.

10. Point to the right border of the **OrderDate** field selector, and when the pointer changes to a two-headed arrow, double-click to widen the field to fit its contents.

    You can now see the entire criterion in this field.

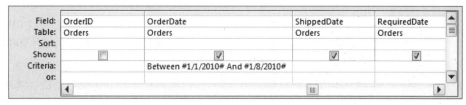

Access has added # signs to designate a date format.

11. Run the query.

Access extracts the matching records.

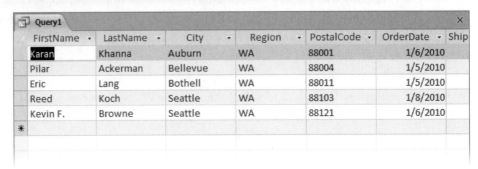

Only five orders were placed in the requested period.

Now let's have the query request the range of dates each time you run it.

12. Switch to Design view. In the **Criteria** row of the **OrderDate** field, type the following exactly as shown, and then press Enter:

Between [Type the beginning date:] And [Type the ending date:]

13. Run the query.

The Enter Parameter Value dialog box opens.

The first Enter Parameter Value dialog box requests the beginning date in the range.

14. In the text box, type **1/8/10**, and click **OK**.

15. In the second **Enter Parameter Value** dialog box, type **1/15/10**, and click **OK**.

Access redisplays the datasheet, this time listing only the nine orders placed between the specified dates.

16. Save the query as **Orders By Date**.

CLEAN UP Close the query. Retain the GardenCompany08 database for use in later exercises.

Using Queries to Summarize Data

You typically use a query to locate all the records that meet some criteria. But sometimes you are not as interested in the details of all the records as you are in summarizing the query results in some way. For example, you might want to know how many orders have been placed this year or the total dollar value of all orders placed.

Tip You don't have to create a query to summarize all the data in a table. You can display the table in Datasheet view and then on the Home tab, in the Records group, click the Totals button to add a Total row at the bottom of the table. (Clicking the Totals button again removes the row from the table.) In the Total row of each field, you can select the type of summary data you want to appear from a list. The types available for each field depend on its data type. For example, you can count all fields, but you can only calculate the sum or average of fields containing numeric data.

The easiest way to extract summary information is by creating a query that groups the necessary fields and does the math for you. The calculations are performed by using one of the following aggregate functions:

- **Sum** Calculates the total of the values in a field

- **Avg** Calculates the average of the values in a field

- **Min** Extracts the lowest value in a field

- **Max** Extracts the highest value in a field

- **Count** Counts the number of values in a field, not counting Null (blank) values

- **StDev** Calculates the standard deviation of the values in a field

- **Var** Calculates the variance of the values in a field

Tip You cannot use aggregate functions in queries in Web databases.

When you use the Simple Query wizard to create a query based on a table that has fields containing numeric data, the wizard gives you the option of creating a summary query. If you click Summary Options, the wizard displays a page on which you can specify the aggregate function you want to use.

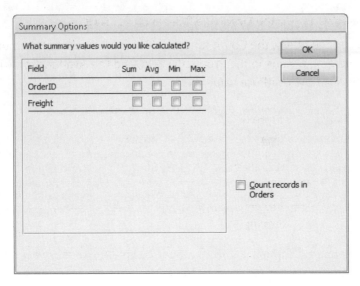

If you are using the Simple Query wizard to build a query with fields that contain numeric data, you can have the wizard add an aggregate function to the query.

When creating a query manually, or modifying an existing query, you can click the Totals button in the Show/Hide group on the Design tab to add a Total row to the grid. You can then select the aggregate function you want from a list.

Tip The list in the Total row also allows you to group fields, select the first or last record that meets the specified criteria, enter an expression, or make additional criteria refinements.

In this exercise, you'll create a query that calculates the total number of products in an inventory, the average price of all the products, and the total value of the inventory.

 SET UP You need the GardenCompany08 database you worked with in the preceding exercise to complete this exercise. Open the GardenCompany08 database, and then follow the steps.

1. Open the **Query Designer**, and add the **Products** field list to the **Diagram** pane.

2. In the **Products** field list, double-click **ProductID**, and then double-click **UnitPrice**.

3. On the **Design** contextual tab, in the **Show/Hide** group, click the **Totals** button.

   Access adds a Total row below the Table row in the Grid pane, and displays the Group By aggregate function in the Total row of each field.

   Tip If you need to adjust the height of the grid after adding the Total row, drag the bar that separates the Diagram and Grid panes upward.

4. Click in the **Total** row of the **ProductID** field, click the arrow, and then in the list, click **Count**.

   Access replaces Group By with the Count aggregate function.

5. Display the **Total** list for the **UnitPrice** field, and click **Avg**.

When you run the query, the Count function will return a count of the number of records containing a value in the ProductID field, and the Avg function will return the average of all the UnitPrice values.

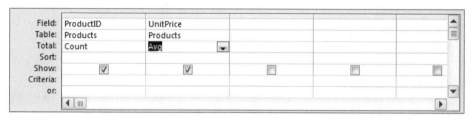

This simple query summarizes the data in two ways.

6. Run the query.

The query returns a single record.

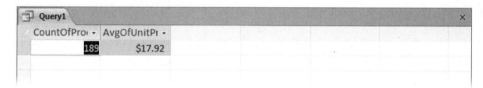

The results show that the average price of 189 products is $17.92.

7. Switch back to Design view.

Now let's add a new field that uses data from two fields in the Products table to perform a calculation.

8. In the **Field** row of the third column, type **UnitPrice*UnitsInStock**, and press Enter.

9. Widen the third column so that you can see the entire contents.

Access has changed the expression you typed to the following:

Expr1: [UnitPrice][UnitsInStock]*

This expression will multiply the price of each product by the number of units in stock.

10. Double-click **Expr1**, and type **Value of Inventory** as the expression's label.

11. Display the **Total** list for the third column, and then click **Sum**.

12. Save the query with the name **Product Analysis**.

13. Run the query.

    The Sum function returns the sum of all the values calculated by the expression.

14. Widen the columns of the results datasheet so that you can see their entire contents.

    Access has summarized the data according to your specifications.

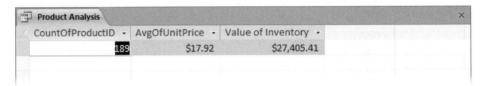

The query has summarized the data in three ways.

 CLEAN UP Close the query. Retain the GardenCompany08 database for use in later exercises.

Using Queries to Perform Calculations

As you saw in the previous exercise, you can not only use a query to summarize data by using built-in aggregate functions but you can also perform a calculation and create a new field in which to store it. For example, you might want to calculate an extended price or how long employees have worked for the company.

One of the basic tenets of good database design is that you should never store information that can be calculated from existing data. Rather than creating a new field in a table and increasing the size of the database with redundant information, you should use the Expression Builder to insert an expression in the design grid that computes the desired information from existing data whenever you need it.

Tip It is possible to use the results of one query as a field in another query. The nested query involves use of a Structured Query Language (SQL) Select statement and is called a *subquery*. For more information about subqueries, search for *Nest a query inside another query or in an expression by using a subquery* in Access Help.

In this exercise, you'll create a query that combines information from two tables into a datasheet and calculates the extended price of an item based on the unit price, quantity ordered, and discount.

SET UP You need the GardenCompany08 database you worked with in the preceding exercise to complete this exercise. Open the GardenCompany08 database, and then follow the steps.

1. Open the **Query Designer**, and add the **Order Details** and **Products** field lists to the **Diagram** pane.

2. Drag the fields in the following table from the field lists to consecutive columns in the design grid.

From this table	Drag this field
Order Details	OrderID
Products	ProductName
Order Details	UnitPrice
Order Details	Quantity
Order Details	Discount

The query will extract information from these five fields.

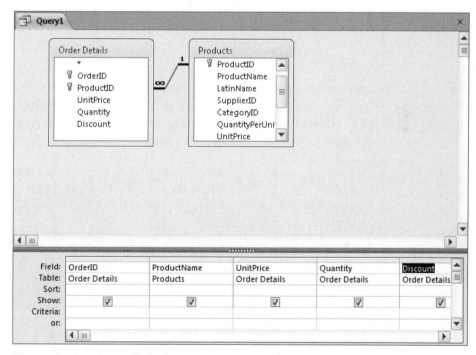

The results datasheet will display the extracted information in the order of the fields in the design grid.

3. Run the query.

Access displays the results in Datasheet view.

OrderID	Product Name	UnitPrice	Quantity	Discount
11091	Autumn crocus	$18.75	4	0
11079	Compost bin	$58.00	1	0
11083	Compost bin	$58.00	1	0
11138	Compost bin	$58.00	1	0
11152	Compost bin	$58.00	1	0
11085	Cactus sand potting mix	$4.50	2	0
11093	Cactus sand potting mix	$4.50	2	0
11121	Cactus sand potting mix	$4.50	1	0
11132	Cactus sand potting mix	$4.50	1	0
11148	Cactus sand potting mix	$4.50	1	0
11114	Weeping Forsythia	$18.00	3	0
11147	Weeping Forsythia	$18.00	1	0
11082	Bat box	$14.75	3	0
11086	Bat box	$14.75	2	0
11159	Bat box	$14.75	3	0.1
11152	Beneficial nematodes	$19.95	1	0
11089	Crown Vetch	$12.95	1	0
11110	Crown Vetch	$12.95	1	0
11089	English Ivy	$5.95	1	0

Record: 1 of 215   No Filter   Search

The results show that the query is working correctly.

4. Save the query with the name **Order Details Extended**.

5. Switch to Design view. Then in the **OrderID** column, display the **Sort** list, and click **Ascending**.

Now in a new field in the design grid, let's use the Expression Builder to insert an expression that computes the extended price by multiplying the unit price by the quantity sold, minus any discount.

6. In the **Field** row, right-click in the first blank column, and then click **Build**.

The Expression Builder dialog box opens.

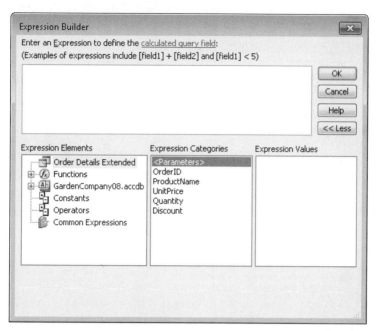

The Expression Builder dialog box.

Here is the expression you are going to build in the expression box:

CCur([Order Details]![UnitPrice]*[Order Details]![Quantity]*(1-[Order Details]![Discount]))

The CCur function converts the results of the math inside its parentheses to currency format.

Tip If you wanted to type this expression directly into the field, you could simplify it to this:

CCur([Order Details]![UnitPrice]*[Quantity]*(1-[Discount]))

The [Order Details]! part is required only for the UnitPrice field, which appears in both tables. It tells the query which table to use.

7. In the **Expression Elements** list, double-click **Functions**, and then click **Built-In Functions**.

8. In the **Expression Categories** list, click **Conversion**. Then in the **Expression Values** list, double-click **CCur**.

Access inserts the currency conversion function into the expression box.

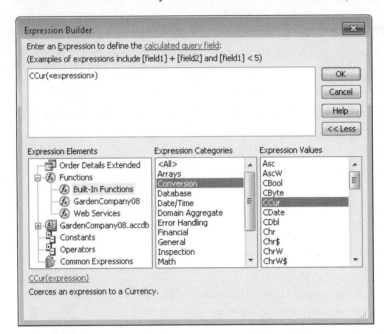

The <<expression>> inside the parentheses represents the expressions that will eventually result in the number Access should convert to currency format.

9. In the expression box, click **<<expression>>** to select it, so that the next thing you enter will replace it.

   The next expression element is the UnitPrice field from the Order Details table.

10. In the **Expression Elements** list, click the minus icon to the left of **Functions** to collapse that element. Then click the plus icon to the left of **GardenCompany08.accdb**, double-click **Tables**, and click **Order Details**.

11. In the **Expression Categories** list, double-click **UnitPrice**.

    Access replaces the <<expression>> placeholder with the table/field information, leaving the cursor after [UnitPrice], which is exactly where you want it. Now you want to multiply the amount in the UnitPrice field by the amount in the Quantity field.

12. In the **Expression Elements** list, click **Operators**; in the **Expression Categories** list, click **Arithmetic**; and in the **Expression Values** list, double-click ***** (multiply).

    Access inserts the multiplication sign and an <<Expr>> placeholder.

13. In the expression box, click **<<Expr>>** to select it. In the **Expression Elements** list, double-click **GardenCompany08.accdb**, double-click **Tables**, and click **Order Details**. Then in the **Expression Categories** list, double-click **Quantity**.

So far, you have entered an expression that calculates the total cost by multiplying the price of an item by the quantity ordered. However, suppose the sale price is discounted due to quantity or another factor. The discount, which is stored in the Order Details table, is expressed as the percentage to deduct. But it is easier to compute the percentage to be paid than it is to compute the discount and subtract it from the total cost.

14. In the expression box, type ***(1-**. In the **Expression Categories** list, double-click **Discount**. Then type **)**.

Although the discount is formatted in the datasheet as a percentage, it is actually stored in the database as a decimal number between 0 and 1. (For example, a discount displayed as 10% is stored as 0.1). So if the discount is 10 percent, the result of (1-Discount) is 0.9. In other words, the formula multiplies the unit price by the quantity and then multiplies that result by 0.9.

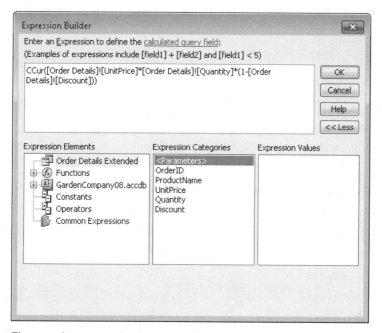

The complete expression.

Tip If an entire expression isn't visible in the expression box, you can widen the Expression Builder dialog box by dragging its left or right border.

15. In the **Expression Builder** dialog box, click **OK**.

Access enters the expression in the design grid.

16. Press Enter to complete the entry of the expression. Then widen the column so that the entire expression is visible.

    Access has assigned the label Expr1 to the field. (This label is known as the *field alias*.)

17. In the design grid, double-click **Expr1**, and then type **ExtendedPrice**.

18. Run the query.

    Access displays the results in a datasheet.

OrderID ▾	Product Name ▾	UnitPrice ▾	Quantity ▾	Discount ▾	ExtendedPrice ▴
11079	Crushed rock	$62.50	1	0	$62.5(
11079	Compost bin	$58.00	1	0	$58.0(
11080	Douglas Fir	$18.75	1	0	$18.75
11080	Fortune Rhododendron	$24.00	2	0.1	$43.2(
11081	Golden Larch	$27.00	1	0	$27.0(
11081	Lawn cart	$85.00	1	0.1	$76.5(
11082	Bat box	$14.75	3	0	$44.25
11083	Compost bin	$58.00	1	0	$58.0(
11083	GrowGood potting soil	$6.35	1	0	$6.35
11083	QwikRoot	$18.00	1	0	$18.0(
11083	Grass rake	$11.95	1	0	$11.95
11084	Gooseberries	$7.50	3	0	$22.5(
11084	Ambrosia	$6.25	1	0	$6.25
11084	Blackberries	$4.50	6	0	$27.0(
11085	Cactus sand potting mix	$4.50	2	0	$9.0(
11086	Bat box	$14.75	2	0	$29.5(
11087	Pea gravel	$24.00	3	0	$72.0(
11088	Grandiflora Hydrangeas	$40.00	1	0	$40.0(
11089	Crown Vetch	$12.95	1	0	$12.95 ▾

Order Details Extended

Record: I◄ ◄ 1 of 215 ► ►I ►☐   ⚑ No Filter   Search

The orders are now sorted by the OrderID field, and the extended price is calculated in the last field.

19. In the few records with discounts, verify that the query calculates the extended price correctly.

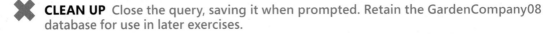

CLEAN UP Close the query, saving it when prompted. Retain the GardenCompany08 database for use in later exercises.

Using Queries to Update Records

As you use a database and as it grows, you might discover that errors creep in or that some information becomes out of date. You can tediously scroll through the records looking for those that need to be changed, but it is more efficient to use the tools and techniques provided by Access for that purpose.

If you want to find or replace multiple instances of the same word or phrase, you can use the Find and Replace commands in the Find group on the Home tab. These commands work much like the same commands in Microsoft Word or Microsoft Excel.

If you want to manipulate information stored in the database only under certain circumstances, you need the power of an action query. An action query performs an action on the results of the selection process in one operation. For example, you can increase the price of all products in one category by a certain percentage, or remove all the items belonging to a specific product line. This type of data manipulation is easy to do with an action query. Not only does using a query save time, but it helps to avoid errors.

Four types of actions are available:

- **Append** These add records from one or more tables to the end of one or more other tables.
- **Delete** These delete records from one or more tables.
- **Make-table** These create a new table from all or part of the data in one or more tables.
- **Update** These make changes to records in one or more tables.

Tip In addition to these queries, you can create SQL queries, such as union, pass through, and data definition queries. SQL queries are beyond the scope of this book. For information, search for *Introduction to Access SQL* in Access Help.

You can't create an action query directly; you must first create a select query and then convert it. With an existing select query open in the Query Designer, you can click the appropriate button in the Query Type group on the Design contextual tab. (You can also right-click the query in the Query Designer, click Query Type, and then click the command you want.)

Important Running an update query makes irreversible changes to the underlying table. You should always create a backup copy of the table before running this type of query. You can quickly create a copy of a table by displaying the Tables list in the Navigation pane, clicking the table you want to copy, pressing Ctrl+C, and then pressing Ctrl+V to paste a copy. In the Paste Table As dialog box, type a name for the new table, and then click OK. The backup table then becomes part of the database. You can delete it when you are sure that the update query produced the results you want.

In this exercise, you'll create an update query to increase the price of selected items by 10 percent.

SET UP You need the GardenCompany08 database you worked with in the preceding exercise to complete this exercise. Open the GardenCompany08 database, and then follow the steps.

1. On the **Create** tab, in the **Queries** group, click the **Query Wizard** button. Then with **Simple Query Wizard** selected in the **New Query** dialog box, click **OK**.

2. Display **Table: Categories** in the **Tables/Queries** list, and in the **Available Fields** list, double-click **CategoryName** to move it to the **Selected Fields** list.

3. Display **Table: Products** in the **Tables/Queries** list, and in the **Available Fields** list, double-click **ProductName** and **UnitPrice** to move them to the **Selected Fields** list.

4. Click **Finish** to create the query using the default detail setting and title.

   Access displays the query results in a datasheet.

Category Nam ▾	Product Name ▾	Unit Pric ▾
Bulbs	Magic Lily	$44.00
Bulbs	Autumn crocus	$20.63
Bulbs	Anemone	$30.80
Bulbs	Lily-of-the-Field	$41.80
Bulbs	Siberian Iris	$14.25
Bulbs	Daffodil	$14.25
Bulbs	Peony	$21.95
Bulbs	Lilies	$11.55
Bulbs	Begonias	$20.85
Bulbs	Bulb planter	$7.65
Cacti	Prickly Pear	$3.30
Ground covers	Crown Vetch	$12.95
Ground covers	English Ivy	$5.95
Ground covers	European Ginger	$6.25
Ground covers	St. John's Wort	$9.75
Ground covers	Fairies Fern	$9.95
Grasses	The Best Bluegrass	$17.95
Grasses	Colonial Bentgrass	$15.50
Grasses	Creeping Bentgrass	$12.05

Categories Query

Record: 1 of 189   No Filter   Search

Only the Category Name, Product Name, and Unit Price fields are displayed.

5. Switch to Design view.

   The current query results include the products in all categories. You want to raise the prices of only the products in the Bulbs and Cacti categories, so your next task is to change the query to select only those categories.

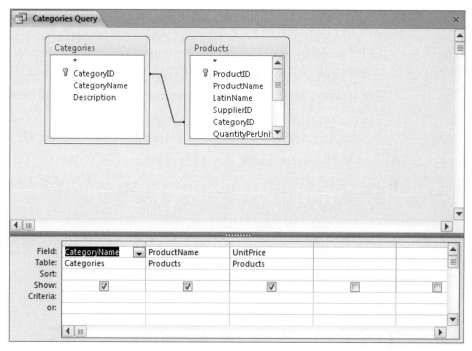

This query was created by the Simple Query wizard.

6. In the **Criteria** row of the **CategoryName** field, type **bulbs**. Then in the **or** row of the same field, type **cacti**. Press Enter.

7. Run the query to confirm that only bulbs and cacti are listed, and then return to Design view.

   The query now selects only the records you want to change. But to actually make a change to the records, you have to convert this select query to an update query.

8. On the **Design** contextual tab, in the **Query Type** group, click the **Update** button.

   Access converts the select query to an update query.

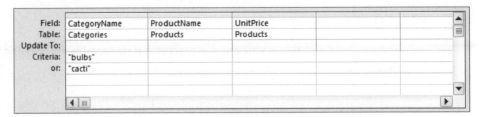

Field:	CategoryName	ProductName	UnitPrice		
Table:	Categories	Products	Products		
Update To:					
Criteria:	"bulbs"				
or:	"cacti"				

In the design grid, the Sort and Show rows disappear and an Update To row appears.

9. In the **Update To** row, under **UnitPrice**, type **[UnitPrice]*1.1**. Then press Enter.

   Tip Enclosing UnitPrice in square brackets indicates it as a database object—in this case, a field in a table. If you use the Expression Builder to insert this expression, it looks like this: *[Products]![UnitPrice]*1.1*. Because this description of the field includes the table in which it is found, you can also insert this expression in other tables.

10. Switch to Datasheet view (don't run the query).

    Important In a select query, clicking the View button or the Datasheet View button is the same as clicking the Run button. But in an update query, clicking the View button or the Datasheet View button simply displays a list of the fields that will be updated.

    You see a list of unit prices. These are the same as those you viewed earlier; they have not been changed yet.

11. Switch to Design view. Then run the query.

    Access asks you to confirm that you want to update the records.

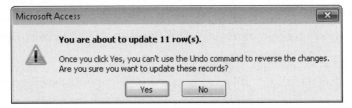

This warning cautions that you can't undo the changes you are about to make.

12. In the message box, click **Yes**. Then switch to Datasheet view.

    The prices in the UnitPrice field have been increased by 10 percent.

✖ CLEAN UP Close the Categories query, saving your changes. Retain the GardenCompany08 database for use in the last exercise.

Using Queries to Delete Records

Over time, some of the information stored in a database might become obsolete. For example, the Products table in our sample database lists all the products the company currently offers for sale or has sold in the past. You can indicate that a product is no longer available for sale by placing a check mark in the Discontinued field. Discontinued products aren't displayed in the catalog or offered for sale, but they are kept in the database for a while in case it becomes practical to sell them again. A similar situation could exist with customers who haven't placed an order in a long time or who have asked to be removed from a mailing list but might still place orders.

To maintain an efficient database, it is a good idea to clean house and discard outdated records from time to time. You could scroll through the tables and delete records manually, but if all the records you want to delete match some pattern, you can use a delete query to quickly get rid of all of them.

It is important to keep two things in mind when deleting records from a database:

- You can't recover deleted records.
- The effects of a delete query can be more far-reaching than you intend.

If the table from which you are deleting records is related to another table, and the Cascade Delete Related Records option for that relationship is selected, records in the second table will also be deleted. (*Cascade Delete* essentially means that the deletion is also applied to related records.) Sometimes this is what you want, but sometimes it isn't. For example, you probably don't want to delete records of previous sales at the same time that you delete discontinued products.

As a precaution, before actually deleting records, you might want to display the Relationships page by clicking the Relationships button in the Relationships group on the Database Tools tab. If the table you are deleting data from has a relationship with any table containing information that shouldn't be deleted, right-click the relationship line, click Edit Relationship, and make sure that if the Enforce Referential Integrity check box is selected, the Cascade Delete Related Records check box is *not* selected.

As a further safeguard against potential problems, you will want to back up your database before deleting the records. You might also want to create a new table (perhaps named *Deleted<file name>*) and then move the records you want to delete to the new table, where you can review them before deleting them permanently.

See Also For information about backing up a database, see "Preventing Database Problems" in Chapter 12, "Protect Databases."

In this exercise, you'll create a delete query that will remove the records of discontinued products from a table.

 SET UP You need the GardenCompany08 database you worked with in the preceding exercise to complete this exercise. Open the GardenCompany08 database, and then follow the steps.

1. Open the **Query Designer**, and add the **Products** field list to the **Diagram** pane.

2. In the **Products** field list, double-click ***** (the asterisk).

   The Field row of the first column of the design grid now contains Products.* and the Table row of the column contains Products.

   Double-clicking the asterisk in the field list is a quick way to move all the fields to the query, without each field taking up a column in the grid and possibly making it necessary to scroll from side to side to see them all. However, selecting all the fields in this way prevents you from setting Sort, Show, and Criteria values for individual fields. To set these values, you have to add the specific fields to the design grid, thereby adding them twice.

   Tip To avoid displaying the fields twice in the results of a select query, clear the check box in the Show row of the duplicate individual fields.

3. In the **Products** field list, double-click **Discontinued** to copy it to the next available column in the design grid.

 4. On the **Design** tab, in the **Query Type** group, click the **Delete** button.

   Access converts this select query to a delete query.

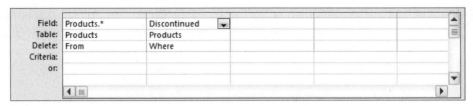

In the design grid, the Sort and Show rows disappear, and a Delete row appears.

In the first column, which contains the reference to all fields in the Products table, the Delete row contains the word *From*, indicating that this is the table from which records will be deleted. When you add individual fields to the remaining columns, as you did with the Discontinued field, the Delete row displays *Where*, indicating that this field can include deletion criteria. The Discontinued field is set to the Yes/No data type, which is represented in the datasheet as a check box that is selected to indicate Yes and cleared to indicate No. To locate all discontinued products, you need to identify records with the Discontinued field set to Yes.

5. In the **Criteria** row of the **Discontinued** field, type **Yes**, and then press Enter.

6. To check the accuracy of the query, switch to Database view.

   Testing the query results in a list of 18 discontinued products that would be deleted if you ran the query.

7. Scroll to the right to verify that for all records, the **Products.Discontinued** check box is selected.

8. Switch back to Design view, and run the query.

   Access displays a warning.

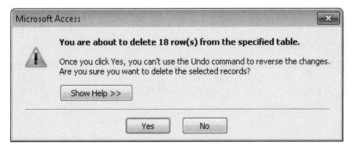

Before deleting the records, Access reminds you of the permanence of this action.

9. In the message box, click **Yes**.

Access displays a warning.

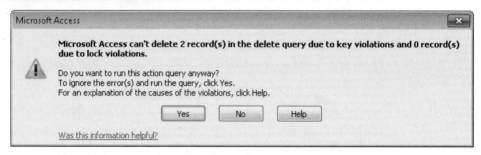

Access cannot delete two of the discontinued records.

Two discontinued records cannot be deleted because they have entries in the Order Details table. You need to decide whether to set the Discontinued field of these products to No (clear their check boxes) or to delete the entries from the Order Details table before allowing the query to delete the product records.

10. In the message box, click **No** to postpone the deletion until you can track down and resolve the two key violations.

Suppose you are concerned that someone might accidentally run this delete query and destroy records you weren't ready to destroy. Let's change the query back to a select query before saving it.

11. On the **Design** tab, in the **Query Type** group, click the **Select** button.

In the design grid, the Delete row disappears, and the Sort and Show rows reappear.

12. Save the query with the name **Delete Discontinued Products**.

You can now open the select query in Design view and change it to a delete query the next time you want to run it.

 **CLEAN UP** Close the query, and then close the GardenCompany08 database.

Key Points

- To display specific fields from specific records from one or more tables, you can create a query. You can save the query for later use.

- You can create a query by using a wizard or by using the Query Designer.

- Queries can use aggregate functions such as Sum and Avg to summarize data.

- You can design queries that perform calculations on matched data.

- An update query performs an updating action on its results, such as replacing the contents of a field.

- A delete query deletes records that meet specific criteria. Use caution with this type of query; the effects can be far reaching, and you can't recover deleted records.

Chapter at a Glance

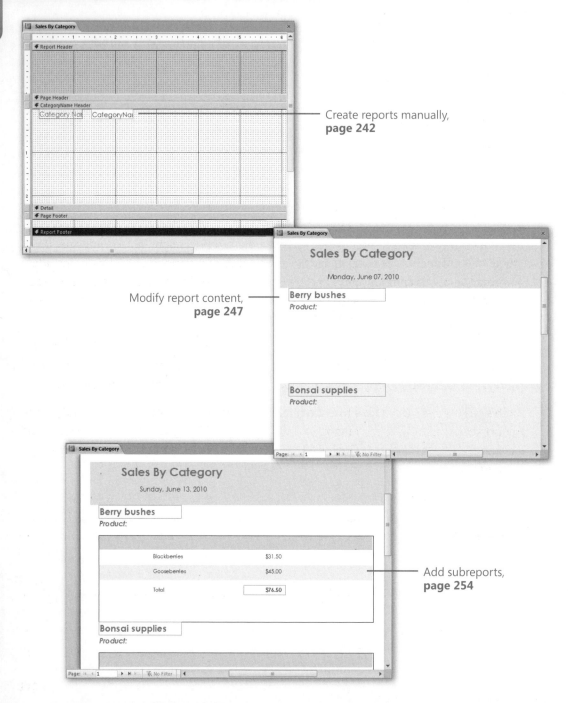

Create reports manually,
page 242

Modify report content,
page 247

Add subreports,
page 254

9 Create Custom Reports

In this chapter, you will learn how to

✔ Create reports manually.

✔ Modify report content.

✔ Add subreports.

Reports often include sets of information that are related to the topic of the report, but not necessarily related to each other. For example, a report might include information about the production, marketing, and sales activities of a company. Or it might include information about compensation and the company's pension plan. Each topic is related to a particular aspect of running the business, but they don't all fit nicely into the structure of an individual Microsoft Access 2010 report.

One solution to this problem is to create separate reports, print them, and store them together in a binder. Another is to save them in electronic format in a folder or on a network. An easier and more graceful solution is to combine them by using subreports.

In this chapter, you'll see how to build a fairly complex report. You'll start by creating the report shell (the main report) manually in Design view. Then you'll modify the layout and content of the shell report. Finally, you'll see how to provide detailed information by embedding a subreport within the main report.

Tip This chapter builds on the discussion of reports in Chapter 5, "Create Simple Reports."

> **Practice Files** Before you can complete the exercises in this chapter, you need to copy the book's practice files to your computer. The practice file you'll use to complete the exercises in this chapter is in the Chapter09 practice file folder. A complete list of practice files is provided in "Using the Practice Files" at the beginning of this book.

Creating Reports Manually

When a report includes controls that are bound to specific fields in one or more tables, usually the most efficient way to create the report is by using the Report wizard. When you include more than one table in a report, the wizard evaluates the relationships between the tables and offers to group the records in any logical manner available. As with multi-table forms, if you haven't already established the relationships between the tables, you have to cancel the wizard and establish them before continuing.

Tip If you are using more than two tables in a report, or if you will be using the same combination of tables in several reports or forms, you can save time by creating a query based on those tables and then using the results of that query as the basis for the report or form. For information about queries, see Chapter 8, "Create Queries."

When a report includes mostly unbound controls, which don't pull information from underlying tables, it is easier to create the report manually in Design view. In this view, you see the structure of the report laid out on a design grid, in much the same arrangement as a form in Design view.

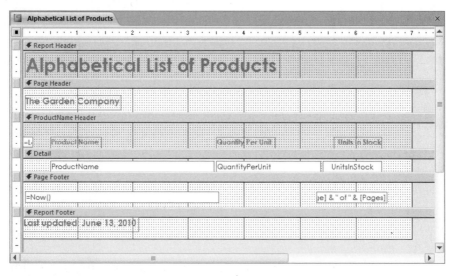

Reports have five main sections, and can include additional grouping sections.

The design grid is divided into five main sections:

- **Detail** This section is usually the main body of the report.

- **Page Header** This section contains information to be displayed at the top of every page of the report, like the header in a Microsoft Word document.

- **Page Footer** This section contains information to be displayed at the bottom of every page, such as a page number.

- **Report Header** This section contains information to be displayed at the top of the first page of the report, such as the report title.

- **Report Footer** This section can contain information to be displayed at the bottom of the last page of the report.

By default, the Report Header and Report Footer sections are not present on the report. You can add and remove the Page Header and Page Footer sections, and the Report Header and Report Footer sections, by right-clicking the design grid and then clicking the respective command. You can also close a section without removing it by setting the Height property in its Property Sheet to 0". (This is sometimes useful if you want to concentrate on one section without being distracted by another.)

To organize a report, you can group and sort its contents. When you group information, such as grouping all customers by region or all products by category, a group header is added to the report for each grouping level you specify. Group headers are identified by the field name in their section bars.

As with forms, you can work with reports In Design view in the following ways:

- Apply a theme.
- Adjust the size of sections.
- Add, size, and arrange controls.
- Adjust the properties of report elements in the Property Sheet.

In this exercise, you'll manually create a shell report that contains a Report Header section, a Page Footer section, and a section where you will add grouped data in a later exercise.

 SET UP You need the GardenCompany09_start database located in your Chapter09 practice file folder to complete this exercise. Open the GardenCompany09_start database, and save it as *GardenCompany09*. Then follow the steps.

Important The database created for this exercise contains queries not present in the databases for previous chapters. Do not continue with the database from a previous exercise.

1. Without selecting a table or query in the **Navigation** pane, on the **Create** tab, in the **Reports** group, click the **Report Design** button.

   Access displays a blank report design grid with the default sections for a new report: Page Header, Detail, and Page Footer. Four Report Design Tools contextual tabs appear on the ribbon.

2. Right-click anywhere in the design grid, and then click **Report Header/Footer**.

   Report Header and Report Footer sections now enclose the Page Header, Detail, and Page Footer sections. (Depending on your program window size and screen resolution, you might have to scroll down to see the footer sections.)

Add Existing
Fields

3. On the **Design** contextual tab, in the **Tools** group, click the **Add Existing Fields** button.

   The Field List opens. Because no source table or query is selected in the Navigation pane, the Field List is currently empty.

4. In the **Field List**, click **Show all tables**.

   The Field List displays a list of the tables whose fields you can add to the report.

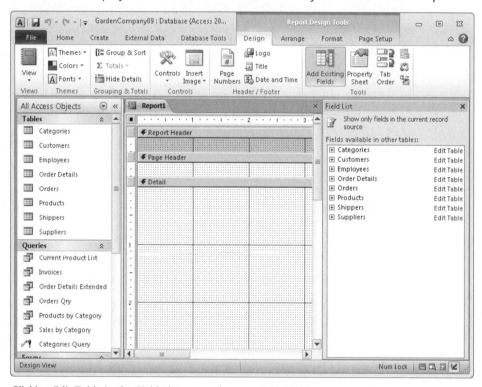

Clicking Edit Table in the Field List opens the associated table.

   Troubleshooting The appearance of buttons and groups on the ribbon changes depending on the width of the program window. For information about changing the appearance of the ribbon to match our screen images, see "Modifying the Display of the Ribbon" at the beginning of this book.

5. In the **Field List**, expand the **Categories** table by clicking the adjacent plus sign, and then double-click the **CategoryName** field.

   Label and text box controls for the selected field appear in the Detail section of the report page.

6. Close the **Field List**.

7. On the **Design** contextual tab, in the **Grouping & Totals** group, click the **Group & Sort** button.

The Group, Sort, And Total pane opens at the bottom of the report page.

8. In the **Group, Sort, and Total** pane, click **Add a group**.

The Group On bar opens, with the Select Field list displayed.

9. In the **select field** list, click **CategoryName**.

A CategoryName Header section appears in the report.

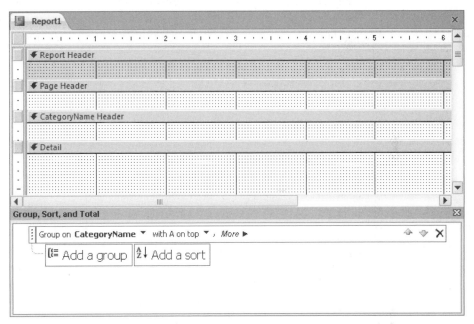

In the final report, records will be grouped by the category whose name appears in the CategoryName Header section.

10. Close the **Group, Sort, and Total** pane.

11. Save the report as **Sales By Category**.

12. Drag the **CategoryName** text box control into the **CategoryName Header** section.

The label control accompanies its associated text box control.

Property Sheet

13. In the **Tools** group, click the **Property Sheet** button.

Keyboard Shortcut Press F4 to open the Property Sheet.

See Also For more information about keyboard shortcuts, see "Keyboard Shortcuts" at the end of this book.

14. Click the **Report Header** section bar, and then on the **Format** page of the **Property Sheet**, set the **Height** property to **1"**.

Tip You can complete the setting of a property by clicking another property or by pressing Enter.

15. Repeat step 14 to set the **Height** property for the other sections of the report as follows:

PageHeader	**0"** (closes the section)
CategoryName Header	**2.2"**
Detail	**0"** (closes the section)
Page Footer	**0.2"**
Report Footer	**0"** (closes the section)

Tip You can manually set the height of a section by dragging its bottom edge up or down.

16. Close the **Property Sheet**.

The shell of the report is now ready for further refinement.

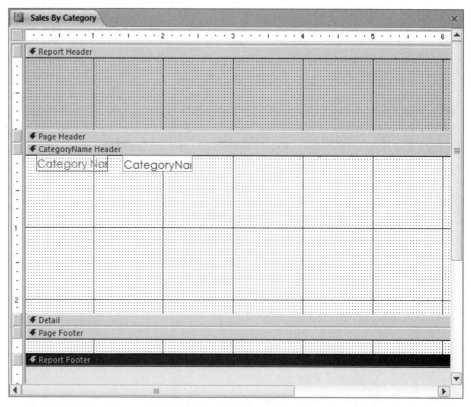

Only the Report Header, CategoryName Header, and Page Footer sections are now open.

17. Switch to Print Preview to see the results of your work.

 CLEAN UP Close the Sales By Category report, saving your changes. Retain the GardenCompany09 database for use in later exercises.

Modifying Report Content

Reports are like forms in the following ways:

- You can create them by using wizards and then modify them in Layout view or Design view.

- You can display information from one or more records from one or more tables or queries.

- You can have multiple sets of headers and footers to group and describe their contents.

Whether you create a report with the Report wizard or manually, you can always modify it by adding controls or changing the layout or formatting of the existing controls. As with forms, you can modify reports in either Layout view or Design view. Layout view is more intuitive because you can see the data while you make adjustments, but Design view gives you more control. In Design view, refining a report can be an iterative process, and you will often find yourself switching back and forth between Design view and Print Preview to evaluate each change and plan the next.

In this exercise, you'll modify the content of a report by inserting a title and date in the report header and page numbers in the report footer. You'll also insert and remove labels and change the appearance of text.

SET UP You need the GardenCompany09 database you worked with in the preceding exercise to complete this exercise. Open the GardenCompany09 database, open the Sales By Category report in Design view, and then follow the steps.

1. In the upper-left corner of the report, double-click the report selector (the box at the junction of the horizontal and vertical rulers).

   Double-clicking the report selector selects the entire report and opens the Property Sheet.

2. On the **Format** page of the **Property Sheet**, set the **Grid X** and **Grid Y** properties to **10**. Then close the **Property Sheet**.

   You might find it easier to align controls against this larger grid.

   Tip You can quickly turn the grid or the rulers on and off by right-clicking the report and then clicking Grid or Ruler.

3. Click the **Report Header** section bar, and on the **Format** contextual tab, in the **Control Formatting** group, click the **Shape Fill** button. Then under **Theme Colors** in the palette, click the third box (**Light Green, Background 2**).

4. On the **Design** tab, in the **Header / Footer** group, click the **Title** button.

Access inserts a control layout identified by a dotted border in the Report Header section and adds a label control containing the report name, along with placeholders for a logo, the date, and the time. (You can click in the layout to the left of the title to see the logo placeholder, in the upper-right corner of the layout to see the date placeholder, and in the lower-right corner to see the time placeholder.)

See Also For information about layouts, see the sidebar "Layouts" later in this chapter.

5. With the title control selected, on the **Format** contextual tab, in the **Font** group, make the title 20 points, bold, and dark green.

6. On the **Arrange** contextual tab, in the **Sizing & Ordering** group, click the **Size/ Space** button, and then click **To Fit**.

Now let's add the date.

7. On the **Design** tab, in the **Header / Footer** group, click the **Date and Time** button.

The Date And Time dialog box opens.

You can specify options for both the data and time controls in this dialog box.

8. With the **Include Date** check box and the first date format option selected, clear the **Include Time** check box, and then click **OK**.

A control containing the =Date() function is inserted in the upper-right corner of the layout in the Report Header section. The function will insert the current date whenever you generate the report.

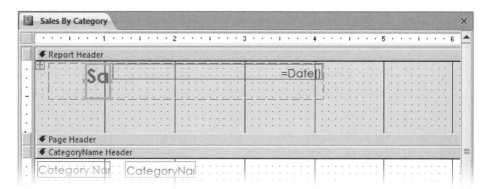

Because the layout constrains the controls, the title control shrinks to make room for the date control.

Tip If you insert a Date And Time control in a report that doesn't have a Report Header section, Access adds the section and inserts the control.

9. Hold down the Shift key, and select all the controls and placeholders in the **Report Header** section. Then right-click the selection, click **Layout**, and click **Remove Layout**.

   Removing the layout will give us more options for arranging the controls.

10. Click the alert button that appears, read the warning about the two controls in this section not being associated, and then in the list, click **Dismiss Error**.

    Tip It is always wise to investigate these alerts, but in this exercise, you can dismiss any alerts displayed about unassociated controls.

11. Click a blank area of the section to release the selection. Then drag the date control below the title control.

    Tip When you release the mouse button, the date control snaps into position against the grid. You can prevent grid snapping by clicking the Size/Space button in the Sizing & Ordering group on the Arrange tab, and then clicking Snap To Grid to turn it off. If you want to override snap to grid and position a control precisely, you can set the Top and Left properties in its Property Sheet.

12. Right-click the title control, click **Size**, and click **To Fit**. Then adjust the width of the date control to match the title control.

13. On the **Format** tab, in the **Font** group, click the **Center** button. Then click away from the control.

    The date will now be centered under the title.

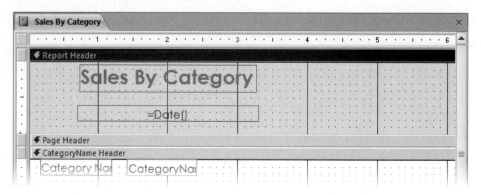

The completed Report Header section.

Tip If you need to format or move several controls in a section, you can group them together by selecting them and clicking the Size/Space button in the Sizing & Ordering group on the Arrange tab, and then clicking Group. Grouped controls can be manipulated as a unit, but not individually. To change just one of the controls, you must first ungroup all the controls.

Now let's turn our attention to the CategoryName Header section.

14. In the **CategoryName Header** section, delete the **Category Name** label.

15. Select the **CategoryName** text box control, and make it 16 points, bold, and dark green. Then open its **Property Sheet**, set the **Height** property to **0.3"** and the **Width** property to **2.0"**, and close the **Property Sheet**.

16. Move the control so that its top sits against the top of the section and its left border sits two grid points in from the left edge of the section.

17. On the **Design** tab, in the **Controls** gallery, click the **Label** button. Then click directly below the lower-left corner of the **CategoryName** text box control.

    Tip To precisely align the left edge of one control with that of another, set their Left properties to the same value.

18. In the label control, type **Product:** (including the colon), and then press Enter.

    The label control expands to fit its contents. Because this label is unassociated, an alert button appears.

19. Click the alert button, and then in the list, click **Ignore Error**.

20. Make the label 12 points, bold, and italic. Then size the control to fit its contents. Here are the results.

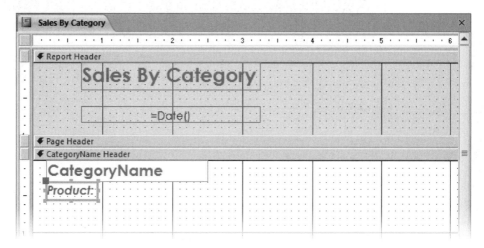

The completed CategoryName Header section.

Now let's add a page number to the Page Footer section.

21. On the **Design** tab, in the **Header / Footer** group, click the **Page Numbers** button. The Page Numbers dialog box opens.

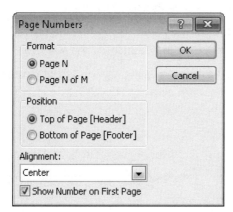

You can set the format, position and alignment of page numbers all in one place.

22. In the **Format** area, click **Page N of M**. In the **Position** area, click **Bottom of Page [Footer]**. Then with **Center** as the **Alignment** setting and the **Show Number on First Page** check box selected, click **OK**.

   Access inserts a control containing "Page " & [Page] & " of " & [Pages] in the center of the Page Footer section. In this expression, "Page" and " of " are literal strings of characters, & is the text concatenation operator, and [Page] and [Pages] are two identifiers derived from the report itself.

   See Also For information about expressions and operators, see "Restricting Data by Using Validation Rules" in Chapter 6, "Maintain Data Integrity."

23. Save the report, and then switch to Print Preview.

   Here are the results.

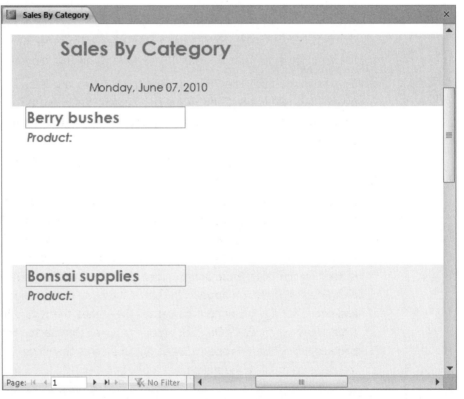

   You can page through the report to see all the product categories.

 CLEAN UP Close the Sales By Category report. Retain the GardenCompany09 database for use in the last exercise.

Adding Hyperlinks, Charts, and Buttons

A variety of additional controls are available to enhance the usefulness of reports and forms, such as the following:

- **Hyperlink and Web Browser** Clicking the Hyperlink button in the Controls gallery displays the Insert Hyperlink dialog box. You can insert a static link to a file, a Web page, another object in the database, or an e-mail message window by using the same techniques you would use to insert a hyperlink in other Office 2010 programs. For example, you might want to add a link to the company's Web site in the Page Footer section of a report.

  In forms, you can use a Web Browser control to insert a dynamic hyperlink that changes depending on the data displayed. To set up dynamic links, you click Hyperlink Builder in the Link To bar of the Insert Hyperlink dialog box to separate the target address into its component parts. For more information about the Web Browser Control, search for *Add Web browsing to a form* in Access Help.

- **Chart** You can use the Chart wizard to plot the data in an existing table or query (or both). In the Controls gallery, click the Chart button, and then drag to create the control that will hold the chart and start the Chart wizard. Follow the wizard's instructions to select the data that will be plotted, the type of chart, and the layout. When you click Finish, the chart appears in the control, which you can move and size like any other control.

- **Button** On a form, you can use the Command Button wizard to create a button that performs a specific task, such as displaying the Print dialog box. In the Controls gallery, click the Button button, and then click to create the button control and start the Command Button wizard. Follow the wizard's instructions to select the action, icon, and name for the button. When you click Finish, the button appears in the location you clicked, and you can move and size it like any other control. Behind the scenes, the wizard has embedded a macro in the control's On Click property. To see the macro, display the Event page of the button's Property Sheet, and then click the Ellipsis button to open the page containing the macro.

  Tip The Command Button wizard does not currently work with reports. To add a button to a report, click the Button button, and click to create the button control. Right-click the control, and click Build Event. Double-click Macro Builder, and under Actions in the Action Catalog, expand the type of action you want. Then double-click the action, and close the macro page. You can assign a name and picture to the button on the Format page of its Property Sheet.

Adding Subreports

A subreport is a report inserted within another report. For a subreport to work, there must be a relationship between the two reports. You create a subreport as you would any other report. Then you use a wizard to insert either the subreport itself or a subreport control into the main report. In either case, both the main report and the subreport appear as objects in the Reports group of the Navigation pane.

Depending on the nature of the information in a report or subreport, you might be able to enhance the usefulness of both types of reports by performing calculations in them. You can insert unbound controls and then use the Expression Builder to create expressions that tell Access what to calculate and how, thereby making summary information and statistics readily available in one report.

Tip After establishing the correct relationships, you can quickly insert an existing report as a subreport of another by opening the main report in Design view and then dragging the second report from the Reports group of the Navigation pane to the appropriate section of the main report.

In this exercise, you'll select a query as a record source for a report and insert a subreport into a main report to display sales by product within category. Then you'll display calculated totals for each category.

SET UP You need the GardenCompany09 database you worked with in the preceding exercise to complete this exercise. Open the GardenCompany09 database, open the Sales By Category report in Design view, and then follow the steps.

1. Double-click the report selector to select the report and open the **Property Sheet**.

2. On the **Data** page of the **Property Sheet**, click the **Record Source** arrow, and in the list, click **Sales By Category**. Then close the **Property Sheet**.

3. On the **Design** contextual tab, in the **Controls** gallery, click the **Subform/Subreport** button, and then click in the **CategoryName Header** section about two grid points below the lower-left corner of the **Product** label control.

   Access inserts a blank, unbound subreport control into the main report, and the SubReport wizard starts.

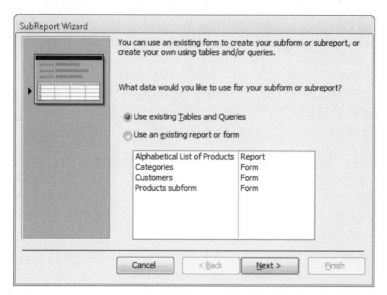

The first step is to choose the object on which the subreport will be based.

4. With **Use existing Tables and Queries** selected, click **Next**.

5. In the **Tables/Queries** list, click **Query: Sales By Category**.

6. In the **Available Fields** list, double-click **CategoryID**, **ProductName**, and **ProductSales** to move them to the **Selected Fields** list, and then click **Next**.

7. With **Choose from a list** and **Show Sales By Category for each record in Sales By Category using CategoryID** selected, click **Next**.

   Tip The selected option is displayed in its entirety in the box at the bottom of the dialog box.

8. Click **Finish** to create a subreport named Sales by Category subreport.

   The Sales By Category subreport control appears in the place of the unbound subreport control in the main report.

9. With the entire subreport control selected, display the **Property Sheet**.

   Troubleshooting If the subreport control is not selected, click its top edge to select it.

10. On the **Format** page of the **Property Sheet**, set the **Width** property to **6.6"** and the **Height** property to **2.0"**. Then close the **Property Sheet**.

We don't need some of the controls in the subreport, so let's delete them.

11. In the vertical ruler of the subreport, point to the **Report Header** section, and when the pointer changes to a black right arrow, click to select all the controls in the section. Then press Delete.

The Report Header section is now empty.

12. In the main report, delete the partially hidden **Sales by Category subreport** label.

Tip If you accidentally delete a control, click the Undo button on the Quick Access Toolbar to undo the deletion.

13. In the **Detail** section of the subreport, delete the **CategoryID** text box control.

Here are the results so far.

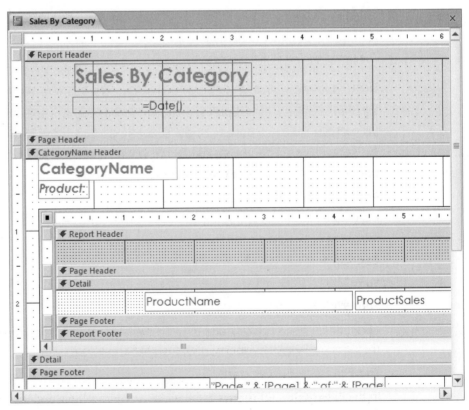

The sales for each product will appear in the Detail section.

Now we'll make some formatting changes to the controls in the Detail section.

14. Click the **ProductName** text box control, display the **Format** page of the **Property Sheet**, change the **Font Size** property to **9**, and change the **Width** property to **2.125"**.

15. Click the **ProductSales** text box control, and in the **Property Sheet**, change the **Font Size** property to **9**, change the **Left** property to **3.5"**, and change the **Width** property to **1"**.

The two controls sit neatly side by side.

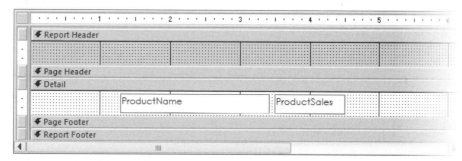

The formatted Detail section controls.

Next, we'll add a summarizing function in the Report Footer section.

16. Scroll the subreport to display the **Report Footer** section, and then set its **Height** property to **0.333"**.

17. On the **Design** tab, in the **Controls** gallery, click the **Text Box** button, and click in the center of the **Report Footer** section.

Access inserts an unbound control and its label.

18. Click the label of the unbound control, open the **Property Sheet**, and set the following properties:

Caption   Total:

Font Size   9

Font Weight   Bold

19. Click the unbound control, and then on the **Data** page of the **Property Sheet**, in the **Control Source** property, click the **Ellipsis** button.

The Expression Builder starts.

20. In the **Expression Elements** list, double-click **Functions**, and then click **Built-In Functions**.

21. In the **Expression Values** list, double-click **Sum**.

    Access displays Sum (<<expression>>) in the expression box.

22. Click **<<expression>>**. In the **Expression Elements** list, click **Sales By Category subreport**, and then in the **Expression Categories** list, double-click **ProductSales**.

    ProductSales replaces <<expression>> in the parentheses.

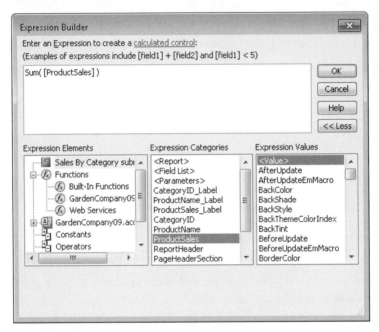

The expression now calculates the total of the ProductSales values.

23. Click **OK** to close the **Expression Builder**.

    Access has entered the calculation in the unbound control and as the Control Source property in the Property Sheet.

24. With the calculated control still selected, on the **Format** page, set **Font Size** to **9** and **Font Weight** to **Bold**.

25. Set the **Format** property to **Currency**, and change the **Left** property to **3.5"**.

26. Click the **Total** label control, and change its **Left** property to **1.3"** and its **Width** property to **2.125"**.

    These two controls now match the locations and sizes of the controls in the Detail section.

27. Switch to Print Preview.

    You can now see the results of your work.

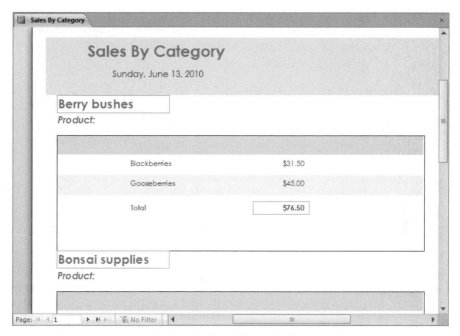

For each product category, the report shows the total of the sales per product.

28. Switch back to Design view, and click the subreport to select it. Then on the **Format** page of the **Property Sheet**, change the **Border Style** property to **Transparent**.

29. Preview the report, noting that the subreport no longer has a border.

    Tip Several factors affect the layout of the subreport. The width of the subreport sets the width of the space available for the display of text. The minimum height of the area where field values (in this case, product information) are displayed is the height you set for the subreport (because the Can Shrink property for the subreport is set to No). The maximum height of the field value display area is the length of the list (because the Can Grow property is set to Yes) plus the space between the bottom of the subreport and the bottom of the Detail section. You might want to experiment with these settings to understand how they interact.

 CLEAN UP Close the Sales By Category report, saving both the main report and subreport when prompted. Then close the GardenCompany09 database.

Layouts

Layouts control the alignment of controls. If you are building a non-Web database, they are optional; but if you are building a Web database that will be published to Access Services, you must use layouts for reports and forms that will be accessed through a Web browser. You work with layouts in Layout view.

See Also A discussion of Web databases is beyond the scope of this book. For a brief overview, see the sidebar "Web Databases" in Chapter 2, "Create Databases and Simple Tables."

By default, Access provides two layout formats:

- **Tabular** This layout arranges controls in columns and rows. The label controls are always in the section above the text box controls so that they resemble column headings. By default, Access uses the tabular layout for reports created with the Report tool and for blank reports populated by dragging fields from the Field List.

- **Stacked** This layout arranges controls in two columns, with label controls in the left column and text box controls in the right column. By default, Access uses the stacked layout for forms created with the Form tool and for blank forms populated by dragging fields from the Field List.

To switch between these two layouts:

- On the Arrange contextual tab, in the Table group, click the button for the layout you want.

To remove a layout:

- Select all the controls in the layout, right-click the selection, click Layout, and then click Remove Layout.

To impose a new layout on selected controls or to move selected controls out of an existing layout and into a new one:

- On the Arrange contextual tab, in the Table group, click the button for the layout you want.

To add a row to an existing layout:

- Select an adjacent cell, and on the Arrange tab, in the Rows & Columns group, click the Insert Above or Insert Below button.

To add a column to an existing layout:

- Select an adjacent cell, and on the Arrange tab, in the Rows & Columns group, click the Insert Left or Insert Right button.

To delete a row or column:

- Right-click a cell in the row or column, and click Delete Row or Delete Column. Or select the column or row, and then press Delete.

To merge two "cells" in a layout (so that one control can span two columns or two rows):

- Select the cells, and on the Arrange tab, in the Merge/Split group, click the Merge button.

To split a "cell" in a layout (so that two controls can fit in one column or one row):

- Select the cells, and on the Arrange tab, in the Merge/Split group, click the Split Horizontally or Split Vertically button.

To move a control within a layout:

- Drag the control, or select it and then press the Arrow keys.

Key Points

- When a report includes mostly unbound controls, it is easier to create the report manually in Design view.

- Refining a report in Design view gives you more control than working in Layout view, but be prepared to switch back and forth between Design view and Print Preview to evaluate each change.

- Inserting a subreport within another report enables you to show grouped information in meaningful ways.

- You can often enhance the usefulness of a subreport by performing calculations in unbound controls to summarize its data.

Part 3

Database Management and Security

Chapter at a Glance

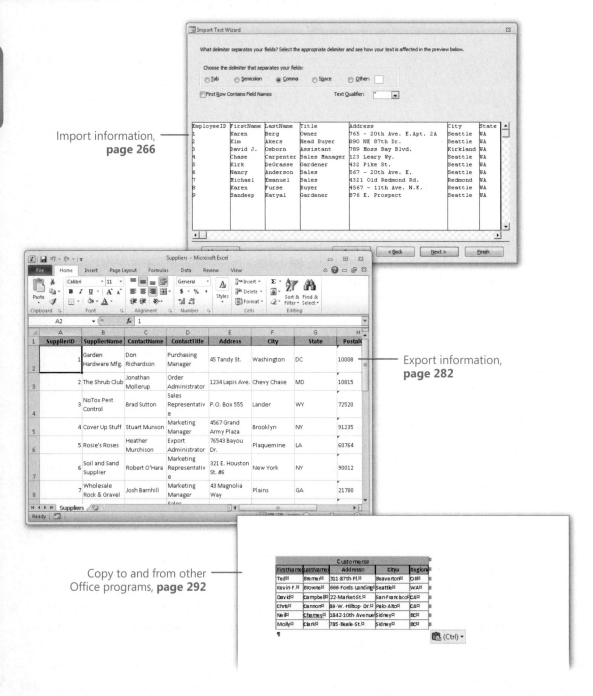

Import information, **page 266**

Export information, **page 282**

Copy to and from other Office programs, **page 292**

10 Import and Export Data

In this chapter, you will learn how to

✔ Import information.

✔ Export information.

✔ Copy to and from other Office programs.

From the moment you set out to create a database, you have to think about how you will manage its data. Good database design saves keystrokes when you're entering new information and maintaining the database. But when you are populating a database, you can save even more time and effort in another way: by importing data from existing files in other formats.

When you import information into a Microsoft Access 2010 database, the data being imported usually needs to match certain patterns, or the import process will fail. There aren't any such restrictions when exporting data from an Access database, and the process rarely fails. However, some exported database objects aren't very useful in certain formats.

All the methods of importing and exporting data described in this chapter work well, but they aren't the only ways to share information with other programs. Sometimes simple copy and paste techniques are the most efficient methods, especially when you want to make Access data available to other Microsoft Office 2010 programs.

Tip Importing from and exporting to SQL Server (the OBDC Database options in the Import & Link and Export groups on the External Data tab) is beyond the scope of this book. For information, search for *SQL Server* in Access Help.

In this chapter, you'll experiment with getting information into and out of an Access database. After an overview of the import processes for various types of files, you'll import data from various sources. Then you'll export data to other Office 2010 programs. Finally, you'll copy and paste data directly from an Access database into a Microsoft Word document and an Excel worksheet.

> **Practice Files** Before you can complete the exercises in this chapter, you need to copy the book's practice files to your computer. The practice files you'll use to complete the exercises in this chapter are in the Chapter10 practice file folder. A complete list of practice files is provided in "Using the Practice Files" at the beginning of this book.

Importing Information

If the information you intend to store in an Access database already exists in almost any other electronic document, it is quite likely that you can move it into Access without retyping it, by using the Get External Data wizard. With this wizard, the standard steps for importing data into an Access 2010 database are as follows:

1. On the External Data tab, in the Import & Link group, click the button for the type of source file you want to import.

   The Get External Data wizard starts.

2. On the wizard's first page, specify the source file's location. Depending on the source type, also specify whether to import the source file as a new table, to append the source file's data to an existing table, or to create a linked table. Then click OK.

   Tip If you want to import data into an existing table but the data structure isn't the same as the table structure, it's often easier to import the data into Excel, manipulate it there, and then import it into Access.

   The Get External Data wizard starts the appropriate import wizard or opens the dialog box necessary to complete the next step.

3. Follow the instructions for selecting data from the source file, formatting the data, choosing a primary key, and naming the target object. Then click Finish.

   Tip When the Finish button is active, you can click it at any time to accept the default settings for the remaining wizard pages.

When the import process is complete, you return to the Get External Data wizard, which gives you the opportunity to save the import steps so that you don't have to repeat them for other similar import processes. To save the import steps:

1. In the Get External Data wizard, select the Save Import Steps check box.

   The wizard page displays the settings necessary to save the process.

2. Name the saved import process, and enter a description (optional).

3. If you use Microsoft Outlook and want to create an Outlook task to remind you to run the import process at some specific time in the future, select the Create Outlook Task check box.

4. Click Save Import.

    If you chose to create an Outlook task, Outlook opens a task window that already contains information about the task. You simply set a due date, make any other necessary adjustments to the settings, and click Save & Close in the Actions group on the Task tab.

Tip To run a saved import operation, click the Saved Imports button in the Import & Link group on the External Data tab, click the import you want to run, and then click Run. If you have created an Outlook task for the import process, you can click Run Import in the Microsoft Access group on the Task tab of the task window.

In the sections that follow, we discuss some of the issues to bear in mind when importing data from a specific source.

Importing from Other Access Databases

Suppose you already have an Access database that includes tables of information about products and orders, and another that includes customer contact information, but you want to have just one database containing all the information you use on a regular basis. You can save time by importing the product and order information into the contacts database (or vice versa), rather than re-creating it all.

You can easily import any of the standard Access objects: tables, queries, forms, and reports. (Macros and modules can also be imported, but we don't discuss them in this book.) When importing a table, you have the option of importing only the table definition (the structure that you see in Design view), or both the definition and the data. When importing a query, you can import it as a query or you can import the results of the query as a table.

When you import an Access object, the entire object is imported as an object with the same name into the active database. You can't import only selected fields or records. If the active database already has an object with the same name, Access imports the new object with a number appended to the end of the name.

Tip If you need only some of the fields or records from a table in another database, you can create a query in the other database to select only the information you need and then import the results of the query as a table. Alternatively, you can import the table and either edit it in Design view or clean it up by using queries.

Importing from Excel Worksheets

Access works well with Excel. You can import an entire worksheet or a named range from a worksheet into either a new table (one that is created during the import process) or an existing table. You can also import specific fields from a worksheet or range.

Excel is a good intermediate format to use when importing information that isn't set up to import directly into Access. For example, if you want to add or remove fields, combine or split fields, or use complex mathematical functions to manipulate data before import-ing it into Access, Excel is a great place to do it.

Importing from Text Files

Text files are the common denominator of all document types. Almost every program that works with words and numbers can generate some kind of text file. Access can import tabular data (tables and lists) from text files that contain data structured in two ways:

- **Delimited text file** Each record ends with a paragraph mark, and each field in the table or list is separated from the next by a comma or some other special character, called a *delimiter*. If the data in a field includes one of these special characters, the entire field must be enclosed in quotation marks. (Some people enclose all fields in quotation marks to avoid having to locate those with the special characters.)

- **Fixed-width text file** In every record, the data in a particular field includes the same number of characters. If the actual data doesn't fill the field, the field is padded with spaces so that the starting point of the data in the next field is the same number of characters from the beginning of every record. For example, if the first field contains 12 characters, the second field always starts 13 characters from the beginning of the record, even if the actual data in the first field is only 4 characters.

  Fixed-width text files used to be difficult to import into databases because you had to carefully count the number of characters in each field and then specify the field sizes in the database or in the import program. If the length of any field was even one character off, all records from that point on would be jumbled. That is no longer a problem with Access, because the Import Text wizard makes importing a fixed-width text file simple.

  Tip The only way to import the data from older programs such as Lotus 1-2-3 is to export the data from that program to a fixed-width text file and then import that file into Access.

Importing from Other Database Programs

Importing information from databases created in programs other than Access is usually an all-or-nothing situation, and quite often, what you get isn't in the exact format you need. For example, you might find that transaction records include redundant information, such as the name of the product or purchaser, in every record. A database containing information about people might include the full name and address in one field, when you would prefer to have separate fields for the first name, last name, street address, and so on. You can choose to import information as it is and manipulate it in Access, or you can move it into some other program, such as Excel or Word, and manipulate it there before importing it into Access.

Importing from Outlook Folders

You can import address books and other folders from Outlook into an Access database. This can be particularly useful if you want to import contact information.

Importing from SharePoint Lists

If your organization uses a Microsoft SharePoint site, you can import content from SharePoint lists into Access in one of two ways:

- **Importing** This process creates a copy of the list in the Access database. During the import operation, you can select the lists you want to copy, and for each selected list, you can specify whether you want to import the entire list or only a specific view. The import operation creates a table in Access, and then copies the source list (or view) into that table as fields and records. Changes made to the imported data in either Access or SharePoint are not replicated.

- **Linking** This process is more efficient than importing if you want to work with data from a SharePoint list in Access but keep the information in both locations current. Linked tables are indicated in the Access Navigation pane by a blue arrow pointing to a yellow table. Information you update in Access is reflected in the SharePoint list when you refresh the view, and vice versa.

Whichever method you choose, before you import a SharePoint list into a new table in an Access database, it is a good idea to do the following:

1. Make a note of the SharePoint site's URL.

2. On the SharePoint site, identify the lists you want to copy to the database, and then decide whether you want the entire list or just a particular view.

   You can import multiple lists in a single import operation, but you can import only one view of each list. If one of the standard views doesn't fit your needs, create a custom view containing only the fields and list items you want before proceeding with the import process.

3. Review the columns in the source list or view, and identify the database into which you want to import the lists.

   When you import a SharePoint list, Access creates a table with the same name as the source list. If that name is already in use, Access appends a number to the new table name—for example, Contacts1.

   Tip Access will not overwrite a table in the destination database or append the contents of a list or view to an existing table.

To import the SharePoint list or lists you have identified, follow these steps:

1. Open a new blank database.

2. On the External Data tab, in the Import & Link group, click the More button, and then click SharePoint List.

   The Get External Data wizard starts, displaying a list of known SharePoint sites. You are not limited to the sites in this list.

3. On the Select The Source And Destination Of The Data page, under Specify A SharePoint Site, click the address of the site you want to connect to, or type it in the box.

4. Click either Import The Source Data or Link To The Data Source. Then click Next.

5. If prompted to enter your site credentials, do so.

   The Import Data From List page displays all the lists available on the selected SharePoint site.

6. In the Import column, select the check box of each list you want to import into the database.

7. In the Items To Import column, for each of the selected lists, select the view (arrangement of data) you want to import into the database.

8. With the Import Display Values Instead Of IDs For Fields That Look Up Values Stored In Another List check box selected, click OK.

   This option controls which data is imported for lookup columns in the selected lists.

   Troubleshooting No progress bar appears while Access imports the lists, and this process can take some time. Resist clicking the OK button more than once.

9. When the last page of the wizard appears, click Close. Or choose to save the import steps, provide the necessary information, and then click Save Import.

After you import or link to a list, open the resulting table in Datasheet view. Ensure that all of the fields and records were imported and that there were no errors. You can review the data type and other field properties by switching to Design view.

Importing from HTML Files

Hypertext Markup Language (HTML) is used to create Web pages. HTML uses tags to control the appearance and alignment of the text displayed in a Web browser. For a table to display correctly on a Web page, the table's rows and cells must be enclosed in appropriate HTML tags. For example, a simple HTML table might look like this:

```
.
.
.
<table>
<tr>
   <td>LastName</td><td>FirstName</td>
</tr>
   <td>Anderson</td><td>Nancy</td>
</tr>
</table>
.
.
.
```

In an HTML document, the <table>, <tr> (table row), and <td> (table data) tags and their corresponding </table>, </tr>, and </td> end tags make the data look like a structured table when it is viewed in a Web browser.

All the Office 2010 programs can save a document in HTML format, and to a limited extent, they can read or import a document that was saved in HTML format by another program. When you import an HTML document into Access, the program scans the document and identifies anything that looks like structured data. You can then look at what Access has found and decide whether to import it.

Importing from XML Files

Extensible Markup Language (XML) files are often used for exchanging information between programs, both on and off the Web. XML files are similar to HTML files in two ways: both are plain text files that indicate formatting within tags, and both use start and end tags. However, HTML tags describe how elements should look, whereas XML tags specify the structure of the elements in a document. Also, as its name implies, the XML tag set is extensible—there are ways to add your own tags. Here is an example of a simple XML file:

```
<?xml version="1.0"?>
<ORDER>
    <CUSTOMER>Michelle Martin</CUSTOMER>
    <PRODUCT>
        <ITEM>Sterilized Soil</ITEM>
        <PRICE>$8.65</PRICE>
        <QUANTITY>1 bag</QUANTITY>
    </PRODUCT></ORDER>
```

This simple file describes an order that Michelle Martin (the customer) placed for one bag (the quantity) of Sterilized Soil (the item) at a cost of $8.65 (the price). As you can see, because XML tags the data's *structure* rather than its *appearance*, you can easily import the data from an XML file into a database table. An actual file created for this purpose would contain one instance of the <ORDER> through </ORDER> block for each order.

With XML, the .xml file might store both the data and the structure for a table; or the .xml file might store only the data, while an .xsd file stores the structure. If the structure is stored in an .xsd file (referred to as the *schema*), make sure that file is in the same folder as the corresponding .xml file; otherwise Access will import only the data and assign default properties to all fields.

Tip Access 2010 can apply a transform to XML data as you import or export it. A transform is a type of template used to convert XML data to other formats. When you apply a transform during the import process, the data is transformed before it enters the table, so you can adapt an XML file to a different table structure. The topic of transforms is beyond the scope of this book.

In this exercise, you'll populate a database from multiple sources. You'll import three tables and a form from an Access database. Then you'll import data from a comma-delimited text file into an existing table. Finally, you'll import information from an Excel worksheet into a new table.

SET UP You need the GardenCompany10_start database, the Customers workbook, the Employees text file, and the ProductsAndSuppliers database located in your Chapter10 practice file folder to complete this exercise. Open the GardenCompany10_start database, and save it as *GardenCompany10*. Then follow the steps.

1. On the **External Data** tab, in the **Import & Link** group, click the **Access** button.

   The Get External Data wizard starts.

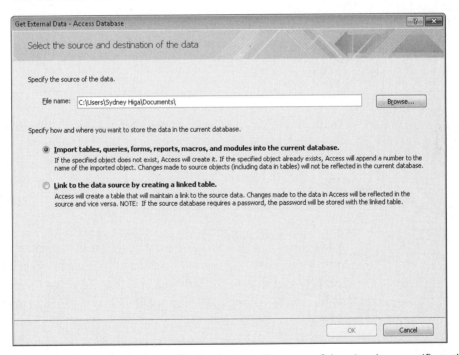

Access Database appears in the title bar because the pages of the wizard are specific to the import process you selected.

2. On the **Select the source and destination of the data** page, click **Browse**.

3. In the **File Open** dialog box, navigate to your **Chapter10** practice file folder, click the **ProductsAndSuppliers** database, and then click **Open**.

4. With **Import tables, queries, forms, reports, macros, and modules into the current database** selected, click **OK**.

   The Import Objects dialog box opens.

The Tables page of the Import Objects dialog box.

5. On the **Tables** page, click **Select All**, and then click **Options** to see additional choices.

   The Categories, Products, and Suppliers tables are selected. The default settings will import any relationships that exist between the selected tables, as well as their data and structure.

The expanded Tables page of the Import Objects dialog box.

6. Click the **Forms** tab, click **Categories**, and then click **OK** to close the dialog box and begin the import process.

   When the import process is complete, Access gives you the option of saving the import steps.

7. On the **Save Import Steps** page, click **Close**.

   The Navigation pane now shows the addition of the three imported tables and one imported form.

8. Open the **Categories**, **Products**, and **Suppliers** tables, review their records, and then close them.

   All three tables have been successfully imported into the database. Now let's populate the empty Employees table.

Text File

9. On the **External Data** tab, in the **Import & Link** group, click the **Text File** button.

The Get External Data wizard starts.

> **Tip** Text files typically have a .txt extension. However, some programs save delimited text files with a .csv or .tab extension. You will also occasionally see text files with an .asc (for ASCII) extension. Some programs save fixed-width text files with a .prn (for printer) extension, which Access doesn't recognize; you would need to change the extension to one that Access does recognize. Access treats text files with all acceptable extensions the same way.

10. Browse to your **Chapter10** practice file folder, click the **Employees** text file, and then click **Open**.

11. Click **Append a copy of the records to the table**. Display the adjacent list, and click **Employees**. Then click **OK**.

The Import Text wizard starts and displays the content of the selected delimited text file.

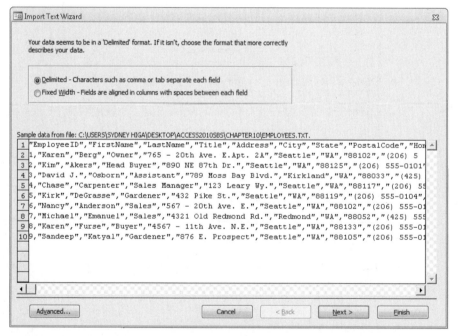

Each field is enclosed in quotation marks, and the fields are separated by commas.

Tip When information is imported into an existing table, all the field names and data types must match exactly; otherwise, Access can't import the file and displays an error. If the structure matches but data in a field is too long or has some other minor problem, Access might import the record containing the field into an ImportError table, rather than into the intended table. You can fix the problem in the ImportError table and then copy and paste the record into the correct table.

12. In the lower-left corner of the page, click **Advanced**.

   The Employees Import Specification dialog box opens.

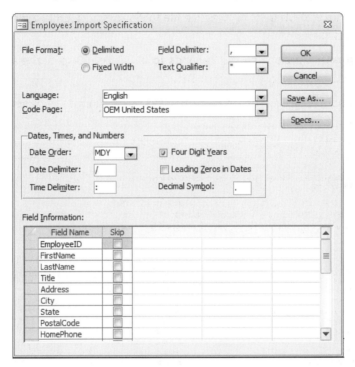

You can make changes to the default settings in this dialog box.

Tip If you want to import several files with the same custom settings, you can specify the settings and save them. Then as you open each file, you can click Specs in this dialog box to apply the saved specifications.

13. In the **Employees Import Specification** dialog box, click **Cancel**. Then in the **Import Text** wizard, click **Next**.

The wizard separates the file into fields at the commas.

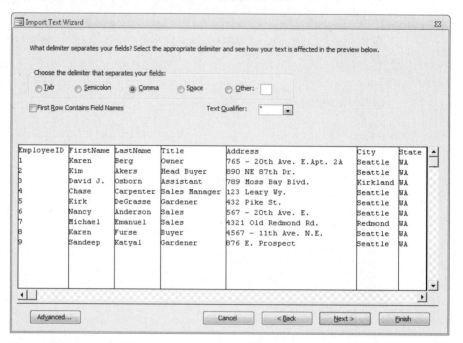

If the columns are jumbled, you can choose a different delimiter from the options at the top of this page to see if that delimiter produces better results.

14. Select the **First Row Contains Field Names** check box, and click **Next**. Then click **Finish**.

Access imports the text file into the Employees table.

15. On the **Save Import Steps** page, click **Close**.

16. Open the **Employees** table to confirm that Access successfully imported the records from the text file. Then close the table.

Now let's import customer information from an Excel worksheet into a new table.

Excel

17. On the **External Data** tab, in the **Import & Link** group, click the **Excel** button.

    The Get External Data wizard starts.

18. Browse to your **Chapter10** practice file folder, click the **Customers** workbook, and then click **Open**.

19. With **Import the source data into a new table in the current database** selected, click **OK**.

    The Import Spreadsheet wizard starts. On this page, you can select any worksheet or named range in the workbook.

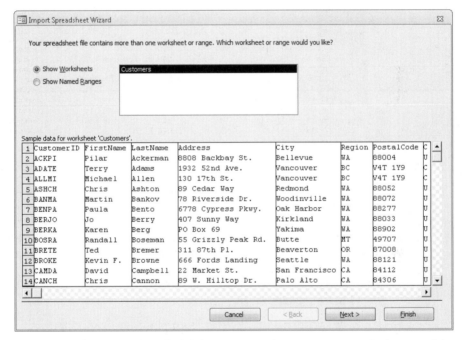

Sample data from the selected worksheet or named range appears at the bottom of the page.

20. With **Show Worksheets** and **Customers** selected, click **Next**.

21. Select the **First Row Contains Column Headings** check box, and then click **Next**.

    On this page, you can click each field in turn and then set its Data Type and Indexed properties.

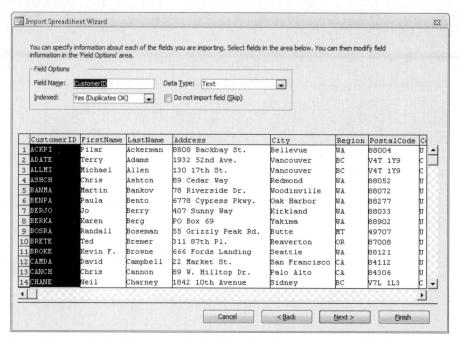

You can select the Do Not Import Field (Skip) check box to exclude a field from the import process.

22. Click **Next**.

23. On the page that sets the primary key, click **Choose my own primary key**. Then with the **CustomerID** field selected in the adjacent box, click **Finish**.

    Access imports the worksheet as the Customers table.

24. On the **Save Import Steps** page, click **Close**.

25. Open the **Customers** table to confirm that Access imported the customer records correctly.

CLEAN UP Close the Customers table. Retain the GardenCompany10 database for use in later exercises.

Linking to Information

If your information is still being actively maintained in another program and you want to bring it into Access to analyze it, create reports, or export it to another format, you should consider linking your Access database to the existing information in its original program rather than importing the information. Although working with data that is stored in your own database is faster, safer, and more flexible, sometimes linking is preferable, especially if it is important that what you see in Access is always up to date.

The most common reason for linking to data in another Access database or a different program is because you don't own the data. Perhaps another department in your organization maintains the data in a SQL database, and that department is willing to give you permission to read the tables and queries but not to change them. Other reasons are security and ease of data distribution.

You can usually link to information in any application from which you can import information. The only difference in the process is that you select the Link To The Data Source By Creating A Linked Table option on the Select The Source And Destination Of The Data page of the Get External Data wizard. Access indicates a linked table by an arrow to the left of the table icon.

Tip If you link to a file stored on your network, be sure to use a universal naming convention (UNC) path, rather than a mapped network drive, because a UNC path is less likely to change.

Exporting Information

You can export Access database objects in all the file formats from which you can import data. You can also export information as Portable Document Format (PDF) and XML Paper Specification (XPS) files. The specific formats available depend on the object you are exporting, as shown in the following table.

Database object	Valid export format
Table	ACCDB, XLS, XLSB, XLSX, SharePoint List, PDF, XPS, RTF, TXT, XML, ODBC, HTML, dBASE, Word Merge
Query	ACCDB, XLS, XLSB, XLSX, SharePoint List, PDF, XPS, RTF, TXT, XML, ODBC , HTML, dBASE, Word Merge
Form	ACCDB, XLS, XLSB, XLSX, PDF, XPS, RTF, TXT, XML, HTML
Report	ACCDB, PDF, XPS, RTF, TXT, XML, HTML

Tip To display a list of the export file formats available for a specific Access object, right-click the object in the Navigation pane, and then point to Export.

Like the import process, the export process for most file types is orchestrated by an easy-to-follow wizard with the following standard steps:

1. In the Navigation pane, select the object you want to export.

2. On the External Data tab, in the Export group, click the button for the program or type of file you want to create.

   The Export wizard starts.

3. On the wizard's first page, depending on export format, specify one or all of the following:

   ○ The destination file's location and format

   ○ Whether to export just data, or data with formatting

   ○ Whether to open the file when the export process is complete

   ○ Whether to export only selected records

4. Click OK.

When the export process is complete, you return to the Export wizard, which gives you the opportunity to save the export steps so that you don't have to repeat them for future similar export processes. The process for saving export steps is nearly identical to the process for saving import steps.

The steps for exporting Access database objects to PDF or XPS files or as e-mail attachments are slightly different but are still quite automated. You can also use an Access table or query as the data source for the Word 2010 mail merge process; this process is not covered in this topic, but if you are familiar with mail merge in Word, it is relatively straightforward.

In the sections that follow, we discuss some of the issues to bear in mind when exporting data to a specific type of file.

Exporting to Other Access Databases

It is very simple to export any single object from one Access 2010 database to either another Access 2010 database or to an Access 2007 or Access 2003 database. You can't, however, export multiple objects in one operation.

Tip Data types that were new in Access 2007, such as Attachment and Rich Text, will not export properly to Access 2003. Rich text is exported as tagged HTML, and attachments are exported to a memo field containing only the file name of the attachment.

Exporting to Excel Worksheets

You can export a single table, form, or query from an Access 2010 database to an Excel 2010 workbook, or to a workbook that can be opened by versions of Excel as early as Excel 5.0/95. However, you cannot export reports.

When you export a table that contains a subdatasheet or a form that contains a subform, Access exports only the main datasheet or form. To export a subdatasheet or subform, you must perform another export operation on that object.

To combine multiple Access objects into a single Excel workbook, you first export the individual objects to different workbooks. Then you merge all the worksheets in Excel.

Exporting to Word Documents

If you need to move a table or the results of a query to an existing Word document, it is often easiest to simply copy and paste the records from the datasheet. But if you want to work with the contents of a report in Word, you need to export the report.

When you export information from Access 2010 to Word, Access creates a Rich Text Format (RTF) document, which can be opened by Word and various other applications.

Exporting to Text Files

Text files are the lowest-common-denominator file format. Most applications can open, display, and save information in text format. The downside to text files is that they don't contain any formatting information, so they look consistently plain in all applications.

Depending on what type of content you are trying to export from a database, you might have the option to export the layout along with the data. If you select this option, the unformatted text will be arranged in the text file much as it is in the Access object. If you don't choose this option, the information will be saved in either delimited or fixed-length lines.

Exporting to PDF and XPS Files

If you want people to be able to view a database object but not change it, you can save the object in the Portable Document Format (PDF) format or XML Paper Specification (XPS) format. Use the PDF format if you know that recipients have a PDF reader, such as Adobe Acrobat Reader, installed on their computer. Use the XPS format if you need all fonts, images, and colors to render precisely on recipients' computers.

Both the PDF and XPS formats are designed to deliver objects as electronic representations of the way they look when printed. The data in .pdf and .xps files is essentially static, and content cannot be easily edited, so these formats are ideal for objects that will be part of legal documents. Both types of files can easily be sent by e-mail to many recipients and can be made available on a Web page for downloading by anyone who wants them. However, the files cannot be opened, viewed, or edited in Office 2010 programs.

When you indicate that you want to export a database object in PDF or XPS format by clicking the PDF Or XPS button in the Export group on the External Data tab, the Publish As PDF Or XPS dialog box opens so that you can select the destination location and format, assign a name, and optimize the size of the file for your intended distribution method. You can click Options to display a dialog box where you can specify the records or pages to include in the .pdf or .xps version of the object and whether to include or exclude accessibility structure tags. When you click Publish, the object is saved with your specifications, and the Export wizard gives you the opportunity to save the export steps.

Tip Another way to create an .xps file or a .pdf file is to display the Backstage view, and in the left pane, click Save & Publish. Then in the File Types area of the center pane, click Save Object As to display the available formats for this task in the right pane. Clicking PDF Or XPS and then clicking the Save As button displays the Publish As PDF Or XPS dialog box, in which you can save the file in the usual way.

Exporting to SharePoint Lists

If you have permission to create content on a SharePoint site, you can export a table or query database object to the site as a SharePoint list. The list content is static and will not reflect changes made to the source table or query after the export operation. You can't overwrite or add data to an existing list.

Tip You can export only one object to a SharePoint list at a time. However, when Access exports a table, it also exports all related tables.

Exporting to HTML Files

Many organizations that store accounting, manufacturing, marketing, sales, and other information on their computers have discovered the advantages of sharing this information within the company or with the rest of the world through a Web site. With Access, you can export tables, queries, forms, and reports as Web-ready HTML files. You can then view the objects in a Web browser, such as Windows Internet Explorer.

When you export a table, query, or form, Access converts it to an HTML table. When you export a report, Access converts it to a series of linked HTML files (one for each page of the report).

Tip To see the HTML tags that define the structure of the file, you can either view the file in a Web browser or open it in a text editor.

Exporting to XML Files

You can export tables, queries, forms, and reports from Access in an XML format that can be used by other applications. Clicking the XML File button in the Export group on the External Data tab displays the Export wizard, where you specify the destination location and assign a name. Clicking OK displays the Export XML dialog box, where you can do one of the following:

- Select the Data (XML) check box to export the data.
- Select the Schema Of The Data (XSD) check box to create a separate .xsd file containing the structure of the .xml file.
- Select the Presentation Of Your Data (XSL) check box to export an XLS Stylesheet that describes how to display the XML data.

Tip To export a table as a combined data/schema file, in the Export XML dialog box, click More Options, click the Schema tab, click Embed Schema In Exported XML Data Document, and then click OK.

When you click OK, the object is saved with your specifications, and the Export wizard gives you the opportunity to save the export steps. You can then view the tagged .xml file in Internet Explorer and the .xsd file in any text editor.

In this exercise, you'll export an Access table to another Access database and to an Excel workbook. Then you'll export the table as both a formatted and an unformatted text file.

SET UP You need the GardenCompany10 database you worked with in the preceding exercise to complete this exercise. Create a blank database, and save it as Exported. Then open the GardenCompany10 database, and follow the steps.

1. In the **Navigation** pane, under **Tables**, click **Suppliers**.

   We are going to export the entire table, so there is no need to open it first.

2. On the **External Data** tab, in the **Export** group, click the **Access** button.

   The Export – Access Database wizard starts.

3. On the wizard's first page, click **Browse**.

4. In the **File Save** dialog box, navigate to your **Chapter10** practice file folder, click **Exported**, and then click **Save**.

5. In the **Export – Access Database** wizard, click **OK**.

   The Export dialog box opens.

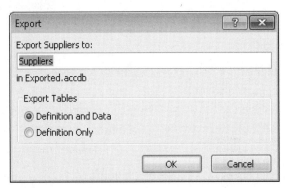

You can export the table's structure and data or only the structure.

6. With **Suppliers** displayed in the **Export Suppliers to** box and **Definition and Data** selected in the **Export Tables** area, click **OK**.

   Access exports the selected table.

7. On the **Save Export Steps** page, click **Close**.

8. In Windows Explorer, navigate to your **Chapter10** practice file folder and double-click **Exported**.

Tip You can open only one database at a time in a single instance of Access. If you open a second database without first closing the one you are working in, Access prompts you to save recent changes and then closes the first database before opening the second. To open two databases at the same time, start a second instance of Access from the Start menu, and then open the second database from the Backstage view. You can also double-click the database file in Windows Explorer.

The Exported database opens in a separate instance of Access 2010.

9. In the **Navigation** pane, under **Tables**, double-click **Suppliers**. Then verify that the table exported correctly, and close this instance of Access.

Now suppose you need to provide the information in the Suppliers table to someone who doesn't have access to the database. Let's export the same table as an Excel workbook.

10. In the **GardenCompany10** database, open the **Suppliers** table in Datasheet view. Then on the **External Data** tab, in the **Export** group, click the **Excel** button.

The Export – Excel Spreadsheet wizard starts.

11. On the wizard's first page, click the **Browse** button. Then in the **File Save** dialog box, navigate to the **Chapter10** practice file folder, and click **Save**.

The File Name setting reflects your specifications.

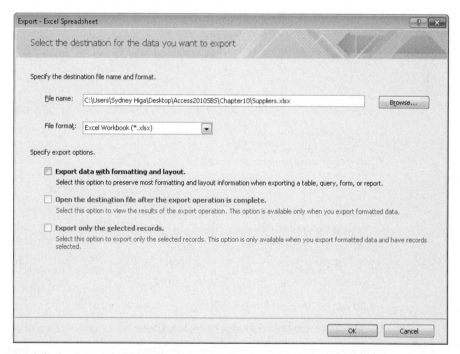

By default, the spreadsheet has the same name as the table it's based on and will be saved in Excel Workbook (*.xlsx) format.

Tip You can change the name and format in the File Save dialog box, or you can edit the name and select a different format in the wizard.

12. Select the **Export data with formatting and layout** check box and the **Open the destination file after the export operation is complete** check box. Then click **OK**.

Access exports the table to an Excel workbook. Excel starts and opens the workbook.

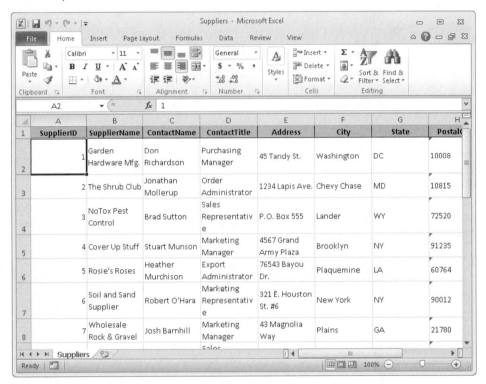

The Suppliers table has been exported to the Suppliers sheet in the workbook.

Troubleshooting The appearance of buttons and groups on the ribbon changes depending on the width of the program window. For information about changing the appearance of the ribbon to match our screen images, see "Modifying the Display of the Ribbon" at the beginning of this book.

13. Close the Excel workbook, and then on the **Save Export Steps** page of the **Export – Excel Spreadsheet** wizard, click **Close**.

Suppose you want to make the data in the Suppliers table available in Outlook. You can't export directly to Outlook, but you can export the data from Access to a text file and then import it into Outlook. Let's export the text file now.

14. With the **Suppliers** table open in Datasheet view, on the **External Data** tab, in the **Export** group, click the **Text File** button.

The Export – Text File wizard starts.

15. With the path to your **Chapter10** practice file folder displayed in the **File name** box, change the default file name from **Suppliers.txt** to **Suppliers_fixed.txt**.

16. Select the **Export data with formatting and layout** check box and the **Open the destination file after the export operation is complete** check box. Then click **OK**.

The Encode 'Suppliers' As dialog box opens.

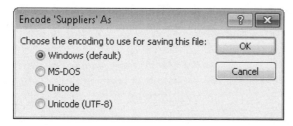

From here, you can select the encoding format options you want.

17. With the **Windows** option selected, click **OK**.

Access exports the table as a formatted text file. Your default text editor starts and opens the Suppliers_fixed text file.

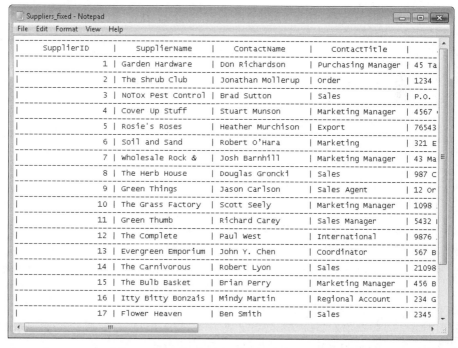

Access has separated the rows and columns of the table with dashes and pipe characters.

18. Close the text file, and then close the wizard without saving the export steps.

19. Repeat steps 14 through 18 to export the table again, but this time change the name to **Suppliers_delim.txt**, and don't select the **Export data with formatting and layout** and **Open the destination file after the export operation is complete** check boxes.

    The Export Text wizard starts.

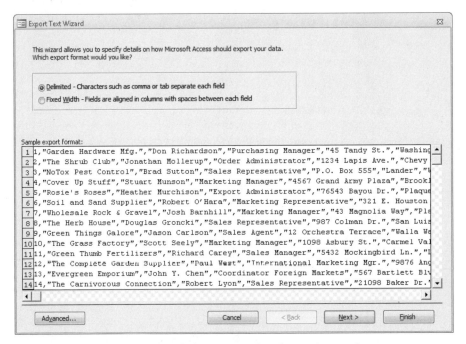

This wizard will guide you through the process of setting various options.

Tip You can experiment with different wizard options, moving as far as the last page before backing up and trying a different approach. At any point, you can click Finish to accept the default settings for all the wizard's remaining options.

20. Switch between the **Delimited** and **Fixed Width** options, noticing the difference in the data in the **Sample export format** box.

21. With **Delimited** selected, click **Next**.

The options on the wizard's next page vary depending on whether you are exporting a delimited or fixed-width file.

22. Leave **Comma** selected, select the **Include Field Names on First Row** check box, and click **Finish**.

Access exports the table as an unformatted text file.

23. Close the wizard without saving the export steps.

24. Start Windows Explorer, navigate to your **Chapter10** practice file folder, and double-click **Suppliers_delim**.

The exported text file opens in your default text editor.

The delimited text file, displayed in Notepad.

 CLEAN UP Close the text file, Windows Explorer, and the Suppliers table. Retain the GardenCompany10 database for use in the last exercise.

Copying to and from Other Office Programs

Sometimes the quickest and easiest way to get information into or out of a database is to just copy it and paste it where you want it. This technique works particularly well for getting data out of an Access table and into Word or Excel. Information that you paste into a Word document becomes a Word table, complete with a heading row containing the field captions as column headings. Information that you paste into an Excel worksheet appears in the normal row-and-column format.

Getting data into an Access table by using this technique is a little more complicated. The data you are pasting must meet all the criteria for entering it by hand (input mask, validation rules, field size, and so on), and you must have the correct table cells selected when you use the Paste command. If Access encounters a problem when you attempt to paste a group of records, it displays an error message and pastes the problem records into a Paste Errors table. You can then troubleshoot the problem in that table, fix whatever is wrong, and try copying and pasting again.

Tip To paste an entire table from one Access database to another, open both databases, copy the table from the source database to the Clipboard, and then paste it in the destination database. You can paste the table data and/or table structure as a new table or append the data to an existing table.

In this exercise, you'll copy and paste records between an Access database table, an Excel worksheet, and a Word document.

 SET UP You need the GardenCompany10 database you worked with in the preceding exercise and the Shippers workbook located in the Chapter10 practice file folder to complete this exercise. Open the GardenCompany10 database, open the Customers table in Datasheet view, and then follow the steps.

1. Point to the row selector of the first record in the table, and when the pointer changes to a right arrow, hold down the mouse button and drag through six records.

 2. On the **Home** tab, in the **Clipboard** group, click the **Copy** button.

   Keyboard Shortcut Press Ctrl+C to copy a selection to the Clipboard.

   See Also For more information about keyboard shortcuts, see "Keyboard Shortcuts" at the end of this book.

3. Start **Excel**.

Paste

4. With cell **A1** selected in the blank worksheet, on the Excel **Home** tab, in the **Clipboard** group, click the **Paste** button.

   Keyboard Shortcut Press Ctrl+V to paste a cut or copied item from the Clipboard.

   Excel pastes the records into the worksheet.

	A	B	C	D	E	F	G	H	I	J
1	CustomerID	FirstName	LastName	Address	City	Region	PostalCode	Country	PhoneNumber	
2	ACKPI	Pilar	Ackerman	8808 Backbay St.	Bellevue	WA	88004	USA	(425) 555-0194	
3	ADATE	Terry	Adams	1932 52nd Ave.	Vancouver	BC	V4T 1Y9	Canada	(604) 555-0193	
4	ALLMI	Michael	Allen	130 17th St.	Vancouver	BC	V4T 1Y9	Canada	(604) 555-0192	
5	ASHCH	Chris	Ashton	89 Cedar Way	Redmond	WA	88052	USA	(425) 555-0191	
6	BANMA	Martin	Bankov	78 Riverside Dr.	Woodinville	WA	88072	USA	(425) 555-0190	
7	BENPA	Paula	Bento	6778 Cypress Pkwy.	Oak Harbor	WA	88277	USA	(360) 555-0189	
8						(Ctrl) ▾				

The Access field names have become Excel column headings.

5. On the Windows Taskbar, click the **Access** button to switch back to Access.

   Now let's copy and paste only a few fields of a few records.

6. In the **FirstName** field, point to the left border of the value **Ted**, and when the pointer changes to a thick cross, hold down the mouse button, and drag down and to the right until the **FirstName** through **Region** fields are selected for six records.

7. In the **Clipboard** group, click the **Copy** button.

8. Switch back to Excel, click cell **A9**, and then in the Excel **Clipboard** group, click the **Paste** button.

   Excel pastes in the new selection, again with column headings. The copied data remains on the Office Clipboard

9. Start **Word**. Then on the **Home** tab, in the **Clipboard** group, click the **Paste** button.

   Word pastes the selection as a nicely formatted table.

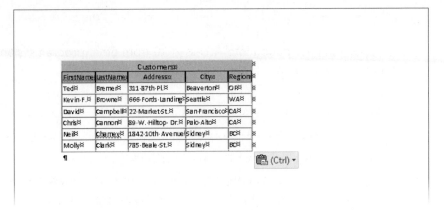

Customers				
FirstName	LastName	Address	City	Region
Ted	Bremer	311·87th·Pl.	Beaverton	OR
Kevin·F.	Browne	666·Fords·Landing	Seattle	WA
David	Campbell	22·Market·St.	San·Francisco	CA
Chris	Cannon	89·W.·Hilltop·Dr.	Palo·Alto	CA
Neil	Charney	1842·10th·Avenue	Sidney	BC
Molly	Clark	785·Beale·St.	Sidney	BC

The Customers title reflects the name of the table from which this data came.

10. Exit Word and Excel, without saving your changes. Then close the **Customers** table.

   Now let's copy the data from an Excel worksheet and paste it into a new table in the current database.

11. Start Windows Explorer, navigate to your **Chapter10** practice file folder, and double-click the **Shippers** Excel workbook.

   Excel starts and opens the Shippers workbook.

12. Select cells **A1:H6**, and on the **Home** tab, in the **Clipboard** group, click the **Copy** button.

13. Switch back to Access, right-click in the **Tables** area of the **Navigation** pane, and click **Paste**.

   Access asks whether the first row of data contains column headings.

14. Click **Yes**.

15. When Access notifies you that the import process was successful, click **OK**.

   The new Shippers table is added to the Tables area of the Navigation pane.

16. Double-click the **Shippers** table to open it, and verify that all records were successfully copied.

 **CLEAN UP** Exit Excel. Then close the Shippers table and the GardenCompany10 database.

Key Points

- Importing information into Access 2010 from other programs is an easy way to enter data without retyping it.

- If data is actively maintained in another program and you want to work with it in Access, you can link the Access database to the data without actually importing it.

- You can export information from an Access database in a variety of formats, depending on the object you are exporting.

- Copying and pasting information from an Access database is often the easiest way to make the data available to other Office programs.

- If the data in other Office programs is set up appropriately, you can copy and paste it into an Access database.

Chapter at a Glance

Create navigation forms, **page 298**

Create custom categories, **page 305**

Control which features are available, **page 309**

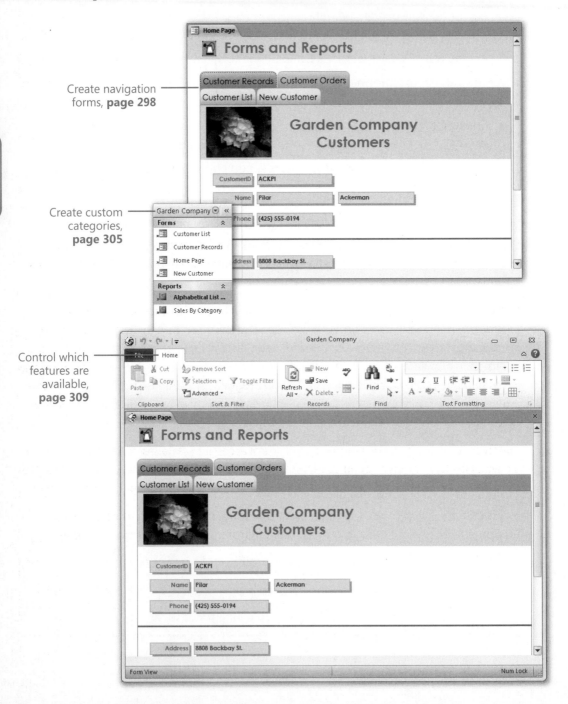

11 Make Databases User Friendly

In this chapter, you will learn how to

✔ Create navigation forms.

✔ Create custom categories.

✔ Control which features are available.

A Microsoft Access 2010 database can be a complex combination of objects and the tools for managing and manipulating them. In the first two parts of this book, you learned how to work with database objects to enter, organize, retrieve, and display information.

If information will be entered and retrieved from your database by people who aren't proficient with Access, the information will be safer and the database users happier if you insulate them from the inner workings of Access. By turning your collection of objects and information into an application that organizes related tasks, you allow users to focus on the job at hand, rather than on learning to use the program the database is running in. With a little extra effort on your part, you can make it easier for them to access and manipulate data, and more difficult for them to unintentionally change or delete it.

In Access 2010, the most common way to control access to a database is either by creating a navigation form or by creating custom categories and groups in the Navigation pane. You can also control which commands and which parts of the database users can interact with.

In this chapter, you'll create a simple navigation form, create a custom category and groups, and set various startup options that control the users' working environment.

> **Practice Files** Before you can complete the exercises in this chapter, you need to copy the book's practice files to your computer. The practice files you'll use to complete the exercises in this chapter are in the Chapter11 practice file folder. A complete list of practice files is provided in "Using the Practice Files" at the beginning of this book.

Creating Navigation Forms

A navigation form appears as a set of navigation buttons that the user can click to display and work with forms and reports. When you create a database based on a Web database template, it includes a navigation form that is the primary interface with the database. (When viewed in a Web browser, a Web database has no Navigation pane.) However, you can add a navigation form to any database to make it easier for users without extensive Access knowledge to enter information and find exactly what they need.

See Also We do not discuss Web databases in detail in this book. For a brief overview, see the sidebar "Web Databases" in Chapter 2, "Create Databases and Simple Tables."

Tip You cannot work with tables and queries directly from a navigation form. If you want users to be able to view a table or the results of a query in a navigation form, you need to create datasheet forms based on those objects and then insert those forms into the navigation form.

When you click the Navigation button in the Forms group on the Create tab, you can choose from the following six navigation form layouts:

- **Horizontal Tabs** Each object is assigned its own button, which looks like a tab, across the top of the form.

- **Vertical Tabs, Left** Each object is assigned its own button down the left side of the form.

- **Vertical Tabs, Right** Each object is assigned its own button down the right side of the form.

- **Horizontal Tabs, 2 levels** Each primary object is assigned its own button at the first level, which appears as a row of buttons across the top of the form. You can assign secondary objects to the buttons on the second row. For example, if the Customers form has a button at the first level, you might assign the New Customer form to a button at the second level. Users can check the Customers form to see if a customer record already exists. If it doesn't, they can click the button for the New Customer form to display a new blank record, where they can enter the customer's information.

- **Horizontal Tabs and Vertical Tabs, Left** Each object is assigned its own button across the top or down the left side of the form, depending on where you insert it. With this arrangement, you can have one navigation form that satisfies the needs of two separate groups—for example, order-related buttons across the top, and inventory-related buttons down the side.

- **Horizontal Tabs and Vertical Tabs, Right** Similar to the Horizontal Tabs and Vertical Tabs, Left layout. Each object is assigned to its own button across the top or down the right side of the form, depending on where you insert it.

The layout you choose depends on the number and type of database objects you want to be available from the form, and the way you want to arrange them.

When you create a navigation form, it is displayed in Layout view so that you can begin to populate it. The functionality of the form is supplied by a navigation control that consists of a placeholder for a navigation button and a subform or subreport control. When you drag a form or report from the Navigation pane to the button placeholder, the Navigation Target Name property on the Data page of the button's Property Sheet is set to the name of the form or report, and that name is also displayed on the button. (You can change the name on the button by changing its Caption property.) The form or report itself is displayed in the subform or subreport control. A new placeholder navigation button is added to the navigation bar, ready to receive the next form or report you insert.

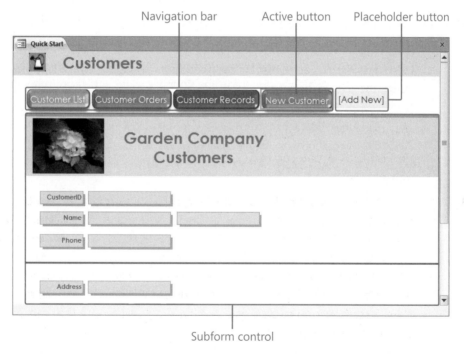

A populated navigation form with the Horizontal Tabs layout in Layout view.

For Web databases, the navigation form is the "home page" of the database and is usually displayed automatically when the database is opened. You should consider making the navigation form the default startup page of non-Web databases so that users can easily access the database objects they are most likely to need to work with.

In this exercise, you'll create a datasheet form for viewing existing customers and a form for entering new customer information. You'll create a simple two-level navigation form to provide easy access to the customer information, and you'll add three forms and a report to it.

SET UP You need the GardenCompany11_start database and the Logo graphic located in your Chapter11 practice file folder to complete this exercise. Open the GardenCompany11_start database, and save it as *GardenCompany11*. Then with All Access Objects displayed in the Navigation pane, follow the steps.

1. Under **Tables** in the **Navigation** pane, click **Customers**. Then on the **Create** tab, in the **Forms** group, click **More Forms**, and in the list, click **Datasheet**.

   Access creates a datasheet form that looks like the Customers table.

2. Save the form as **Customer List**. Then open its **Property Sheet**, and on the **Data** page, set the **Allow Additions**, **Allow Deletions**, and **Allow Edits** properties to **No**.

3. Close the **Property Sheet**, and then close the form, saving your changes.

4. Under **Forms** in the **Navigation** pane, right-click **Customer Records**, and click **Copy**. Then right-click anywhere in the **Forms** group, and click **Paste**. In the **Paste As** dialog box, type **New Customer** as the name of the form, and click **OK**.

5. Open the **New Customer** form in Layout view, right-click the form's title, and click **Form Properties** to open the **Property Sheet** for the form. On the **Data** page, set the **Data Entry**, **Allow Additions**, **Allow Deletions**, and **Allow Edits** properties to **Yes**.

6. Close the **Property Sheet**, and then close the form, saving your changes.

   You've now created two new forms, one exclusively for data lookup and the other exclusively for data entry.

7. On the **Create** tab, in the **Forms** group, click the **Navigation** button, and click **Horizontal Tabs, 2 Levels**. Then if Access opens the **Field List**, close it.

   Access creates the form, adds the navigation control to it, and displays the form in Layout view.

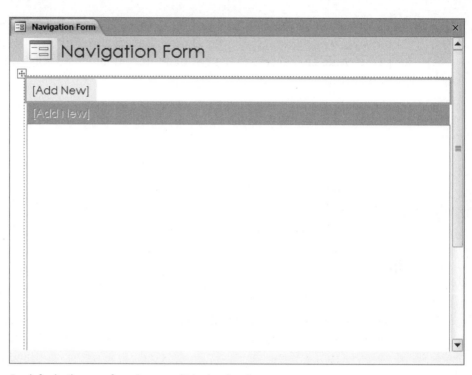

By default, the new form is named Navigation Form.

First let's customize the form's tab and title.

8. Display the **Property Sheet** for the form. On the **Format** page, in the **Caption** property, type Home Page, and press Enter. Then close the **Property Sheet**.

9. In the **Form Header**, click the **Navigation Form** title, click it again to activate it for editing, change the title to Forms and Reports, and press Enter. Then make the title 20 points, bold, and dark green.

10. Click in the **Form Header** away from the title control and logo placeholder, and apply the **Light Green, Background 2** color.

11. On the **Design** contextual tab, in the **Header/Footer** group, click the **Logo** button, and insert the **Logo** graphic from your **Chapter11** practice file folder.

The navigation form now looks similar to other objects in this database.

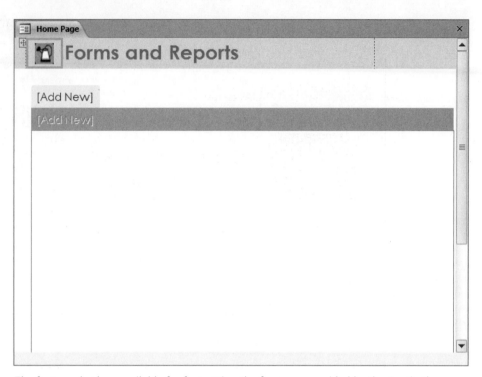

The fonts and colors available for formatting the form are provided by the Austin theme.

12. Save the form with the name **Home Page**.

    Now let's populate the navigation form by adding forms and reports to it. We do this by assigning the forms and reports to the two rows of buttons on the navigation bar above the subform control.

13. Under **Forms** in the **Navigation** pane, click **Customer Records**, and drag it to the first-level placeholder button at the top of the navigation control.

    The first-level button is now labeled Customer Records, and because the button is active, the Customer Records form is displayed in the subform control.

The Customer Records form displays the first record in the Customers table.

14. Under **Forms** in the **Navigation** pane, click **Customer List**, and drag it to the second-level placeholder button under **Customer Records**.

    The second-level button is now labeled Customer List, and because the button is active, the datasheet form appears in the subform control.

15. Under **Forms** in the **Navigation** pane, click **New Customer**, and drag it to the second-level placeholder button to the right of **Customer List**.

    The second-level button is now labeled New Customer, and the data entry form appears in the subform control. The first-level Customer Records button now has two second-level buttons and a second-level placeholder button.

16. Under **Reports** in the **Navigation** pane, click **Customer Orders**, and drag it to the first-level placeholder button to the right of **Customer Records**.

17. Switch to Form view.

    In Layout view, Customer Orders has a second-level placeholder button, but the placeholder button is not visible in this view.

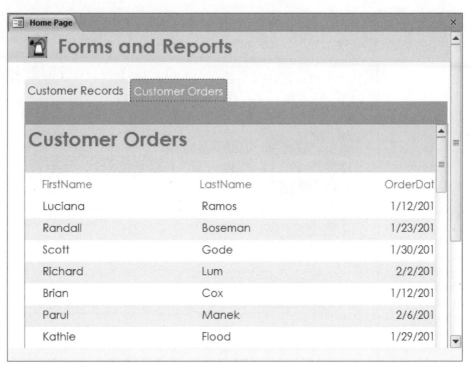

Customer Orders has no second-level objects.

18. Click the **Customer Records** button, and then in turn click the **Customer List** and **New Customer** buttons, observing the effect in the form.

    Now let's format the navigation buttons to more clearly define the hierarchy.

19. Switch back to Layout view. Then click the **Customer Records** button, hold down the Shift key, and click the **Customer Orders** button.

20. On the **Format** contextual tab, in the **Control Formatting** group, click the **Change Shape** button, and then click the second shape in the second column (**Round Same Side Corner Rectangle**).

21. Without changing the selection, in the **Control Formatting** group, click the **Quick Styles** button, and then click the fourth color in the rightmost column (**Subtle Effect – Orange, Accent 6**).

22. Repeat steps 20 and 21 for the second-level buttons, making them the same shape as the first-level buttons but applying the fourth color in the second column (**Subtle Effect – Green, Accent 1**).

23. Switch to Form view, and click the **Customer Records** button.

The buttons now resemble colored tabs.

You can use shapes and colors to categorize forms and reports.

CLEAN UP Close the Home Page form, saving your changes. Retain the GardenCompany11 database for use in later exercises.

Creating Custom Categories

By now, you are accustomed to selecting the database object you want to work with in the Navigation pane, and you know that the Navigation pane is organized into categories and groups. A number of built-in categories are available, and you can filter by group in various ways.

To provide database users with easy access to specific database objects, you can create custom categories, each of which can contain multiple custom groups. You can drag and drop any valid Access object into a custom group to create a shortcut to the object; the object itself remains in its original group. This combination of categories, groups, and object shortcuts can be used to make frequently used objects more accessible. For example, if the accounting department runs a set of reports on the last day of each month, you could create an Accounting category containing a Month End Reports group, and add the reports to that group. Or if the Marketing department routinely works with several forms, queries, and reports, you could create a Marketing category for them. This category could contain one group holding shortcuts to all the objects, or a group for each object type. There are no restrictions on the mix of objects placed in one group.

In this exercise, you'll create a custom category, add two groups to it, and then add shortcuts to database objects to the groups.

SET UP You need the GardenCompany11 database you worked with in the preceding exercise to complete this exercise. Open the GardenCompany11 database, and then follow the steps.

1. Right-click the category at the top of the **Navigation** pane, and then click **Navigation Options**.

   The Navigation Options dialog box opens.

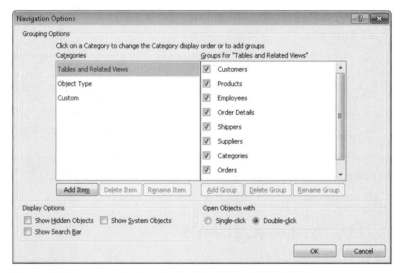

You can hide a group by clearing its check box in the right list.

2. In the **Grouping Options** area, below the **Categories** list, click **Add Item**.

   A new category is added to the Categories list. The category name is selected.

3. Replace **Custom Category 1** with Garden Company, and press Enter.

   The heading above the right list changes to Groups For "Garden Company" to reflect the category selected in the left list.

4. Below the **Groups for "Garden Company"** list, click **Add Group**. Then replace **Custom Group 1** with Forms, and press Enter.

> **Tip** Every category contains a default group named Unassigned Objects. This group contains a list of all objects in the database and is the source for the shortcuts you create in your custom groups.

5. Repeat step 4 to add a group named **Reports**. Then click **OK**.

   Although you can't see it yet, the new category has been added to the Navigation pane.

6. Click the category at the top of the **Navigation** pane to display the list of available categories, and then click the new **Garden Company** category.

   The category contains an empty Forms group, an empty Reports group, and the Unassigned Objects group.

In the Unassigned Objects group, the object icons distinguish items of the same name.

7. In the **Unassigned Objects** group, click the **Customer List** form. Then hold down the Ctrl key, and click the **Customer Records**, **Home Page**, and **New Customer** forms. Drag the selection up to the top of the **Navigation** pane, releasing the mouse button when the selection is on top of the **Forms** group header.

Access removes the selected forms from the Unassigned Objects group and creates shortcuts for them in the custom Forms group.

8. In the **Unassigned Objects** group, select the **Alphabetical List of Products** and the **Sales By Category** reports. Then right-click either selected object, click **Add to group**, and click **Reports**.

Access removes the selected reports from the Unassigned Objects group and creates shortcuts for them in the custom Reports group.

9. Right-click the **Unassigned Objects** group header, and then click **Hide**.

Tip To redisplay the Unassigned Objects group, display the Navigation Options dialog box, click Garden Company, select the Unassigned Objects check box, and then click OK.

Now the forms and reports needed most often are conveniently located in the Garden Company category.

This uncluttered Navigation pane makes it easy for users to spot what they need.

10. Test the new shortcuts by opening each form and report.

 CLEAN UP Retain the GardenCompany11 database for use in the last exercise.

Controlling Which Features Are Available

If your database will be used by people with little or no experience with Access, you might want to control which features are available when a database opens. You can control the user environment by setting startup options for the database. For example, you can use startup options to control whether ribbon tabs and the Navigation pane are available, whether a specified object (such as a navigation form) is displayed on startup, and other features.

Tip Additional control can be achieved by the use of macros and Visual Basic for Applications (VBA) procedures. These topics are beyond the scope of this book. For information, search for *Introduction to Access Programming* in Access Help.

In this exercise, you'll set startup options that create a version of the database that is appropriate for inexperienced users. You'll give the database the appearance of being a custom application, display the Home Page form when the database is opened, and hide program elements that users don't need. Then you'll see how to bypass the startup options.

 SET UP You need the GardenCompany11 database you worked with in the preceding exercise and the Icon image located in your Chapter11 practice file folder to complete this exercise. Open the GardenCompany11 database, and then follow the steps.

1. Display the Backstage view, and click **Options** to open the **Access Options** dialog box. Then in the left pane, click **Current Database**.

   Several options for controlling the database that is open on your screen are available on this page. Setting these options affects this database only.

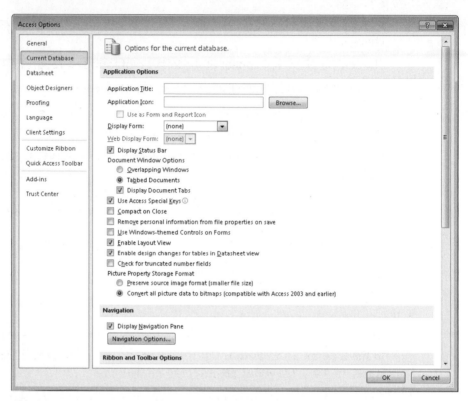

The Current Database page of the Access Options dialog box.

> **See Also** For information about the other pages of the Access Options dialog box, see "Changing Default Program Options" in Chapter 13, "Customize Access."

2. In the **Application Options** area, in the **Application Title** box, type **Garden Company**, and then press the Tab key.

   Access will display this title in the database title bar, in place of the usual Microsoft Access title.

3. To the right of the **Application Icon** box, click **Browse**. Then navigate to your **Chapter11** practice file folder, and double-click the **Icon** image.

   Access enters the path to the icon in the Application Icon box.

4. Below the **Application Icon** box, select the **Use as Form and Report Icon** check box.

   The selected icon will appear at the left end of form and report tabs.

5. Display the **Display Form** list, and then click **Home Page**.

   The Home Page navigation form you created in an earlier exercise will now be displayed by default whenever anyone opens this database.

6. Clear the **Enable Layout View** and **Enable design changes for tables in Datasheet view** check boxes.

   Now users cannot inadvertently make changes to the design of the database objects.

7. In the **Navigation** area, clear the **Display Navigation Pane** check box.

   Now the Navigation pane will not initially be displayed.

   Tip When the Use Access Special Keys check box is selected, database users can show and hide the Navigation pane by pressing the F11 key. If you clear the Display Navigation Pane check box and the Use Access Special Keys check box, users can't display the Navigation pane at all.

8. In the **Ribbon and Toolbar Options** area, clear the **Allow Full Menus** and **Allow Default Shortcut Menus** check boxes.

   This prevents users from using these tools to make inappropriate changes to the database. Now all they will see are the File and Home tabs.

9. Click **OK** to implement the changes and close the **Access Options** dialog box.

10. When Access tells you that you must close and reopen the database for the changes to take effect, click **OK**.

    Initially the only change you see is that *Garden Company* has replaced the file name and program name in the Access program window title bar, and a colorful icon appears at the left end of the title bar.

11. Close the **GardenCompany11** database, and then reopen it.

    The database opens with the Home Page form displayed.

The Navigation pane is completely hidden, and only the File and Home tabs appear on the ribbon.

Troubleshooting The appearance of buttons and groups on the ribbon changes depending on the width of the program window. For information about changing the appearance of the ribbon to match our screen images, see "Modifying the Display of the Ribbon" at the beginning of this book.

12. Press the F11 key.

Because you did not clear the Use Access Special Keys check box, users can still use the F11 keyboard shortcut to display or hide the Navigation pane.

See Also For more information about keyboard shortcuts, see "Keyboard Shortcuts" at the end of this book.

13. Click the **File** tab to display the Backstage view.

    Only the Print page, a Privacy Options button, and an Exit button are available.

    Tip At the time of writing this book, clicking the Privacy Options button displays the Access Options dialog box, where you can easily reverse the changes you have made on the Current Database page. This might be by design, or the functionality of this button might be changed in future updates to the program.

14. Click **Exit** to close the database and exit Access.

15. Restart Access, and in the Backstage view, display the **Recent** page.

16. Hold down the Shift key, and then in the **Recent Databases** list, click **GardenCompany11**.

    Holding down the Shift key while you open the database bypasses all the startup options, so the database starts the same way it did before you set those options.

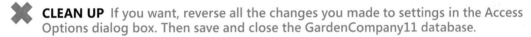 **CLEAN UP** If you want, reverse all the changes you made to settings in the Access Options dialog box. Then save and close the GardenCompany11 database.

Key Points

- Navigation forms provide a Web-like interface that makes it easy for people who are not familiar with Access to enter data and view reports.
- Custom categories and groups provide users with access to the forms, reports, and other objects they need, while restricting access to the objects they don't need.
- Setting startup options is another way to make it more difficult for users to unintentionally change or delete data.

Chapter at a Glance

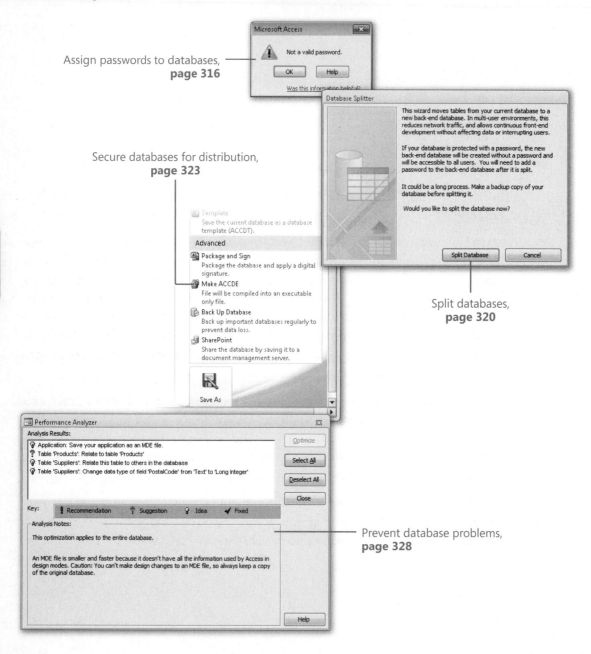

Assign passwords to databases,
page 316

Microsoft Access

⚠ Not a valid password.

OK   Help

Was this information helpful?

Secure databases for distribution,
page 323

Template
Save the current database as a database
template (ACCDT).

Advanced

Package and Sign
Package the database and apply a digital
signature.

Make ACCDE
File will be compiled into an executable
only file.

Back Up Database
Back up important databases regularly to
prevent data loss.

SharePoint
Share the database by saving it to a
document management server.

Save As

Database Splitter

This wizard moves tables from your current database to a
new back-end database. In multi-user environments, this
reduces network traffic, and allows continuous front-end
development without affecting data or interrupting users.

If your database is protected with a password, the new
back-end database will be created without a password and
will be accessible to all users. You will need to add a
password to the back-end database after it is split.

It could be a long process. Make a backup copy of your
database before splitting it.

Would you like to split the database now?

Split Database   Cancel

Split databases,
page 320

Performance Analyzer

Analysis Results:

⚙ Application: Save your application as an MDE file.
? Table 'Products': Relate to table 'Products'
⚙ Table 'Suppliers': Relate this table to others in the database
💡 Table 'Suppliers': Change data type of field 'PostalCode' from 'Text' to 'Long Integer'

Optimize

Select All

Deselect All

Close

Key: ❗ Recommendation   ? Suggestion   💡 Idea   ✔ Fixed

Analysis Notes:

This optimization applies to the entire database.

An MDE file is smaller and faster because it doesn't have all the information used by Access in
design modes. Caution: You can't make design changes to an MDE file, so always keep a copy
of the original database.

Help

Prevent database problems,
page 328

12 Protect Databases

In this chapter, you will learn how to

✔ Assign passwords to databases.

✔ Split databases.

✔ Secure databases for distribution.

✔ Prevent database problems.

Database protection takes two forms: ensuring that the database's data is secure and ensuring that its data is available and useable.

The need for database security is an unfortunate fact of life. As with your house, car, office, or briefcase, the level of security required for your database depends on the value of what you have and whether you are trying to protect it from curious eyes, accidental damage, malicious destruction, or theft. The security of a company's business information can be critical to its survival. For example, you might not be too concerned if a person gained unauthorized access to your products list, but you would be very concerned if a competitor managed to see—or worse, steal—your customer list. And the destruction or deletion of your critical order information would be a disaster.

Ongoing database maintenance is unavoidable if you want to prevent, at best, decreased performance and, at worst, data corruption. In the day-to-day use of a Microsoft Access 2010 database—adding and deleting records, modifying forms and reports, and so on—various problems can develop. This is especially true if the database is stored on a network share, rather than on a local drive, and is accessed by multiple users.

Your goal is to provide adequate protection without imposing unnecessary restrictions on the people who need access to your database. The protection techniques you choose depend to a large extent on how many people are using the database and where it is stored.

In this chapter, you'll assign a password to a database, protect data from accidental or intentional corruption by splitting the database, and prepare the database for broader distribution. You'll also back up a database and see how to run various utilities to identify database problems.

> **Practice Files** Before you can complete the exercises in this chapter, you need to copy the book's practice files to your computer. The practice file you'll use to complete the exercises in this chapter is in the Chapter12 practice file folder. A complete list of practice files is provided in "Using the Practice Files" at the beginning of this book.

Assigning Passwords to Databases

You can prevent unauthorized users from opening a database by assigning it a password. Then Access prompts anyone attempting to open the database to enter the password, and will open it only if the password is correct.

To assign a password to or remove a password from a database, you must first open the database for exclusive use, meaning that no one else can have the database open. This will not be a problem for a database stored on your local computer and used only by you, but if you want to set or remove a password for a database that is located on a network, you will first need to make sure nobody else is using it.

You can use any word or phrase as a database password, but to create a secure password, keep the following in mind:

● Passwords are case sensitive.

● You can include letters, accented characters, numbers, spaces, and most punctuation marks.

A good password includes uppercase letters, lowercase letters, and symbols or numbers, and isn't a word found in a dictionary.

Assigning a password to a database has an important secondary benefit. A database created in Access is a binary file (a file that stores instructions and data in such a way that it can usually be understood only by a computer). If you open the file in a word processor or a text editor, its content is mostly unreadable, but if you look closely enough at the file, you can discover quite a bit of information. It is unlikely that enough information will be exposed to allow anyone to steal anything valuable. However, people can and do scan files with computer tools designed to look for key words that lead them to restricted information. When you assign a password to a database, the database is automatically encrypted each time it is closed, making it really unreadable. Opening the file in Access with the correct password decrypts the file and makes its data readable again.

A caveat: It is easy to assign a database password, and certainly better than providing no protection at all, in that it keeps most unauthorized people out of the database. However, many inexpensive password recovery utilities are available, theoretically to help people recover a lost password. Anyone can buy one of these utilities and "recover" the password to your database. Also, because the same password works for all users (and nothing prevents one person from giving the password to many other people), simple password protection is most appropriate for a single-user database.

In this exercise, you'll assign a password to a database, test it, and then remove it.

 SET UP You need the GardenCompany12_start database located in your Chapter12 practice file folder to complete this exercise. Open the GardenCompany12_start database, and save it as *GardenCompany12*. Close the file, and then follow the steps.

1. With Access running but no database open, display the Backstage view, and in the left pane, click **Open**.

2. In the **Open** dialog box, navigate to your practice file folder, and click (don't double-click) the **GardenCompany12** database. Then click the **Open** arrow, and in the list, click **Open Exclusive**.

   Access opens the database for your exclusive use. (In other words, if the database were shared with other users, no one else would be able to open it until you closed it.)

3. Display the Backstage view, and if the Info page is not displayed, click **Info** in the left pane.

   From this page, you can run utilities to help prevent database problems, assign a password, and assign file properties that help identify the file.

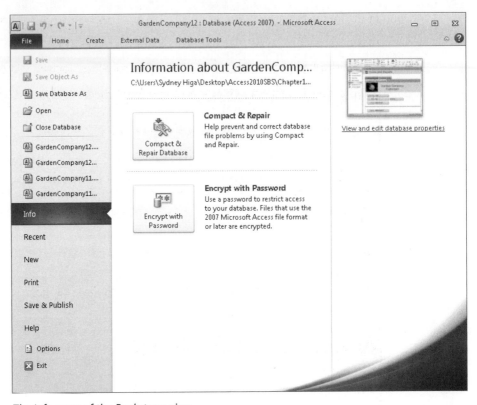

The Info page of the Backstage view.

Tip Clicking View And Edit Database Properties in the right pane doesn't display the Property Sheet. It displays the GardenCompany12.accdb Properties dialog box, where you can assign properties to the file, such as a title, subject, and keywords, that help identify it and make it easier to find in browsing dialog boxes and programs such as Windows Explorer.

4. Click **Encrypt with Password**.

The Set Database Password dialog box opens.

In this dialog box, Access will disguise the characters of the password as asterisks as you type them.

5. In the **Password** box, type **2010D@t@b@se!**, and then press the Tab key.

6. In the **Verify** box, type **2010D@t@b@se!**. Then click **OK**.

   Access displays a message box warning that row-level locking will be ignored.

   Row-level locking is one of the settings that prevent two people from making changes to the same record (row) at the same time.

   Tip If you have not enrolled in the Microsoft Customer Experience Improvement Program, you will not see the Was This Information Helpful link.

7. Click **OK** to close the message box, and then close and reopen the database.

   The Password Required dialog box opens.

   You cannot work with the database unless you know the password.

8. In the **Enter database password** box, type **2010_D@tabase**, and then click **OK**.

   A message box opens.

   Access warns that the password is not valid.

9. In the message box, click **OK**.

10. When the **Password Required** dialog box is redisplayed, type the correct password, **2010D@t@b@se!**, and then click **OK**.

   The database opens. Now let's remove the password.

11. Display the **Info** page of the Backstage view, and click **Decrypt Database**.

   Oops! The password cannot be removed unless the database is open for exclusive use.

12. Close the database, and then open it for exclusive use, entering the password when prompted.

13. On the **Info** page of the Backstage view, click **Decrypt Database**. Then in the **Unset Database Password** dialog box, enter the password, and click **OK**.

   Access removes the password, allowing anyone to open the database.

✖ **CLEAN UP** Retain the GardenCompany12 database for use in later exercises.

Splitting Databases

When a database user works over a network on a database that is not stored on his or her local computer, Access has to move database objects over the network from the computer where the objects are stored to the computer where the user is working on them. If several people are working on the database at the same time, processing times can get noticeably slower. Under these circumstances, you should consider splitting the database to speed up performance.

Splitting a database involves organizing the database into two parts: a back-end database containing the tables that store all the data, and a front-end database containing the forms, queries, and reports that people use to work with the data. The back end remains on the central computer, and the front end can be copied to the local computer of any user who needs to work with the database. Because Access can move the data required by a database object over the network much faster than it can move the entire object, database performance is improved. But another major benefit of splitting the database is that it helps protect the core data from problems that might affect its reliability and usability.

You split a database by using the Database Splitter wizard, which you start by clicking the Access Database button in the Move Data group on the Database Tools tab.

In this exercise, you'll use the Database Splitter wizard to organize a database into back-end and front-end components.

SET UP You need the GardenCompany12 database you worked with in the preceding exercise to complete this exercise. Open the GardenCompany12 database, and then follow the steps.

1. Save the database as **GardenCompany12_split**.

   Important You should ALWAYS make a local copy of a database you want to split. Then if the results are not what you expected, you have an unsplit version available for use.

2. Close the **Home Page** navigation form.

   You cannot split a database if any of the tables are being accessed by open database objects.

3. On the **Database Tools** tab, in the **Move Data** group, click the **Access Database** button.

   The Database Splitter wizard starts.

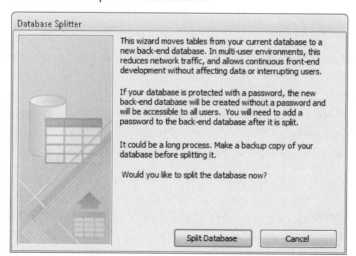

The wizard explains the process before you begin.

4. Click **Split Database**.

   The Create Back-end Database dialog box opens. The wizard suggests the name GardenCompany12_split_be for the back-end part of the database.

5. If the contents of your practice file folder are not displayed in the dialog box, navigate to that folder now.

In practice, you would navigate to the central location in which you want to store the back-end database. Or you could avoid including a drive letter in the path to the back-end database location by typing the UNC path (\\<*server*>\<*share*>) of the storage location in the File Name box, before the file name. Either way, this location must be specified at this time in order for the links that the wizard establishes between the back-end and front-end databases to work.

6. Click **Split**.

   The splitting operation for the practice file is very short, but for some working databases, the process can take quite some time. When the process is complete, the wizard displays a message that the database has been successfully split.

7. Click **OK** to close the message box and the wizard.

   The GardenCompany12_split file (the one you started with) is now the front-end file.

8. In the **Navigation** pane, right-click the active category (which for this database is **Garden Company**), click **Category**, and click **Object Type**.

   The All Access Objects category is displayed.

The Tables group now contains shortcuts to the tables in the back-end database, as indicated by the arrows to the left of the table icons.

You can now distribute the GardenCompany12_split database to anyone who needs to use it. Provided that person has a connection to the computer on which the associated back-end database is stored, the front-end database will automatically connect to the back-end to retrieve data as needed.

 CLEAN UP Close the GardenCompany12_split database. Retain the GardenCompany12 database for use in later exercises.

Securing Databases for Distribution

When a database is used on your local computer or on your company's network, it is not difficult to control who has access to it. But if you send the database out into the world, on its own or as part of a larger application, you lose that control. There is no way you can know who is using the database or what tools they might have available to hack into it. If this is of concern to you, consider distributing your database as an Access Database Executable (ACCDE) file.

Suppose you want to make a database available for use by several organizations, but the organizations don't want their members to be able to change the database objects and perhaps "break" things. You can save the database as an ACCDE file and distribute that file instead of the ACCDB file.

Saving a database as an ACCDE file compiles and compacts the resulting database. Users of the ACCDE file can view forms and reports, update information, and run queries, but they cannot change the design of forms and reports.

Tip ACCDE files also restrict what can be done with macros, modules, and VBA code.

You can't save a database in ACCDE format back to the source ACCDB format, so after saving a database as an ACCDE file, be sure to retain the original ACCDB file in a safe place. If you need to change a form or report in the database, you will need to make the change in the original database and then save it as an ACCDE file again.

Important When creating an ACCDE file for a database that is accessed by multiple users, first make sure that no user has the database open. In Windows Explorer, navigate to the location of the file, and verify that there is no file of the same name with an .laccdb (locked Access database) extension. If you attempt to create an ACCDE file for an open database, you will be warned that the database has already been opened by someone else (the username and computer name are provided) and told to try again later.

In this exercise, you'll create a secure database by saving it as a distributable ACCDE file. You'll then test the file.

SET UP You need the GardenCompany12 database you worked with in the preceding exercise to complete this exercise. Open the GardenCompany12 database (not the GardenCompany12_split database), and then follow the steps.

1. Display the Backstage view, and in the left pane, click **Save & Publish**.

   The Save & Publish page provides several options for saving and distributing the database.

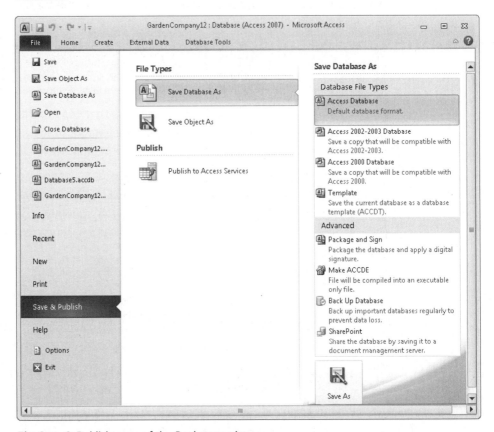

The Save & Publish page of the Backstage view.

2. Below **Advanced** in the right pane, click **Make ACCDE**, and then click **Save As**.

3. In the **Save As** dialog box, verify that the contents of your practice file folder are displayed, and then click **Save**.

   No message alerts you when the save process is complete.

4. When the **Save As** dialog box closes, close the database.

5. Display the Backstage view, and then click **Open**.

6. In the **Open** dialog box, ensure that the contents of your practice file folder are displayed.

   Access has created a database executable file. (You might need to turn off the Navigation task pane and adjust column widths to see the file types in the practice file folder.)

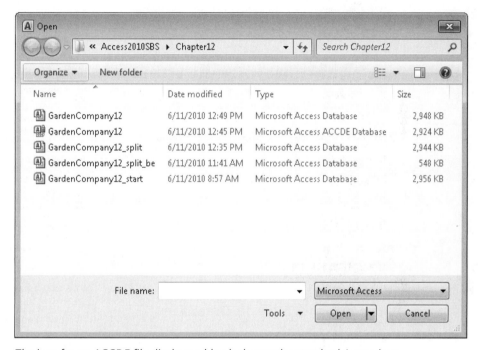

The icon for an ACCDE file displays a blue lock over the standard Access icon.

7. Double-click the **GardenCompany12** database executable file that is identified as a Microsoft Access ACCDE Database.

   Access displays a somewhat scary security notice.

This security warning is displayed when you open an executable file that is from an untrusted publisher or that is stored in an untrusted location.

8. Because you trust the source of this file (you!), click **Open**.

9. In the **Navigation** pane, right-click each object in the **Garden Company** category, and notice that the **Design View** command is not available.

   Because Design view is inactive, you cannot make any design changes to forms or reports.

 CLEAN UP If you want, delete the GardenCompany12.accde file. Retain the GardenCompany12.accdb file for use in the last exercise.

Packaging and Signing Databases

If you want to convey to users of a database executable file that they can trust the file, you might want to use the Package And Sign tool to create an Access Deployment (ACCDC) file. An ACCDC file contains one database that has been compressed. The file is signed with a digital signature, signifying that no changes have been made since the package was created.

Tip You can either purchase a digital signature from a third-party company or you can create your own signature. For information, search for *digital signature* in Access Help.

To package the current database as a signed ACCDC file:

1. Display the Save & Publish page of the Backstage view.

2. Below Advanced in the right pane, click Package And Sign, and then click Save As.

3. When a security message asks you to confirm that you want to use the installed certificate, click OK.

4. In the Create Microsoft Access Signed Package dialog box, specify a location for the package and assign a name. Then with Save As Type set to Microsoft Access Signed Package, click Create.

To use the packaged file:

1. In Windows Explorer, navigate to the location where the signed ACCDC file is stored.

   You can turn on file name extensions so that you can see them.

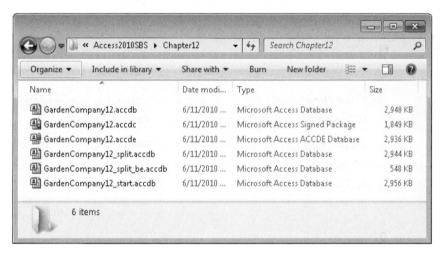

The signed package is considerably smaller that the source database file.

2. Double-click the package, and when Access displays a security notice, click Show Signature Details.

3. Check the signature in the Digital Signature Details dialog box, and then click OK.

   Tip To trust all files originating from this publisher, you can click Trust All From Publisher to add the source to the Trusted Publishers list in the Trust Center. For information, see "Changing Default Program Options" in Chapter 13, "Customize Access."

4. In the security notice box, click Open.

5. In the Extract Database To dialog box, navigate to the location to which you want to extract the database, and click OK.

You can then work on the database as you normally would.

Preventing Database Problems

Normal database use causes the internal structure of a database to become fragmented, resulting in a bloated file and inefficient use of disk space. Access monitors the condition of database files as you open and work with them. If a problem develops, Access attempts to fix it. If Access can't fix the problem, it usually provides additional information to help you to find a solution. But Access doesn't always spot problems before they affect the database, so you need to pay attention, particularly if the performance of the database seems slow or erratic.

There are various things you can do to help keep a database healthy and running smoothly. Your first line of defense against damage or corruption in any kind of file is the maintenance of backups. Database files can rapidly become very large, so you need to choose an appropriate place to store a backup copy, such as a DVD, another computer on your network, or removable media such as a USB flash drive or external hard disk.

In addition to regularly backing up the database, you can use the following Access utilities to keep it running smoothly:

- **Compact and Repair Database** This utility first optimizes performance by rearranging how the file is stored on your hard disk, and then attempts to repair any corruption in tables, forms, and reports.

   Tip It's a good idea to compact and repair a database often. You can have Access run this utility automatically each time the database is closed. Display the Backstage view, and click Options to open the Access Options dialog box. Display the Current Database page, and in the Application Options area, select the Compact On Close check box. Then click OK.

- **Database Documenter** This tool produces a detailed report containing enough information to rebuild the database structure if that is ever necessary.

- **Analyze Performance** This utility analyzes the objects in your database and offers three types of feedback: ideas, suggestions, and recommendations. You can instruct Access to optimize the file by following through on any of the suggestions or recommendations.

- **Analyze Table** This wizard tests database tables for compliance with standard database design principles, suggests solutions to problems, and implements those solutions at your request.

In this exercise, you'll first back up a database. Then you'll run the Compact And Repair Database, Analyze Performance, and Database Documenter utilities.

SET UP You need the GardenCompany12 database you worked with in the preceding exercise to complete this exercise. Open the GardenCompany12.accdb file FOR EXCLUSIVE USE, and then follow the steps.

See Also For information about opening a file for exclusive use, see the previous exercise.

1. Display the **Save & Publish** page of the Backstage view.

2. In the right pane, click **Back Up Database**, and then click **Save As**.

3. In the **Save As** dialog box, verify that the contents of your practice file folder are displayed, and then click **Save**.

    Access creates a copy of the database with the current date appended to the file name in the specified folder. As with any file name, you can change the name to suit your needs.

4. Display the Backstage view, and if the Info page is not displayed, click **Info**.

5. In the center pane of the **Info** page, click **Compact & Repair Database**.

    Tip You can also click the Compact And Repair Database button in the Tools group on the Database Tools tab.

    Troubleshooting If you don't have enough space on your hard disk to store a temporary copy of the database, you don't have appropriate permissions, or another user also has the database open, the Compact And Repair Database utility will not run.

    The utility takes only a few seconds to run, and you see no difference in the appearance of the database. If you have been using a database regularly and have not compacted it for a while, running the Compact And Repair Database utility can sometimes reduce the file size by as much as 25 percent.

6. Close all open database objects, and then under **Forms** in the **Navigation** pane, click **Home Page**.

7. On the **Database Tools** tab, in the **Analyze** group, click the **Analyze Performance** button.

    The Performance Analyzer dialog box opens. Each type of database object is represented by a page, and there are also pages for all objects and for the database as a whole.

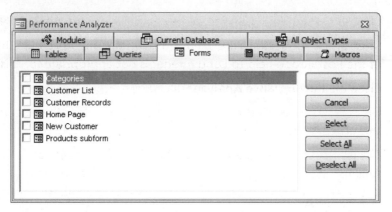

The active page reflects the object that is selected in the Navigation pane when you start the utility.

8. Click the **All Object Types** tab, click **Select All**, and then with the check boxes for all the objects in the database selected, click **OK** to start the analyzer.

   When it finishes, the Performance Analyzer displays its results. (The results you see might be different from those shown here.)

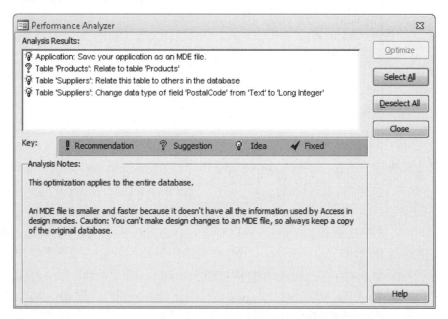

The Key tells you the nature of each item in the Analysis Results list.

Tip In previous versions of Access, Access Database Executable (ACCDE) files were called *Microsoft Database Executable (MDE)* files, hence the use of the MDE acronym in the first item in the Analysis Results list shown in this graphic.

9. Click each entry in turn, and read the information in the **Analysis Notes** area.

   Most of the suggestions are valid, although the one to change the data type of the PostalCode field to Long Integer is not appropriate for this database.

10. Close the **Performance Analyzer** dialog box.

11. On the **Database Tools** tab, in the **Analyze** group, click the **Database Documenter** button.

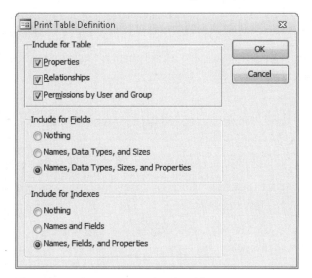

   The Documenter dialog box opens. This dialog box is identical to the Performance Analyzer dialog box. It contains a page for each type of object the utility can document, and a page displaying all the existing database objects.

12. Click the **Tables** tab, and then click **Options**.

   The Print Table Definition dialog box opens.

The print options associated with tables.

   The options associated with each object type vary, but they all enable you to specify what items you want to include in the documentation for that type of object.

13. In the **Print Table Definition** dialog box, click **Cancel**.

14. Click the **All Object Types** tab, click **Select All**, and then click **OK** to start the documentation process.

   When the process finishes, Access displays a report in Print Preview.

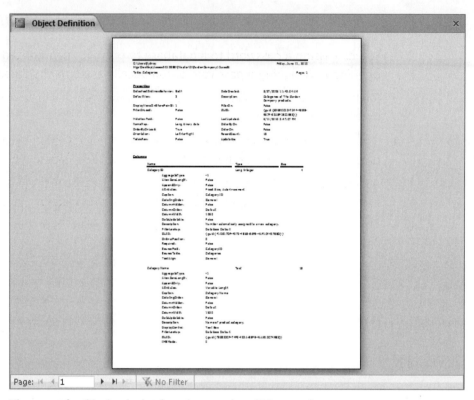

The report for this simple database is more than 200 pages long.

15. Zoom in on the report to see the kinds of things included in the documentation. Then scroll through a few pages.

    You probably don't want to print this long report, but it is a good idea to create and save a report such as this one for your own databases, in case you ever need to reconstruct them.

    Tip You can't save the report generated by the Documenter utility, but you can export it in a variety of formats. Right-click the report, click Export, and then click the format you want.

 CLEAN UP Close the Object Definition report and the GardenCompany12 database.

Key Points

- You can assign a password to a database to prevent unauthorized users from opening it. Assigning a password automatically encrypts the database.

- Splitting a database can enhance database performance and safeguard data in a multiuser environment.

- If you save the database as an ACCDE file, people using the file can view and update data and run queries, but they can't create or change database objects.

- Access automatically fixes many problems that can arise with a database. You can prevent problems by regularly using the utilities provided for that purpose.

- The simplest way to protect your database is to back it up regularly.

Chapter at a Glance

Change default program options, **page 336**

Customize the ribbon, **page 346**

Customize the Quick Access Toolbar, **page 351**

13 Customize Access

In this chapter, you will learn how to

✔ Change default program options.

✔ Customize the ribbon.

✔ Customize the Quick Access Toolbar.

If you use Microsoft Access 2010 only occasionally, you might be perfectly happy creating new databases with the wide range of tools we have already discussed in this book. And you might be comfortable with the default working environment options and behind-the-scenes settings.

However, if you create a lot of databases of various types, you might find yourself wishing that you could streamline the development process or change aspects of the program to make it more suitable for the kinds of databases you create.

In this chapter, you'll take a tour of the pages of the Access Options dialog box to understand the ways in which you can customize the program. Then you'll manipulate the ribbon and the Quick Access Toolbar to put the tools you need for your daily work at your fingertips.

> **Practice Files** Before you can complete the exercises in this chapter, you need to copy the book's practice files to your computer. The practice file you'll use to complete the exercises in this chapter is in the Chapter13 practice file folder. A complete list of practice files is provided in "Using the Practice Files" at the beginning of this book.

Changing Default Program Options

In earlier chapters, we accomplished common database tasks by working with the default Access program settings. After you work with Access for a while, you might want to refine these settings to tailor the program to the way you work. Knowing which settings are where in the Access Options dialog box makes the customization process more efficient.

In this exercise, you'll take a closer look at the Access Options dialog box and explore several of the available pages.

 SET UP You don't need any practice files to complete this exercise. Open a blank database, and then follow the steps.

Tip Don't be concerned if the pages of your Access Options dialog box look different from ours. Some pages might have changed when you installed a program on your machine, or a system administrator might have configured some settings to comply with company policy.

1. Click the **File** tab to display the Backstage view, and then click **Options**.

   The Access Options dialog box opens, displaying the General page.

   Important Some of the options on the General page apply to all Microsoft Office applications, not just Access.

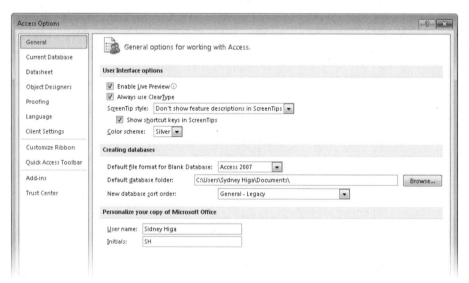

The options on this page control the user interface appearance, the availability of Live Preview, the default file format and storage location, and owner identification.

2. In the left pane, click **Current Database**.

This page controls the display of the current database.

The options on this page apply only to the active database, not to all databases.

See Also For information and practice using several of the options on the Current Database page, see "Controlling Which Features Are Available" in Chapter 11, "Make Databases User Friendly."

3. Under **Navigation**, click **Navigation Options**.

The Navigation Options dialog box opens.

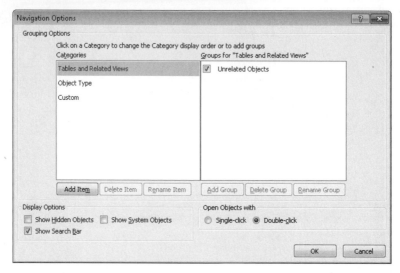

In this dialog box, you can change the display and behavior of the Navigation pane.

4. Click **Cancel**. Then in the **Access Options** dialog box, display the **Datasheet** page.

On this page, you can change the display of gridlines, cells, and fonts.

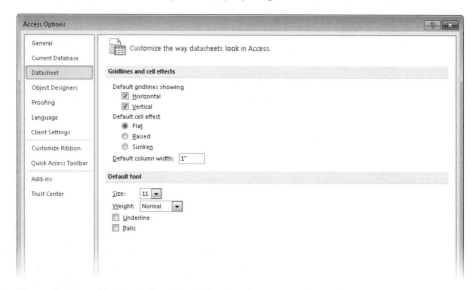

The options on this page affect the default appearance of tables and query results in Datasheet view.

5. Display the **Object Designers** page.

This page controls the database object design environments.

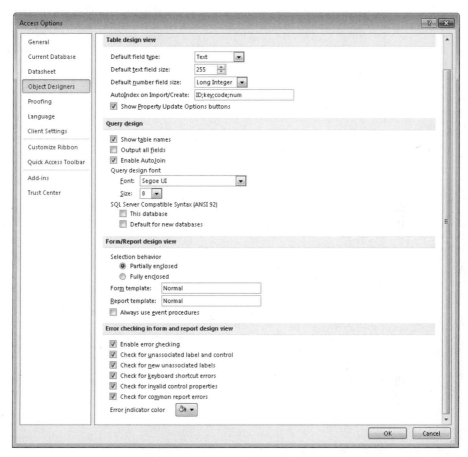

The options on this page affect the way Design view looks and behaves when you are manipulating tables, queries, forms, and reports.

Tip Most of the settings on this page do not apply when the object is open in Datasheet or Layout views.

6. Display the **Proofing** page.

This page provides AutoCorrect and spell checking options.

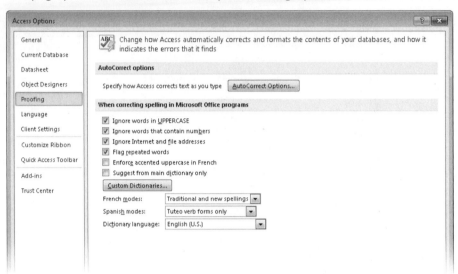

Access includes the same tools for checking spelling as the other Office 2010 programs.

7. Display the **Language** page.

If you create databases for international audiences, you might find the settings on this page useful for making additional languages available.

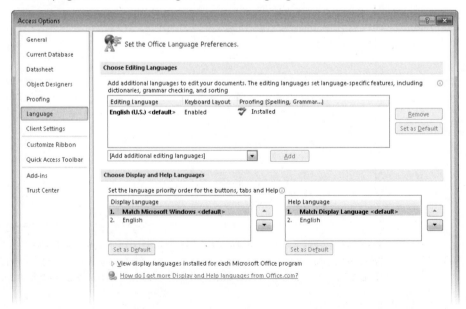

The options on this page enable you to specify the editing, display, and Help languages.

8. Display the **Client Settings** page.

These settings apply to the local computer; they do not affect Web databases.

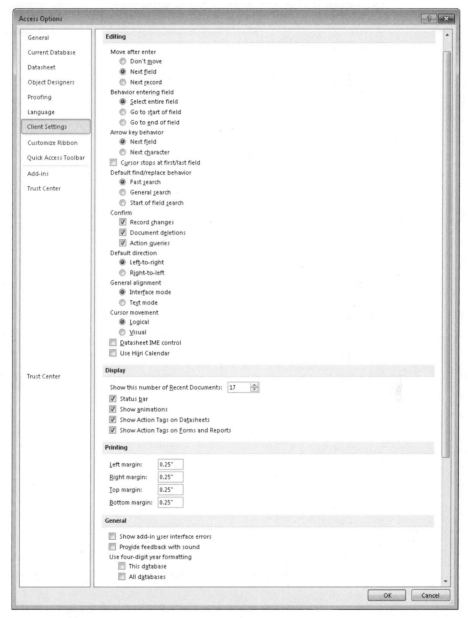

The options on this page affect default behaviors of Access on your local computer.
(The Advanced options at the bottom of the page are not shown in this graphic.)

9. Skipping over Customize Ribbon and Quick Access Toolbar, which we discuss in later topics in this chapter, click **Add-Ins**.

This page displays all the active and inactive add-ins installed on your computer. (Don't worry if your Add-Ins page looks different from ours. We have no installed add-ins on this computer.)

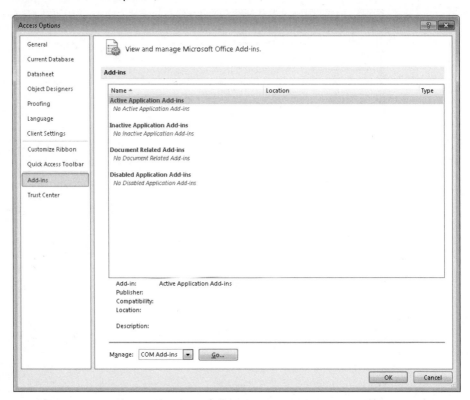

You can use the Manage options at the bottom of the page to add and remove add-ins.

See Also For information about add-ins, see the sidebar "Using Add-Ins" at the end of this topic.

10. Display the **Trust Center** page.

This page provides links to information about privacy and security. It also provides access to the Trust Center settings that control the actions Access takes in response to databases that are provided by certain people or companies, that are saved in certain locations, or that contain ActiveX controls or macros.

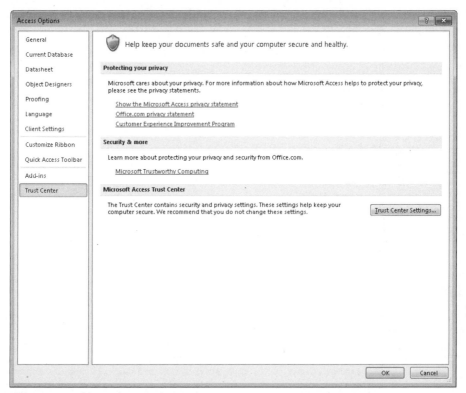

The links on this page provide information concerning the privacy and security of your databases.

11. Under **Microsoft Access Trust Center**, click **Trust Center Settings**, and then in the left pane of the **Trust Center** dialog box, click **Trusted Locations**.

On this page, you can specify the locations from which Access will not block content.

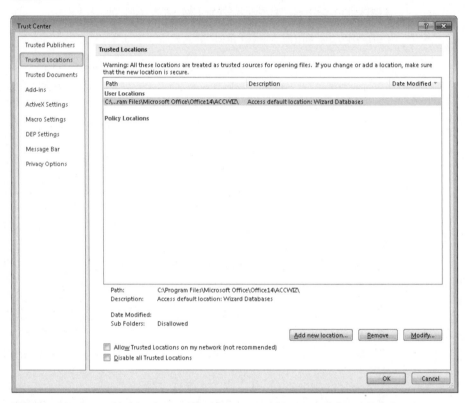

This graphic shows that the Access wizards are stored in a trusted user location, meaning that Access will not block them from running on your computer.

12. Explore the other pages of the **Trust Center** dialog box, and then click **Cancel** to return to the **Access Options** dialog box.

 **CLEAN UP** Close the Access Options dialog box.

Using Add-Ins

Add-ins are utilities that add specialized functionality to a program (but aren't full-fledged programs themselves). Access includes two primary types of add-ins: Component Object Model (COM) add-ins and Access add-ins.

There are several sources of add-ins:

- You can purchase add-ins from third-party vendors—for example, you can purchase an add-in that creates forms with controls automatically sized to fit their data.
- You can download free add-ins from the Microsoft Web site or other Web sites.
- When installing a third-party program, you might install an add-in to allow it to interface with Microsoft Office 2010 programs.

Important Be careful when downloading add-ins from Web sites other than those you trust. Add-ins are executable files that can easily be used to spread viruses and otherwise wreak havoc on your computer. For this reason, default settings in the Trust Center intervene when you attempt to download or run add-ins.

To use some add-ins, you must first install them on your computer and then load them into your computer's memory, as follows:

1. At the bottom of the Add-Ins page of the Access Options dialog box, display the Manage list, click either COM Add-Ins or Access Add-Ins, and then click Go.

   An Add-Ins dialog box corresponding to the type of add-in you chose opens.

2. In the dialog box, click Add or Add New.

3. In the dialog box that opens, navigate to the folder where the add-in you want to install is stored, and double-click its name.

   In the Add-Ins dialog box, the new add-in appears in the list of those that are available for use.

4. In the list, select the check box of the new add-in, and then click OK or an option to load the add-in.

   For example, you might be given the option of always loading the add-in when you start your computer.

Tip You can also manage add-ins in the Add-In Manager dialog box displayed when you click the Add-Ins button in the Add-Ins group on the Database Tools tab.

Customizing the Ribbon

Even if Access 2010 is the first version of the program you have ever worked with, you will by now be accustomed to working with commands represented as buttons on the ribbon. The ribbon was designed to make all the commonly used commands visible, so that people could more easily discover the full potential of the program. But many people use Access to perform the same set of tasks all the time, and for them, the visibility of buttons (or even entire groups of buttons) that they never use is just another form of clutter.

See Also For information about minimizing and expanding the ribbon, see "Customizing the Quick Access Toolbar" later in this chapter.

Would you prefer to see fewer commands, not more? Or would you prefer to see more specialized groups of commands? Well, you can. Clicking Customize Ribbon in the left pane of the Access Options dialog box displays the Customize Ribbon page, which is new in Access 2010.

The Customize Ribbon page of the Access Options dialog box.

On this page, you can customize the ribbon in the following ways:

● If you rarely use a tab, you can turn it off.

● If you use the commands in only a few groups on each tab, you can remove the groups you don't use. (The group is not removed from the program, just from its tab.)

● You can move a predefined group by removing it from one tab and then adding it to another.

● You can duplicate a predefined group by adding it to another tab.

● You can create a custom group on any tab and then add commands to it. (You cannot add commands to a predefined group.)

● For the ultimate in customization, you can create a custom tab. For example, you might want to do this if you use only a few commands from each tab and you find it inefficient to flip between them.

Don't be afraid to experiment with the ribbon to come up with the configuration that best suits the way you work. If at any point you find that your new ribbon is harder to work with rather than easier, you can always reset everything back to the default configuration.

Tip If you have upgraded from Access 2003 or an earlier version, you might have identified a few commands that no longer seem to be available. A few old features have been abandoned, but others that people used only rarely have simply been pushed off to one side. If you sorely miss one of these sidelined features, you can make it a part of your Access environment by adding it to the ribbon. You can find a list of all the commands that do not appear on the ribbon but are still available in Access by displaying the Customize Ribbon page of the Access Options dialog box and then clicking Commands Not In The Ribbon in the Choose Commands From list.

In this exercise, you'll turn off tabs, remove groups, create a custom group, and add commands to the new group. Then you'll create a tab and move predefined groups of buttons to it. Finally, you'll reset the ribbon to its default state.

 SET UP You need the GardenCompany13_start database located in your Chapter13 practice file folder to complete this exercise. Open the GardenCompany13_start database, and save it as *GardenCompany13*. Then follow the steps.

1. Display the **Customize Ribbon** page of the **Access Options** dialog box.

2. In the right pane, clear the check boxes of the **External Data** and **Database Tools** tabs. Then click **OK**.

   The ribbon now displays only the File, Home, and Create tabs.

You cannot turn off the File tab.

Troubleshooting The appearance of buttons and groups on the ribbon changes depending on the width of the program window. For information about changing the appearance of the ribbon to match our screen images, see "Modifying the Display of the Ribbon" at the beginning of this book.

3. Redisplay the **Customize Ribbon** page of the **Access Options** dialog box, and in the right pane, select the **Database Tools** check box. Then click the plus sign to display the groups on this tab.

4. Display the **Choose commands from** list, and click **Main Tabs**. Then in the list box below, click the plus sign adjacent to **Database Tools** to display the groups that are predefined for this tab.

5. In the right list box, click the **Move Data** group, and then click **Remove**.

   The group is removed from the Database Tools tab on the ribbon (the list box on the right), but is still available in the list box on the left. You can add it back to the Database Tools tab, or add it to a different tab, at any time.

6. If the **Home** group is not expanded in the right list box, click the plus sign adjacent to **Home** to displays its groups, and then click the word **Home**.

7. Below the right list box, click **New Group**. When the **New Group (Custom)** group is added to the bottom of the Home group list, click **Rename**, type **Final** in the **Display name** box, and click **OK**. Then click the **Move Up** button until the **Final (Custom)** group is above **Views** in the group list.

   Because of its location in the hierarchy, the new group will appear at the left end of the Home tab.

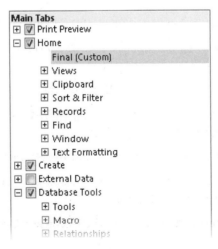

You have created a custom group on the Home tab.

8. Display the **Choose commands from** list, and click **File Tab**.

   The available commands list changes to include only the commands that are available in the Backstage view, which you display by clicking the File tab.

9. In the available commands list, click **Encode/Decode Database**, and click **Add**. Then repeat this step to add **Package and Sign**.

   The two commands are added to the custom group.

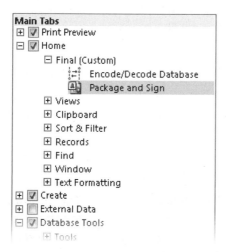

You can add commands to a custom group, but not to a predefined group.

10. In the right list box, remove the **Find** and **Sort & Filter** groups from the **Home** tab.

11. Click the word **Home**, and then below the list box, click **New Tab**.

    A new tab is added to the right list box and is selected for display on the ribbon. It has automatically been given one custom group.

12. Remove the custom group from the **New Tab (Custom)** tab.

13. Click **New Tab (Custom)**, and then click **Rename**. In the **Rename** dialog box, type Search in the **Display name** box, and click **OK**.

14. Display **Main Tabs** in the left list box, and then expand the **Home** tab.

15. With the **Search (Custom)** tab selected in the right list box, add the **Sort & Filter** and **Find** groups from **Home** in the left list box.

    The right list box shows the new configuration of the Home and Search tabs.

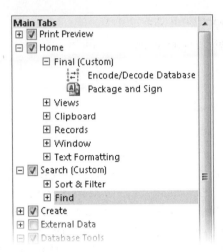

You have created a new tab containing two predefined groups.

16. In the **Access Options** dialog box, click **OK**.

The Home tab displays the new Final group.

The custom Home tab.

17. Display the **Customers** table in Datasheet view, and then click the **Search** tab.

The filter, sort, and find commands are now collected on the Search tab.

The custom Search tab.

18. Display the **Customize Ribbon** page of the **Access Options** dialog box. Below the right list box, click **Reset**, and then click **Reset all customizations**. Then in the message box asking you to confirm that you want to delete all ribbon and Quick Access Toolbar customizations, click **Yes**.

19. Click **OK** to close the **Access Options** dialog box.

   The default ribbon configuration is restored.

 **CLEAN UP** Close the Customers table. Retain the GardenCompany13 database for use in the last exercise.

Customizing the Quick Access Toolbar

By default, the Save, Undo, and Repeat/Redo buttons appear on the Quick Access Toolbar. If you regularly use a few buttons that are scattered on various tabs of the ribbon and you don't want to switch between tabs to access the buttons or crowd your ribbon with a custom tab, you might want to add these frequently used buttons to the Quick Access Toolbar. They are then always visible in the upper-left corner of the program window.

Clicking Quick Access Toolbar in the left pane of the Access Options dialog box displays the page where you specify which commands you want to appear on the toolbar.

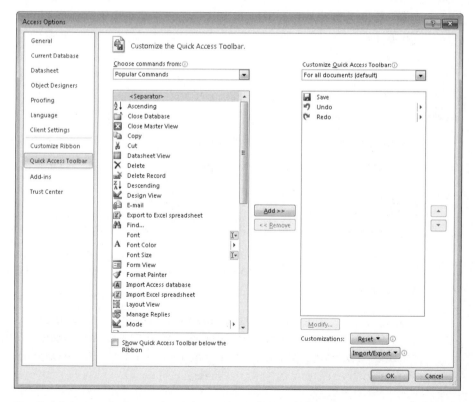

The Quick Access Toolbar page of the Access Options dialog box.

On this page, you can customize the Quick Access Toolbar in the following ways:

● You can define a custom Quick Access Toolbar for all databases, or you can define a custom Quick Access Toolbar for a specific database.

● You can add any command from any group of any tab, including contextual tabs, to the toolbar.

● You can display a separator between different types of buttons.

● You can move buttons around on the toolbar until they are in the order you want.

● You can reset everything back to the default Quick Access Toolbar configuration.

If you never use more than a few buttons, you can add those buttons to the Quick Access Toolbar and then hide the ribbon by double-clicking the active tab or by clicking the Minimize The Ribbon button. Only the Quick Access Toolbar and tab names remain visible. You can temporarily redisplay the ribbon by clicking the tab you want to view. You can permanently redisplay the ribbon by double-clicking any tab or by clicking the Expand The Ribbon button.

As you add buttons to the Quick Access Toolbar, it expands to accommodate them. If you add many buttons, it might become difficult to view the text in the title bar, or some of the buttons on the Quick Access Toolbar might not be visible, defeating the purpose of adding them. To resolve this problem, you can move the Quick Access Toolbar below the ribbon by clicking the Customize Quick Access Toolbar button and then clicking Show Below The Ribbon.

In this exercise, you'll add a few buttons to the Quick Access Toolbar for all databases, and then you'll test some of the buttons.

SET UP You need the GardenCompany13 database you worked with in the preceding exercise to complete this exercise. Open the GardenCompany13 database, open the Customers table in Datasheet view, and then follow the steps.

1. Display the **Quick Access Toolbar** page of the **Access Options** dialog box.

   A list of popular commands appears in the left list box, and a list of the commands currently displayed on the Quick Access Toolbar appears in the right list box.

   Tip If you want to create a Quick Access Toolbar that is specific to the active database, display the Customize Quick Access Toolbar list, and click For *<path of database>*. Then any command you select will be added to that specific toolbar instead of the toolbar for all databases.

2. Display the **Choose commands from** list, and click **All Commands**.

3. At the top of the available commands list, double-click **Separator**.

   A separator line will appear on the Quick Access Toolbar, dividing the default Save, Undo, and Redo commands from the custom commands you are about to add to the toolbar.

4. Scroll about two-thirds of the way down the available commands list, click **Quick Print**, and then click **Add**.

5. Repeat step 4 to add the **Reports**, **Tables**, and **Forms** ribbon groups. Then rearrange these groups so that they appear in this order: **Tables**, **Forms**, and then **Reports**.

   In addition to the three default commands, a separator bar, one custom command, and three custom groups now appear in the right list box.

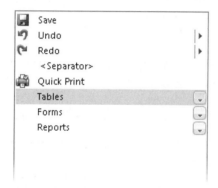

The down-arrows to the right of Tables, Forms, and Reports indicate that clicking any of these buttons on the Quick Access Toolbar will display the associated group's commands.

6. Click **OK** to close the **Access Options** dialog box.

   The Quick Access Toolbar now includes the default Save, Undo, and Repeat/Redo buttons, the custom Quick Print button, and the Tables, Forms, and Reports group buttons, separated by a line.

You have added a button and three groups to the Quick Access Toolbar.

To print a database with the default settings, you no longer have to click the File tab to display the Backstage view, click Print in the left pane, and then click the appropriate printing button in the right pane. And you can access the commands in the Tables, Forms, and Reports groups without having to display the Create tab of the ribbon.

7. If you want to test printing from the Quick Access Toolbar, verify that your printer is turned on, and then on the Quick Access Toolbar, click the **Quick Print** button.

8. Close the **Customers** table.

9. With **Customers** selected in the **Navigation** pane, on the Quick Access Toolbar, click the **Forms** button.

The Forms group is displayed.

All of the buttons in the Forms group are active because the Customers table is selected in the Navigation pane.

10. Display the **Quick Access Toolbar** page of the **Access Options** dialog box.

11. Below the right pane, click **Reset**, and then click **Reset only Quick Access Toolbar**.

12. In the **Reset Customizations** message box, click **Yes** to return the Quick Access Toolbar to its default contents. Then click **OK** to close the **Access Options** dialog box.

✖ **CLEAN UP** Close the GardenCompany13 database.

Key Points

- The Access environment is flexible and can be customized to meet your needs.
- Most of the settings that control the working environment are gathered on the pages of the Access Options dialog box.
- You can customize the ribbon to put precisely the database development tools you need at your fingertips.
- You can provide one-click access to any Access 2010 command by adding a button for it to the Quick Access Toolbar, either for all databases or for one database.

Glossary

Access Database Executable (ACCDE) file An Access database file that has been compiled and compacted for distribution. The ACCDE file format allows users to view forms and reports, update information, and run queries, but prevents them from changing database objects.

Access Deployment (ACCDC) file An Access database file that has been compressed and digitally signed for distribution.

application parts Predefined database objects that you can add to an existing database. Access comes with 10 types of forms and several Quick Start parts.

action query A type of query that performs an action on matched records, such as updating fields or deleting the records. See also *select query*.

aggregate function A function that performs a calculation, such as Sum or Avg (average), on multiple values and returns a single summary value.

append query A query that adds, or appends, records from one or more tables to the end of one or more tables.

arithmetic operator An operator that is used with numerals: + (addition), - (subtraction), * (multiplication), or / (division).

back-end database The portion of a split database that contains the tables that store all the data. The back-end database is kept on a central computer. See also *front-end database* and *split database*.

binary file A file that contains encoded information that is interpreted by a computer according to the application that created it. In general, a binary file can be edited only by the application in which it was created. A binary file is not encrypted and is therefore not secure.

bound Linked, as when a text box control is linked to a specific field in a table. See also *unbound*.

combo box A control that combines a text box with a list box. This allows the user to type an entry or choose one from a list.

comma-delimited text file A text file in which each field is separated from the next by a comma.

command button Any button with which users initiate an immediate action. You can add command button controlss to forms and reports.

comparison operator An operator that compares two expressions, expressed as > (greater than), < (less than), = (equal to), >= (greater than or equal to), <= (less than or equal to), <> (not equal to), or like (pattern matching).

constant A value that is not calculated and, therefore, does not change. For example, the number 210 and the text *Quarterly Earnings* are constants. An expression, or a value resulting from an expression, is not a constant.

control A graphical user interface object, such as a text box, combo box, or command button, that displays data or choices, performs an action, or makes a database object easier to use.

control property A setting in the control's Property Sheet that determines the control's appearance, what kind of data it can display, and its behavior.

control source The element, such as a field, table, or query, to which a control is bound. See also *record source*.

crosstab query A type of query that displays data for summarized values from a field or table and then groups them by two sets of facts: one down the left side, and the other across the top of the datasheet.

database application A database that is made easier to use by the inclusion of queries, forms, reports, custom categories and groups, and various other tools.

database object One of the components of an Access database, such as a table, query, form, report, macro, or module.

database program An application for creating databases, ranging from simple databases that can store one table per file (referred to as *flat databases*) to more complex databases that can store information in multiple related tables (referred to as *relational databases*).

database security Measures adopted to protect data from accidental or intentional corruption and make it difficult for unauthorized people to gain access to private information; for example, passwords, encryption, and ACCDE files.

Datasheet view The view in which you can see and modify information in a table or query. Along with Design view, this is one of the two most common views for tables. See also *Design view* and *view*.

delete query A query that deletes records that match a specified pattern from one or more tables.

delimited text file A text file that contains data in which individual field values are separated by a character, such as a comma or a tab.

delimiter A character, such as a comma (,), semicolon (;), or backslash (\), that is used to separate records and fields in a delimited text file.

deselect To click away from selected data or controls to release a selection.

design grid In Design view, the grid in which you can manually work with advanced filters and queries.

Design view The view in which you can see and modify the structure of a table, query, form, or report.

dialog box launcher On the ribbon, a button at the bottom of some groups that opens a dialog box with features related to the group.

duplicate query A type of select query that finds records containing identical information in one or more specified fields. Can be created with the assistance of the Find Duplicates Query wizard.

empty string A string with the value "" (two quotation marks with nothing between them).

encrypting To encode (scramble) information in such a way that it is unreadable to all but those individuals possessing the key to the code.

exclusive use A setting that permits only one person to have a database open. Generally used when setting or removing a database password.

exporting The process of converting an Access table or database into a format that can be used by other programs. See also *importing*.

expression A combination of functions, field values, constants, and operators that can be used to assign properties to tables or forms, to determine values in fields or reports, as a part of a query, and in many other places. Also known as a *formula*.

Expression Builder A tool used to create an expression. The Expression Builder includes a list of common expressions that you can select from to define the properties you want to target.

Extensible Markup Language (XML) A format for delivering rich, structured data in a standard, consistent way. XML tags describe the content of a Web document, whereas HTML tags describe how the document looks. XML allows designers to create their own customized tags. See also *Hypertext Markup Language (HTML)*.

field An element of a table that contains a specific item of information, such as a last name. A field is represented in Access as a column in a database table. See also *record*.

field property A property that controls what can be put into a field and how it can be placed there.

filter A set of criteria you can use to specify the information you want to display.

fixed-width text file A common text file format that is often used to transfer data from older programs. The same field in every record contains the same number of characters. If the actual data doesn't fill a field, the field is padded with spaces so that the starting point of the data in the next field is the same number of characters from the beginning of every record.

flat database A simple database that can store information in only one table. See also *relational database*.

form An organized and formatted view of some or all of the fields from one or more tables or queries. Forms work interactively with the tables in a database and are often used to simplify data entry.

form selector The box at the intersection of the vertical and horizontal rulers when a form is displayed in Design view. You click the form selector to select the entire form.

front-end database The portion of a split database that contains the forms, queries, and reports people use to work with data. The front end can be copied to the local computer of any user who needs to work with the database. See also *back-end database* and *split database*.

function A named procedure or routine, often used for mathematical or financial calculations.

group On a ribbon tab, an area containing buttons related to a specific database element or function. On the Navigation bar, a list that is part of a category.

grouping level The level by which records are grouped in a report. When you group on a field, the report adds a group header and footer around each group of records that have the same value in that field.

HTML tag A code that identifies an element in an HTML document, such as a heading or a paragraph, for the purposes of formatting, indexing, and linking information in the document.

Hypertext Markup Language (HTML) A simple markup language used to create hypertext documents that are portable from one platform to another. HTML files are simple ASCII text files with embedded markup tags that control formatting and hypertext links. See also *Extensible Markup Language (XML)*.

importing The process of converting external data into a format that can be used by Access. See also *exporting*.

input mask A property that controls the appearance, format, and type of data in a field.

label control A control that contains text as it will appear on a form or report.

linking The process of connecting to data in other programs so that you can view and edit it both in Access and the originating program.

logical operator An operator, such as AND, OR, or NOT, that is used in queries and filters to extract matching records from tables.

Lookup wizard An Access wizard with which you can create a lookup list.

main form A form that contains other embedded subforms. See also *subform*.

main report A report that serves as a shell for one or more embedded subreports. See also *subreport*.

make-table query A query that combines all or part of the data from one or more tables into a new table.

many-to-many relationship A relationship between two tables in which records in each table have multiple matching records in the related table. For example, each sales invoice can contain multiple products, and each product can appear on multiple sales invoices. See also *one-to-many relationship* and *one-to-one relationship*.

mapped network drive A network drive to which you have assigned a drive letter so that it can be accessed as a hard drive on your local computer. See also *Universal Naming Convention (UNC)*.

Microsoft Database Executable (MDE) file The equivalent of an ACCDE file created by previous versions of Access. See *Access Database Executable (ACCDE) file*.

named range A group of related spreadsheet cells defined by a single name.

navigation control A control on a navigation form that consists of a placeholder for a navigation button and a subform or subreport control.

navigation form A form that presents the user with a set of navigation buttons that can be clicked to display and work with forms and reports. Database designers can use navigation forms to make it easier for users to access and manipulate data and more difficult for them to unintentionally change or delete it.

Navigation pane An area of the Access program window that enables the user to quickly open database objects.

network share A storage location on a network that is shared with and accessible from authorized computers on the network

normalization rules A set of database design rules that minimizes data redundancy and results in a database in which referential integrity can be enforced.

Null Nothing; a field with no entry.

one-to-many relationship In relational databases, a relationship between two tables in which a single record in the first table can be related to one or more records in the second table, but a record in the second table can be related to only one record in the first table. See also *many-to-many relationship* and *one-to-one relationship*.

one-to-one relationship In relational databases, a relationship between two tables in which a single record in the first table can be related to only one record in the second table, and a record in the second table can be related to only one record in the first table. See also *many-to-many relationship* and *one-to-many relationship*.

operator See *arithmetic operator, comparison operator,* and *logical operator.*

option button A control that allows a user to select from a fixed set of mutually exclusive choices.

parameter query A type of query that, when run, prompts for the values (criteria) to use to select the records for the result set so that the same query can be used to retrieve different result sets. See also *action query, crosstab query,* and *select query.*

parsing The process of analyzing an imported document, such as an HTML document, and identifying anything that looks like structured data.

password A string of characters used to access information or log on to a computer. Passwords help prevent unauthorized people from accessing files, programs, and other resources. See also *secure password.*

populating To add data to a table or other object.

primary key One or more fields whose value or values uniquely identify each record in a table. A primary key cannot allow Null values and must always have a unique index. In related tables, the primary key field in one table corresponds with the foreign key field in the other table.

property A named attribute of a control, a field, or an object that you set to define one of the object's characteristics (such as size, color, or screen location) or an aspect of its behavior (such as whether the object is hidden).

publisher The person or entity who digitally signs a database or other file, thereby guaranteeing its source.

query A database object that locates specific information stored in a table and allows you to view and manipulate the results. The results of a query can be used as the basis for forms and reports.

Quick Access Toolbar A small, customizable toolbar that displays frequently used commands.

record All the related information about a person or item in a table. A record in Access is represented as a row in a database table. See also *field*.

record selector The gray bar along the left edge of a form in Form view. You can select an entire record by clicking its record.

record source The source from which the data in a bound record originates. See also *control source*.

referential integrity A restriction on data, requiring that in two related tables, an entry will not be allowed in one table unless it already exists in the other table.

relational database A type of database that stores information in tables. Relational databases use matching values from two tables to relate data in one table to data in the other table. In a relational database, you typically store a specific type of data just once. See also *flat database*.

relationship An association between common fields in two or more tables.

report A database object used to display table information in a formatted, easily accessible manner, either on the screen or on paper. It can include items from multiple tables and queries, values calculated from information in the database, and formatting elements such as headers, footers, titles, and headings.

report selector The box at the intersection of the vertical and horizontal rulers when a report is displayed in Design view. You click the report selector to select the entire report.

results datasheet The presentation of the records matched by a query and any specified calculations in a table-like structure.

ribbon A user interface design that organizes commands into logical groups, which appear on separate tabs.

row selector The gray box at the left end of each row in the field definition area when a table's structure is displayed in Design view.

schema The definition of the structure of an XML file. A schema contains property information as it pertains to the records and fields within the structure.

secure password A password that includes uppercase letters, lowercase letters, and symbols or numbers, and is not a word found in a dictionary. Also called a *strong password*.

security warning A warning that appears when a database that contains one or more macros is opened.

select query A query that matches records from one or more tables and displays them in a results datasheet. Can contain specifications for which fields to display in what order and how to group (summarize) their values. See also *action query*.

signing The act of guaranteeing the source and content of a file by attaching a digital signature.

sorting A method of arranging data based on the order of specified information.

split database A database that has been organized into two parts: a back-end database containing the tables that store all the data, and a front-end database containing the forms, queries, and reports that people use to work with the data. See also *back-end database* and *front-end database*.

SQL database A database based on Structured Query Language (SQL).

subdatasheet A datasheet that is contained within another datasheet.

subform A form that is contained within another form. See also *main form*.

subreport A report that is contained within another report. See also *main report*.

syntax The required format in which expressions must be entered.

tab A tabbed page on the ribbon that contains buttons organized in groups. Also a navigation button attached to a database object that is open in the Access program window workspace. You click the button to display the object's page.

tabbed pages The default display of objects in the Access program window. Alternatively, you can display objects in their own windows.

table A structured arrangement of one or more rows and one or more columns. The intersection of each row and column is a cell. All the items of information in a row constitute a record, and all the items of information in a column constitute a field.

tag A code in HTML or XML that gives instructions for formatting or defining the structure of a document.

template A ready-made pattern that can be used to create a specific type of database. Access 2010 comes with several templates, all of which can be customized.

text box control A control on a form or report in which text can be viewed, entered or edited. A text box control is bound to a field in the underlying table.

transform A type of template used to convert XML data to other formats.

unbound Not linked. An unbound control is not linked to a field in an underlying table; instead it might be used, for example, to calculate values from multiple fields. See also *bound*.

undocking To drag a toolbar, task pane, or similar item so that it floats in the program window.

Universal Naming Convention (UNC) The system of naming files among computers on a network so that a file on a given computer will have the same path when it is accessed from any of the other computers on the network. See also *mapped network drive*.

unmatched query A select query that locates records in one table that do not have any related records in another table. This query can be created with the assistance of the Find Unmatched Query wizard.

update query A query that changes the values in one or more fields of matched records in a table.

validation rule A field property that ensures entries contain only the correct type, size, or range of data.

view The display of information from a specific perspective. Each Access object has two or more views, such as Datasheet view and Design view.

wildcard character A keyboard character that can be used to represent one or many characters in a search. The question mark (?) represents a single character, and the asterisk (*) represents one or more characters.

Keyboard Shortcuts

This section presents a comprehensive list of all the keyboards shortcuts built into Microsoft Access 2010. The list has been excerpted from Access Help and formatted in tables for convenient lookup. Some of these shortcuts might not be available for your edition of Access 2010 or for your keyboard layout.

In the following tables, keys you press at the same time are separated by a plus sign (+), and keys you press sequentially are separated by a comma (,).

General Shortcut Keys

Work with Global Access Keys

Opening Databases

Action	Keyboard shortcut
Open a new database.	Ctrl+N
Open an existing database.	Ctrl+O
Exit Access 2010.	Alt+F4

Printing and Saving

Action	Keyboard shortcut
Print the current or selected object.	Ctrl+P
Open the Print dialog box from Print Preview.	P or Ctrl+P
Open the Page Setup dialog box from Print Preview.	S
Cancel Print Preview or Layout Preview.	C or Esc
Save a database object.	Ctrl+S or Shift+F12
Open the Save As dialog box.	F12

Using a Combo Box or List Box

Action	Keyboard shortcut
Open a combo box.	F4 or Alt+Down Arrow
Refresh the contents of a list box or combo box.	F9
Move up or down one line.	Up Arrow or Down Arrow
Move up or down one page.	Page Up or Page Down
Exit the combo box or list box.	Tab

Finding and Replacing Text or Data (Datasheet View or Form View)

Action	Keyboard shortcut
Open the Find tab in the Find And Replace dialog box.	Ctrl+F
Open the Replace tab in the Find And Replace dialog box.	Ctrl+H
Find the next occurrence of the text specified in the Find And Replace dialog box when the dialog box is closed.	Shift+F4

Working in Design View

Action	Keyboard shortcut
Switch between Edit mode (with the cursor displayed) and Navigation mode in a datasheet. When working in a form or report, press Esc to leave Navigation mode.	F2
Switch to the Property Sheet (form or report Design view in both Access databases and Access projects).	F4
Switch to Form view from form Design view.	F5
Switch between the upper and lower panes (query Design view, and the Advanced Filter/Sort window).	F6
Cycle through the field grid, field properties, the Navigation pane, access keys in the Keyboard Access System, Zoom controls, and the security bar (table Design view).	F6
Open the Choose Builder dialog box (form or report Design view).	F7
Open the Visual Basic Editor from a selected property in the Property Sheet for a form or report.	F7
Switch from the Visual Basic Editor to form or report Design view.	Shift+F7 or Alt+F11

Editing Controls in Form and Report Design View

Action	Keyboard shortcut
Copy the selected control to the Clipboard.	Ctrl+C
Cut the selected control and copy it to the Clipboard.	Ctrl+X
Paste the contents of the Clipboard in the upper-left corner of the selected section.	Ctrl+V
Move the selected control to the right (except controls that are part of a layout).	Right Arrow or Ctrl+Right Arrow
Move the selected control to the left (except controls that are part of a layout).	Left Arrow or Ctrl+Left Arrow
Move the selected control up.	Up Arrow or Ctrl+Up Arrow
Move the selected control down.	Down Arrow or Ctrl+Down Arrow
Increase the height of the selected control.	Shift+Down Arrow
Increase the width of the selected control. Note: If used with controls that are in a layout, the entire layout is resized.	Shift+Right Arrow
Reduce the height of the selected control.	Shift+Up Arrow
Reduce the width of the selected control. Note: If used with controls that are in a layout, the entire layout is resized.	Shift+Left Arrow

Working with Windows

By default, Access 2010 databases display as tabbed documents. To use windowed documents, click the File tab, and then click Options. In the Access Options dialog box, click Current Database and, under Document Window Options, click Overlapping Windows.

Tip You will have to close and reopen the current database for the option to take effect.

Action	Keyboard shortcut
Toggle the Navigation pane.	F11
Cycle between open windows.	Ctrl+F6
Restore the selected minimized window when all windows are minimized.	Enter
Turn on Resize mode for the active window when it is not maximized; press the Arrow keys to resize the window.	Ctrl+F8
Display the control menu.	Alt+Spacebar
Display the shortcut menu.	Shift+F10

(continued)

Action	Keyboard shortcut
Close the active window.	Ctrl+W or Ctrl+F4
Switch between the Visual Basic Editor and the previous active window.	Alt+F11

Working with Wizards

Action	Keyboard shortcut
Toggle the focus forward between controls in the wizard.	Tab
Move to the next page of the wizard.	Alt+N
Move to the previous page of the wizard.	Alt+B
Complete the wizard.	Alt+F

Miscellaneous

Action	Keyboard shortcut
Display the complete hyperlink address for a selected hyperlink.	F2
Check spelling.	F7
Open the Zoom box to conveniently enter expressions and other text in small input areas.	Shift+F2
Display a Property Sheet in Design view.	Alt+Enter
Exit Access or close a dialog box.	Alt+F4
Invoke a Builder.	Ctrl+F2
Toggle forward between views when in a table, query, form, report, page, PivotTable list, PivotChart report, stored procedure, or Access project (.adp) function. If there are additional views available, successive keystrokes will move to the next available view.	Ctrl+Right Arrow or Ctrl+Comma (,)
Toggle back between views when in a table, query, form, report, page, PivotTable list, PivotChart report, stored procedure, or .adp function. If there are additional views available, successive keystrokes will move to the previous view. Note: Ctrl+Period (.) does not work under all conditions with all objects.	Ctrl+Left Arrow or Ctrl+Period (.)

Work with the Navigation Pane

Action	Keyboard shortcut
Go to the Navigation pane Search box from anywhere in the database.	Alt+Ctrl+F

Editing and Navigating the Object List

Action	Keyboard shortcut
Rename a selected object.	F2
Move down one line.	Down Arrow
Move down one window.	Page Down
Move to the last object.	End
Move up one line.	Up Arrow
Move up one window.	Page Up
Move to the first object.	Home

Navigating and Opening Objects

Action	Keyboard shortcut
Open the selected table or query in Datasheet view.	Enter
Open the selected form or report.	Enter
Run the selected macro.	Enter
Open the selected table, query, form, report, macro, or module in Design view.	Ctrl+Enter
Display the Immediate window in the Visual Basic Editor.	Ctrl+G

Work with Menus

Action	Keyboard shortcut
Show the shortcut menu.	Shift+F10
Show the access keys.	Alt or F10
Show the program icon menu (on the program title bar).	Alt+Spacebar
With the menu or submenu visible, select the next or previous command.	Down Arrow or Up Arrow
Select the menu to the left or right; or, when a submenu is visible, to switch between the main menu and the submenu.	Left Arrow or Right Arrow
Select the first or last command on the menu or submenu.	Home or End
Close the visible menu and submenu at the same time.	Alt
Close the visible menu; or, with a submenu visible, to close the submenu only.	Esc

Work in Windows and Dialog Boxes

Using a Program Window

Action	Keyboard shortcut
Switch to the next program.	Alt+Tab
Switch to the previous program.	Alt+Shift+Tab
Show the Windows Start menu.	Ctrl+Esc
Close the active database window.	Ctrl+W
Switch to the next database window.	Ctrl+F6
Switch to the previous database window.	Ctrl+Shift+F6
Restore the selected minimized window when all windows are minimized.	Enter

Using a Dialog Box

Action	Keyboard shortcut
Switch to the next tab in a dialog box.	Ctrl+Tab
Switch to the previous tab in a dialog box.	Ctrl+Shift+Tab
Move to the next option or option group.	Tab
Move to the previous option or option group.	Shift+Tab
Move between options in the selected drop-down list box, or to move between some options in a group of options.	Arrow keys
Perform the action assigned to the selected button; select or clear the check box.	Spacebar
Move to the option by the first letter in the option name in a drop-down list box.	Letter key for the first letter in the option name you want (when a drop-down list box is selected)
Select the option, or to select or clear the check box by the letter underlined in the option name.	Alt+letter key
Open the selected drop-down list box.	Alt+Down Arrow
Close the selected drop-down list box.	Esc
Perform the action assigned to the default button in the dialog box.	Enter
Cancel the command and close the dialog box.	Esc
Close a dialog box.	Alt+F4

Editing in a Text Box

Action	Keyboard shortcut
Move to the beginning of the entry.	Home
Move to the end of the entry.	End
Move one character to the left or right.	Left Arrow or Right Arrow
Move one word to the left or right.	Ctrl+Left Arrow or Ctrl+Right Arrow
Select from the cursor to the beginning of the text entry.	Shift+Home
Select from the cursor to the end of the text entry.	Shift+End
Change the selection by one character to the left.	Shift+Left Arrow
Change the selection by one character to the right.	Shift+Right Arrow
Change the selection by one word to the left.	Ctrl+Shift+Left Arrow
Change the selection by one word to the right.	Ctrl+Shift+Right Arrow

Work with Property Sheets

Using a Property Sheet with a Form or Report in Design View

Action	Keyboard shortcut
Toggle the Property Sheet tab.	F4
Move among choices in the control drop-down list one item at a time.	Down Arrow or Up Arrow
Move among choices in the control drop-down list five items at a time.	Page Down or Page Up
Move to the Property Sheet tabs from the control drop-down list.	Tab
Move among the Property Sheet tabs with a tab selected, but no property selected.	Left Arrow or Right Arrow
With a property already selected, move down one property on a tab.	Tab
With a property selected, move up one property on a tab; or if already at the top, move to the tab.	Shift+Tab
Toggle forward between tabs when a property is selected.	Ctrl+Tab
Toggle backward between tabs when a property is selected.	Ctrl+Shift+Tab

Using a Property Sheet with a Table or Query

Action	Keyboard shortcut
Toggle the Property Sheet tab.	F4
With a tab selected, but no property selected, move among the Property Sheet tabs.	Left Arrow or Right Arrow
Move to the Property Sheet tabs when a property is selected.	Ctrl+Tab
Move to the first property of a tab when no property is selected.	Tab
Move down one property on a tab.	Tab
Move up one property on a tab; or if already at the top, select the tab itself.	Shift+Tab
Toggle forward between tabs when a property is selected.	Ctrl+Tab
Toggle backward between tabs when a property is selected.	Ctrl+Shift+Tab

Working with the Field List Pane

Action	Keyboard shortcut
Toggle the Field List pane.	Alt+F8
Add the selected field to the form or report detail section.	Enter
Move up or down the Field List pane.	Up Arrow or Down Arrow
Move to the upper Field List pane from the lower pane.	Shift+Tab
Move to the lower Field List pane from the upper pane.	Tab

Work with the Help Window

Action	Keyboard shortcut
Select the next hidden text or hyperlink, or Show All or Hide All at the top of a topic.	Tab
Select the previous hidden text or hyperlink, or the Browser View button at the top of a Microsoft Office Web site article.	Shift+Tab
Perform the action for the selected Show All, Hide All, hidden text, or hyperlink.	Enter
Move back to the previous Help topic.	Alt+Left Arrow
Move forward to the next Help topic.	Alt+Right Arrow
Open the Print dialog box.	Ctrl+P

Action	Keyboard shortcut
Scroll small amounts up and down, respectively, within the currently displayed Help topic.	Up Arrow and Down Arrow
Scroll larger amounts up and down, respectively, within the currently displayed Help topic.	Page Up and Page Down
Display a menu of commands for the Help window; requires that the Help window have active focus (click an item in the Help window).	Shift+F10

Keys for Working with Text and Data

Select Text and Data

Selecting Text in a Field

Action	Keyboard shortcut
Change the size of the selection by one character to the right.	Shift+Right Arrow
Change the size of the selection by one word to the right.	Ctrl+Shift+Right Arrow
Change the size of the selection by one character to the left.	Shift+Left Arrow
Change the size of the selection by one word to the left.	Ctrl+Shift+Left Arrow

Selecting a Field or Record

Tip To cancel a selection, use the opposite Arrow key.

Action	Keyboard shortcut
Select the next field.	Tab
Switch between Edit mode (with the cursor displayed) and Navigation mode in a datasheet. When using a form or report, press Esc to leave Navigation mode.	F2
Switch between selecting the current record and the first field of the current record, in Navigation mode.	Shift+Spacebar
Extend selection to the previous record, if the current record is selected.	Shift+Up Arrow
Extend selection to the next record, if the current record is selected.	Shift+Down Arrow
Select all records.	Ctrl+A or Ctrl+Shift+Spacebar

Extending a Selection

Action	Keyboard shortcut
Turn on Extend mode (in Datasheet view, Extended Selection appears in the lower-right corner of the window); pressing F8 repeatedly extends the selection to the word, the field, the record, and all records.	F8
Extend a selection to adjacent fields in the same row in Datasheet view.	Left Arrow or Right Arrow
Extend a selection to adjacent rows in Datasheet view.	Up Arrow or Down Arrow
Undo the previous extension.	Shift+F8
Cancel Extend mode.	Esc

Selecting and Moving a Column in Datasheet View

Action	Keyboard shortcut
Select the current column or cancel the column selection, in Navigation mode only.	Ctrl+Spacebar
Select the column to the right, if the current column is selected.	Shift+Right Arrow
Select the column to the left, if the current column is selected.	Shift+Left Arrow
Turn on Move mode; then press the Right Arrow or Left Arrow key to move selected column(s) to the right or left.	Ctrl+Shift+F8

Edit Text and Data

Tip If the cursor is not visible, press F2 to display it.

Moving the Cursor in a Field

Action	Keyboard shortcut
Move the cursor one character to the right.	Right Arrow
Move the cursor one word to the right.	Ctrl+Right Arrow
Move the cursor one character to the left.	Left Arrow
Move the cursor one word to the left.	Ctrl+Left Arrow
Move the cursor to the end of the field, in single-line fields; or to move it to the end of the line in multiple-line fields.	End
Move the cursor to the end of the field, in multiple-line fields.	Ctrl+End
Move the cursor to the beginning of the field, in single-line fields; or to move it to the beginning of the line in multiple-line fields.	Home
Move the cursor to the beginning of the field, in multiple-line fields.	Ctrl+Home

Copying, Moving, or Deleting Text

Action	Keyboard shortcut
Copy the selection to the Clipboard.	Ctrl+C
Cut the selection and copy it to the Clipboard.	Ctrl+X
Paste the contents of the Clipboard at the cursor.	Ctrl+V
Delete the selection or the character to the left of the cursor.	Backspace
Delete the selection or the character to the right of the cursor.	Delete
Delete all characters to the right of the cursor.	Ctrl+Delete

Undoing Changes

Action	Keyboard shortcut
Undo typing.	Ctrl+Z or Alt+Backspace
Undo changes in the current field or current record; if both have been changed, press Esc twice to undo changes, first in the current field and then in the current record.	Esc

Entering Data in Datasheet or Form View

Action	Keyboard shortcut
Insert the current date.	Ctrl+Semicolon (;)
Insert the current time.	Ctrl+Shift+Colon (:)
Insert the default value for a field.	Ctrl+Alt+Spacebar
Insert the value from the same field in the previous record.	Ctrl+Apostrophe (')
Add a new record.	Ctrl+Plus Sign (+)
In a datasheet, delete the current record.	Ctrl+Minus Sign (-)
Save changes to the current record.	Shift+Enter
Switch between the values in a check box or option button.	Spacebar
Insert a new line.	Ctrl+Enter

Refreshing Fields with Current Data

Action	Keyboard shortcut
Recalculate the fields in the window.	F9
Requery the underlying tables; in a subform, this requires the underlying table for the subform only.	Shift+F9
Refresh the contents of a Lookup field list box or combo box.	F9

Keys for Navigating Records

Navigate in Design View

Action	Keyboard shortcut
Switch between Edit mode (with cursor displayed) and Navigation mode.	F2
Toggle the Property Sheet.	F4
Switch to Form view from form Design view.	F5
Switch between the upper and lower portions of a window (Design view of macros, queries, and the Advanced Filter/Sort window). Use F6 when the Tab key does not take you to the section of the screen you want.	F6
Toggle forward between the design pane, properties, Navigation pane, access keys, and Zoom controls (Design view of tables, forms, and reports).	F6
Open the Visual Basic Editor from a selected property in the Property Sheet for a form or report.	F7
Invokes the Field List pane in a form or report. If the Field List pane is already open, focus moves to the Field List pane.	Alt+F8
When you have a code module open, switch from the Visual Basic Editor to form or report Design view.	Shift+F7
Switch from a control's Property Sheet in form or report Design view to the design surface without changing the control focus.	Shift+F7
Display a Property Sheet.	Alt+Enter
Copy the selected control to the Clipboard.	Ctrl+C
Cut the selected control and copy it to the Clipboard.	Ctrl+X
Paste the contents of the Clipboard in the upper-left corner of the selected section.	Ctrl+V
Move the selected control to the right by a pixel along the page grid.	Right Arrow
Move the selected control to the left by a pixel along the page grid.	Left Arrow
Move the selected control up by a pixel along the page grid. Note: For controls in a stacked layout, this switches the position of the selected control with the control directly above it, unless it is already the uppermost control in the layout.	Up Arrow
Move the selected control down by a pixel along the page grid. Note: For controls in a stacked layout, this switches the position of the selected control with the control directly below it, unless it is already the lowermost control in the layout.	Down Arrow

Action	Keyboard shortcut
Move the selected control to the right by a pixel (irrespective of the page grid).	Ctrl+Right Arrow
Move the selected control to the left by a pixel (irrespective of the page grid).	Ctrl+Left Arrow
Move the selected control up by a pixel (irrespective of the page grid). Note: For controls in a stacked layout, this switches the position of the selected control with the control directly above it, unless it is already the uppermost control in the layout.	Ctrl+Up Arrow
Move the selected control down by a pixel (irrespective of the page grid). Note: For controls in a stacked layout, this switches the position of the selected control with the control directly below it, unless it is already the lowermost control in the layout.	Ctrl+Down Arrow
Increase the width of the selected control (to the right) by a pixel. Note: For controls in a stacked layout, this increases the width of the whole layout.	Shift+Right Arrow
Decrease the width of the selected control (to the left) by a pixel. Note: For controls in a stacked layout, this decreases the width of the whole layout.	Shift+Left Arrow
Decrease the height of the selected control (from the bottom) by a pixel.	Shift+Up Arrow
Increase the height of the selected control (from the bottom) by a pixel.	Shift+Down Arrow

Navigate in Datasheet View

Going to a Specific Record

Action	Keyboard shortcut
Move to the record number box; then type the record number and press Enter.	F5

Navigating Between Fields and Records

Action	Keyboard shortcut
Move to the next field.	Tab or Right Arrow
Move to the last field in the current record, in Navigation mode.	End
Move to the previous field.	Shift+Tab, or Left Arrow

(continued)

Action	Keyboard shortcut
Move to the first field in the current record, in Navigation mode.	Home
Move to the current field in the next record.	Down Arrow
Move to the current field in the last record, in Navigation mode.	Ctrl+Down Arrow
Move to the last field in the last record, in Navigation mode.	Ctrl+End
Move to the current field in the previous record.	Up Arrow
Move to the current field in the first record, in Navigation mode.	Ctrl+Up Arrow
Move to the first field in the first record, in Navigation mode.	Ctrl+Home

Navigating to Another Screen of Data

Action	Keyboard shortcut
Move down one screen.	Page Down
Move up one screen.	Page Up
Move right one screen.	Ctrl+Page Down
Move left one screen.	Ctrl+Page Up

Navigate in Subdatasheets

Going to a Specific Record

Action	Keyboard shortcut
Move from the subdatasheet to move to the record number box; then type the record number and press Enter.	Alt+F5

Expanding and Collapsing a Subdatasheet

Action	Keyboard shortcut
Move from the datasheet to expand the record's subdatasheet.	Ctrl+Shift+Down Arrow
Collapse the subdatasheet.	Ctrl+Shift+Up Arrow

Navigating Between the Datasheet and Subdatasheet

Action	Keyboard shortcut
Enter the subdatasheet from the last field of the previous record in the datasheet.	Tab
Enter the subdatasheet from the first field of the following record in the datasheet.	Shift+Tab

Action	Keyboard shortcut
Exit the subdatasheet and move to the first field of the next record in the datasheet.	Ctrl+Tab
Exit the subdatasheet and move to the last field of the previous record in the datasheet.	Ctrl+Shift+Tab
From the last field in the subdatasheet to enter the next field in the datasheet.	Tab
From the datasheet to bypass the subdatasheet and move to the next record in the datasheet.	Down Arrow
From the datasheet to bypass the subdatasheet and move to the previous record in the datasheet.	Up Arrow

Tip You can navigate between fields and records in a subdatasheet with the same shortcut keys used in Datasheet view.

Navigate in Form View

Going to a Specific Record

Action	Keyboard shortcut
Move to the record number box; then type the record number and press Enter.	F5

Navigating Between Fields and Records

Action	Keyboard shortcut
Move to the next field.	Tab
Move to the previous field.	Shift+Tab
Move to the last control on the form and remain in the current record, in Navigation mode.	End
Move to the last control on the form and set focus in the last record, in Navigation mode.	Ctrl+End
Move to the first control on the form and remain in the current record, in Navigation mode.	Home
Move to the first control on the form and set focus in the first record, in Navigation mode.	Ctrl+Home
Move to the current field in the next record.	Ctrl+Page Down
Move to the current field in the previous record.	Ctrl+Page Up

Navigating in Forms with More Than One page

Action	Keyboard shortcut
Move down one page; at the end of the record, moves to the equivalent page on the next record.	Page Down
Move up one page; at the end of the record, moves to the equivalent page on the previous record.	Page Up

Navigating Between the Main Form and Subform

Action	Keyboard shortcut
Enter the subform from the preceding field in the main form.	Tab
Enter the subform from the following field in the main form.	Shift+Tab
Exit the subform and move to the next field in the master form or next record.	Ctrl+Tab
Exit the subform and move to the previous field in the main form or previous record.	Ctrl+Shift+Tab

Navigate in Print Preview

Working with Dialog Boxes and Windows

Action	Keyboard shortcut
Open the Print dialog box from the Print page of the Backstage view, or from datasheets, forms, and reports.	Ctrl+P
Open the Page Setup dialog box (forms and reports only).	S
Zoom in or out on a part of the page.	Z
Cancel Print Preview or Layout Preview.	C or Esc

Viewing Different Pages

Action	Keyboard shortcut
Move to the page number box; then type the page number and press Enter.	Alt+F5
View the next page (when Fit To Window is selected)..	Page Down or Down Arrow
View the previous page (when Fit To Window is selected).	Page Up or Up Arrow

Navigating in Print Preview

Action	Keyboard shortcut
Scroll down in small increments.	Down Arrow
Scroll down one full screen.	Page Down
Move to the bottom of the page.	Ctrl+Down Arrow
Scroll up in small increments.	Up Arrow
Scroll up one full screen.	Page Up
Move to the top of the page.	Ctrl+Up Arrow
Scroll to the right in small increments.	Right Arrow
Move to the right edge of the page.	End
Move to the lower-right corner of the page.	Ctrl+End
Scroll to the left in small increments.	Left Arrow
Move to the left edge of the page.	Home
Move to the upper-left corner of the page.	Ctrl+Home

Navigate in the Database Diagram Window

Action	Keyboard shortcut
Move from a table cell to the table's title bar.	Esc
Move from a table's title bar to the last cell you edited.	Enter
Move from table title bar to table title bar, or from cell to cell inside a table.	Tab
Expand a list inside a table.	Alt + Down Arrow
Scroll through the items in a drop-down list from top to bottom.	Down Arrow
Move to the previous item in a list.	Up Arrow
Select an item in a list and move to the next cell.	Enter
Change the setting in a check box.	Spacebar
Go to the first cell in the row, or to the beginning of the current cell.	Home
Go to the last cell in the row, or to the end of the current cell.	End
Scroll to the next "page" inside a table, or to the next "page" of the diagram.	Page Down
Scroll to the previous "page" inside a table, or to the previous "page" of the diagram.	Page Up

Navigate in the Query Designer

Any Pane

Action	Keyboard shortcut
Move among the Query Designer panes.	F6, Shift+F6

Diagram Pane

Action	Keyboard shortcut
Move among tables, views, and functions, (and to join lines, if available).	Tab, or Shift+Tab
Move between columns in a table, view, or function.	Arrow keys
Choose the selected data column for output.	Spacebar or Plus key
Remove the selected data column from the query output.	Spacebar or Minus key
Remove the selected table, view, or function, or join line from the query.	Delete

Tip If multiple items are selected, pressing the Spacebar affects all selected items. Select multiple items by holding down the Shift key while clicking them. Toggle the selected state of a single item by holding down the Ctrl key while clicking it.

Grid Pane

Action	Keyboard shortcut
Move among cells.	Arrow keys or Tab or Shift+Tab
Move to the last row in the current column.	Ctrl+Down Arrow
Move to the first row in the current column.	Ctrl+Up Arrow
Move to the upper-left cell in the visible portion of the grid.	Ctrl+Home
Move to the lower-right cell.	Ctrl+End
Move in a drop-down list.	Up Arrow or Down Arrow
Select an entire grid column.	Ctrl+Spacebar
Toggle between edit mode and cell selection mode.	F2
Copy selected text in cell to the Clipboard (in edit mode).	Ctrl+C
Cut selected text in a cell and place it on the Clipboard (in edit mode).	Ctrl+X
Paste text from the Clipboard (in edit mode).	Ctrl+V
Toggle between insert and overstrike mode while editing in a cell.	Ins

Action	Keyboard shortcut
Toggle the check box in the Output column. Note: If multiple items are selected, pressing this key affects all selected items.	Spacebar
Clear the selected contents of a cell.	Delete
Remove a row containing a selected data column from the query. Note: If multiple items are selected, pressing this key affects all selected items.	Delete
Clear all values in a selected grid column.	Delete
Insert a row between existing rows (after selecting a row).	Ins
Add an Or column (after selecting any Or column).	Ins

SQL Pane

You can use the standard Windows editing keys when working in the SQL pane, such as Ctrl+Arrow keys to move between words, and the Cut, Copy, and Paste commands on the Edit menu.

Tip You can only insert text; there is no overstrike mode.

Work with PivotTable Views

PivotTable View

Selecting Elements

Action	Keyboard shortcut
Move the selection from left to right, and then down.	The Tab key
Move the selection from top to bottom, and then to the right.	Enter
Select the cell to the left. If the current cell is the leftmost cell, Shift+Tab selects the last cell in the previous row.	Shift+Tab
Select the cell above the current cell. If the current cell is the topmost cell, Shift+Enter selects the last cell in the previous column.	Shift+Enter
Select the detail cells for the next item in the row area.	Ctrl+Enter
Select the detail cells for the previous item in the row area.	Shift+Ctrl+Enter
Move the selection in the direction of the Arrow key. If a row or column field is selected, press the Down Arrow key to move to the first item of data in the field, and then press an Arrow key to move to the next or previous item or back to the field. If a detail field is selected, press the Down Arrow key or Right Arrow key to move to the first cell in the detail area.	Arrow keys

(continued)

Action	Keyboard shortcut
Extend or reduce the selection in the direction of the Arrow key.	Shift+Arrow keys
Move the selection to the last cell in the direction of the Arrow key.	Ctrl+Arrow keys
Move the selected item in the direction of the Arrow key.	Shift+Alt+Arrow keys
Select the leftmost cell of the current row.	Home
Select the rightmost cell of the current row.	End
Select the leftmost cell of the first row.	Ctrl+Home
Select the last cell of the last row.	Ctrl+End
Extend selection to the leftmost cell of the first row.	Shift+Ctrl+Home
Extend selection to the last cell of the last row.	Shift+Ctrl+End
Select the field for the currently selected item of data, total, or detail.	Ctrl+Spacebar
Select the entire row containing the currently selected cell.	Shift+Spacebar
Select the entire PivotTable view.	Ctrl+A
Display the next screen.	Page Down
Display the previous screen.	Page Up
Extend the selection down one screen.	Shift+Page Down
Reduce the selection by one screen.	Shift+Page Up
Display the next screen to the right.	Alt+Page Down
Display the previous screen to the left.	Alt+Page Up
Extend the selection to the page on the right.	Shift+Alt+Page Down
Extend the selection to the page on the left.	Shift+Alt+Page Up

Carrying Out Commands

Action	Keyboard shortcut
Display Help topics.	F1
Display the shortcut menu for the selected element of the PivotTable view. Use the shortcut menus to carry out commands in the PivotTable view.	Shift+F10
Carry out a command on the shortcut menu.	Underlined letter
Close the shortcut menu without carrying out a command.	Esc
Display the Properties dialog box.	Alt+Enter
Close the Properties dialog box.	Alt+F4
Cancel a refresh operation in progress.	Esc
Copy the selected data from the PivotTable view to the Clipboard.	Ctrl+C
Export the contents of the PivotTable view to Excel 2010.	Ctrl+E

Keys for Displaying, Hiding, Filtering, or Sorting Data

Action	Keyboard shortcut
Show or hide the expand indicators (plus and minus boxes) beside items.	Ctrl+8
Expand the currently selected item.	Ctrl+Plus Sign (on the numeric keypad)
Hide the currently selected item.	Ctrl+Minus Sign (on the numeric keypad)
Open the list for the currently selected field.	Alt+Down Arrow
Alternately move to the most recently selected item, the OK button, and the Cancel button in the drop-down list for a field.	The Tab key
Move to the next item in the drop-down list for a field.	Arrow keys
Select or clear the check box for the current item in the drop-down list for a field.	Spacebar
Close the drop-down list for a field and apply any changes you made.	Enter
Close the drop-down list for a field without applying your changes.	Esc
Turn AutoFilter on or off.	Ctrl+T
Sort data in the selected field or total in ascending order (A–Z 0–9).	Ctrl+Shift+A
Sort data in the selected field or total in descending order (Z–A 9–0).	Ctrl+Shift+Z
Move the selected member up or left.	Alt+Shift+Up Arrow or Alt+Shift+Left Arrow
Move the selected member down or right.	Alt+Shift+Down Arrow or Alt+Shift+Right Arrow

Adding Fields and Totals and Changing the Layout

Working with the Field List Pane

Action	Keyboard shortcut
Display the Field List pane, or activate it if it is already displayed.	Ctrl+L
Move to the next item in the Field List pane.	Arrow keys
Move to the previous item and include it in the selection.	Shift+Up Arrow
Move to the next item and include it in the selection.	Shift+Down Arrow
Move to the previous item, but don't include it in the selection.	Ctrl+Up Arrow
Move to the next item, but don't include it in the selection.	Ctrl+Down Arrow

(continued)

Action	Keyboard shortcut
Remove the item from the selection, if the item that has focus is included in the selection, and vice versa.	Ctrl+Spacebar
Expand the current item in the Field List pane to display its contents. Or expand Totals to display the available total fields.	Plus Sign (numeric keypad)
Collapse the current item in the Field List pane to hide its contents. Or collapse Totals to hide the available total fields.	Minus Sign (numeric keypad)
Move between the most recently selected item, the Add To button, and the list next to the Add To button in the Field List pane.	Tab
Display the list next to the Add To button in the Field List pane. Use the Arrow keys to move to the next item in the list, and then press Enter to select an item.	Alt+Down Arrow
Add the highlighted field in the Field List pane to the area in the PivotTable view that is displayed in the Add To list.	Enter
Close the Field List pane.	Alt+F4

Adding Fields and Totals

Action	Keyboard shortcut
Add a new total field for the selected field in the PivotTable view by using the Sum function.	Ctrl+Shift+S
Add a new total field for the selected field in the PivotTable view by using the Count function.	Ctrl+Shift+C
Add a new total field for the selected field in the PivotTable view by using the Min function.	Ctrl+Shift+M
Add a new total field for the selected field in the PivotTable view by using the Max function.	Ctrl+Shift+X
Add a new total field for the selected field in the PivotTable view by using the Average function.	Ctrl+Shift+E
Add a new total field for the selected field in the PivotTable view by using the Standard Deviation function.	Ctrl+Shift+D
Add a new total field for the selected field in the PivotTable view by using the Standard Deviation Population function.	Ctrl+Shift+T
Add a new total field for the selected field in the PivotTable view by using the Variance function.	Ctrl+Shift+V
Add a new total field for the selected field in the PivotTable view by using the Variance Population function.	Ctrl+Shift+R
Turn subtotals and grand totals on or off for the selected field in the PivotTable view.	Ctrl+Shift+B
Add a calculated detail field.	Ctrl+F

Changing the Layout

Action	Keyboard shortcut
Move the selected field in the PivotTable view to the row area.	Ctrl+1
Move the selected field in the PivotTable view to the column area.	Ctrl+2
Move the selected field in the PivotTable view to the filter area.	Ctrl+3
Move the selected field in the PivotTable view to the detail area.	Ctrl+4
Move the selected row or column field in the PivotTable view to a higher level.	Ctrl+Left Arrow
Move the selected row or column field in the PivotTable view to a lower level.	Ctrl+Right Arrow

Tip The first four shortcuts do not work if you press the 1, 2, 3, or 4 keys on the numeric pad of your keyboard.

Formatting Elements

To use the following shortcuts, first select a detail field or a data cell for a total field.

The first seven keyboard shortcuts change the number format of the selected field.

Action	Keyboard shortcut
Apply the general number format to values in the selected total or detail field.	Ctrl+Shift+~ (tilde)
Apply the currency format, with two decimal places and negative numbers in parentheses, to values in the selected total or detail field.	Ctrl+Shift+$
Apply the percentage format, with no decimal places, to values in the selected total or detail field.	Ctrl+Shift+%
Apply the exponential number format, with two decimal places, to values in the selected total or detail field.	Ctrl+Shift+^
Apply the date format, with the day, month, and year, to values in the selected total or detail field.	Ctrl+Shift+#
Apply the time format, with the hour, minute, and AM or PM, to values in the selected total or detail field.	Ctrl+Shift+@
Apply the numeric format, with two decimal places, thousands separator, and a minus sign for negative values, to values in the selected total or detail field.	Ctrl+Shift+!
Make text bold in the selected field of the PivotTable view.	Ctrl+B
Make text underlined in the selected field of the PivotTable view.	Ctrl+U
Make text italic in the selected field of the PivotTable view.	Ctrl+I

PivotChart View

Selecting Items in a Chart

Action	Keyboard shortcut
Select the next item in the chart.	Right Arrow
Select the previous item in the chart.	Left Arrow
Select the next group of items.	Down Arrow
Select the previous group of items.	Up Arrow

Working with Properties and Options

Action	Keyboard shortcut
Display the Properties dialog box.	Alt+Enter
Close the Properties dialog box.	Alt+F4
When the Properties dialog box is active, select the next item on the active tab.	The Tab key
When a tab in the Properties dialog box is active, select the next tab.	Right Arrow
When a tab in the Properties dialog box is active, select the previous tab.	Left Arrow
Display a list or palette when a button that contains a list or palette is selected.	Down Arrow
Display the shortcut menu.	Shift+F10
Carry out a command on the shortcut menu.	Underlined letter
Close the shortcut menu without carrying out a command.	Esc

Working with Fields

Action	Keyboard shortcut
Open the list for the currently selected field.	Alt+Down Arrow
In the drop-down list for a field, alternately move to the most recently selected item, the OK button, and the Cancel button.	The Tab key
In the drop-down list for a field, move to the next item.	Arrow keys
In the drop-down list for a field, select or clear the check box for the current item.	Spacebar
Close the drop-down list for a field and apply any changes you made.	Enter
Close the drop-down list for a field without applying your changes.	Esc

Working with the Fields List Pane

Action	Keyboard shortcut
Display the Field List pane, or activate it if it is already displayed.	Ctrl+L
Move to the next item in the Field List pane.	Arrow keys
Move to the previous item and include it in the selection.	Shift+Up Arrow
Move to the next item and include it in the selection.	Shift+Down Arrow
Move to the previous item, but don't include the item in the selection.	Ctrl+Up Arrow
Move to the next item, but don't include the item in the selection.	Ctrl+Down Arrow
Remove the item from the selection if the item that has focus is included in the selection, and vice versa.	Ctrl+Spacebar
Expand the current item in the Field List pane to display its contents, or expand Totals to display the available total fields.	Plus Sign (numeric keypad)
Collapse the current item in the Field List pane to hide its contents, or collapse Totals to hide the available total fields.	Minus Sign (numeric keypad)
In the Field List pane, alternately move to the most recently selected item, the Add To button, and the list next to the Add To button.	The Tab key
Open the drop-down list next to the Add To button in the Field List pane. Use the Arrow keys to move to the next item in the list, and then press Enter to select an item.	Alt+Down Arrow
Add the highlighted field in the Field List pane to the drop area that is displayed in the Add To list.	Enter
Close the Field List pane.	Alt+F4

Keys for Working with the Ribbon

1. Press Alt.

   The KeyTips are displayed over each feature that is available in the current view.

2. Press the letter shown in the KeyTip over the feature that you want to use.

3. Depending on which letter you press, you might be shown additional KeyTips. For example, if the External Data tab is active and you press C, the Create tab is displayed, along with the KeyTips for the groups on that tab.

4. Continue pressing letters until you press the letter of the command or control that you want to use. In some cases, you must first press the letter of the group that contains the command.

Tip To cancel the action that you are taking and hide the KeyTips, press Alt.

Keys for Working with Online Help

The Help window provides access to all Office Help content. The Help window displays topics and other Help content.

Action	Keyboard shortcut
Open the Help window.	F1
Close the Help window	Alt+F4
Switch between the Help window and the active program.	Alt+Tab
Go back to <program name> Home.	Alt+Home
Select the next item in the Help window.	Tab
Select the previous item in the Help window.	Shift+Tab
Perform the action for the selected item.	Enter
In the Browse <program name> Help section of the Help window, select the next or previous item, respectively.	Tab or Shift+Tab
In the Browse <program name> Help section of the Help window, expand or collapse the selected item, respectively.	Enter
Select the next hidden text or hyperlink, including Show All or Hide All at the top of a topic.	Tab
Select the previous hidden text or hyperlink.	Shift+Tab
Perform the action for the selected Show All, Hide All, hidden text, or hyperlink.	Enter
Move back to the previous Help topic (Back button).	Alt+Left Arrow or Backspace
Move forward to the next Help topic (Forward button).	Alt+Right Arrow
Scroll small amounts up or down, respectively, within the currently displayed Help topic.	Up Arrow, Down Arrow
Scroll larger amounts up or down, respectively, within the currently displayed Help topic.	Page Up, Page Down
Display a menu of commands for the Help window. This requires that the Help window have the active focus (click in the Help window).	Shift+F10
Stop the last action (Stop button).	Esc
Refresh the window (Refresh button).	F5
Print the current Help topic. Note: If the cursor is not in the current Help topic, press F6, and then press Ctrl+P.	Ctrl+P

Action	Keyboard shortcut
Change the connection state.	F6, and then press Enter to open the list of choices
Switch among areas in the Help window; for example, switch between the toolbar and the Search list.	F6
In a Table of Contents in tree view, select the next or previous item, respectively.	Up Arrow, Down Arrow
In a Table of Contents in tree view, expand or collapse the selected item, respectively.	Left Arrow, Right Arrow

Keys for Basic Office Tasks

Display and Use Windows

Action	Keyboard shortcut
Switch to the next window.	Alt+Tab
Switch to the previous window.	Alt+Shift+Tab
Close the active window.	Ctrl+W or Ctrl+F4
Move to a task pane from another pane in the program window (clockwise). You might need to press F6 more than once. Note: If pressing F6 doesn't display the task pane you want, try pressing Alt to place focus on the ribbon and then pressing Ctrl+Tab to move to the task pane.	F6
When multiple windows are open, switch to the next window.	Ctrl+F6
Switch to the previous window.	Ctrl+Shift+F6
When a window is not maximized, invoke the Size command (on the Control menu for the window). Press the Arrow keys to resize the window, and, when finished, press Enter.	Ctrl+F8
Minimize a window to an icon (works for only some Microsoft Office programs).	Ctrl+F9
Maximize or restore a selected window.	Ctrl+F10
Copy a picture of the screen to the Clipboard.	Print Screen
Copy a picture of the selected window to the Clipboard.	Alt+Print Screen

Move Around in Text or Cells

Action	Keyboard shortcut
Move one character to the left.	Left Arrow
Move one character to the right.	Right Arrow
Move one line up.	Up Arrow
Move one line down.	Down Arrow
Move one word to the left.	Ctrl+Left Arrow
Move one word to the right.	Ctrl+Right Arrow
Move to the end of a line.	End
Move to the beginning of a line.	Home
Move up one paragraph.	Ctrl+Up Arrow
Move down one paragraph.	Ctrl+Down Arrow
Move to the end of a text box.	Ctrl+End
Move to the beginning of a text box.	Ctrl+Home
Repeat the last Find action.	Shift+F4

Move Around in and Work in Tables

Action	Keyboard shortcut
Move to the next cell.	Tab
Move to the preceding cell.	Shift+Tab
Move to the next row.	Down Arrow
Move to the preceding row.	Up Arrow
Insert a tab in a cell.	Ctrl+Tab
Start a new paragraph.	Enter
Add a new row at the bottom of the table.	Tab at the end of the last row

Access and Use Task Panes

Action	Keyboard shortcut
Move to a task pane from another pane in the program window. (You might need to press F6 more than once.)	F6
Note: If pressing F6 doesn't display the task pane you want, try pressing Alt to place focus on the menu bar and then pressing Ctrl+Tab to move to the task pane.	

Action	Keyboard shortcut
When a menu or toolbar is active, move to a task pane. (You might need to press Ctrl+Tab more than once.)	Ctrl+Tab
When a task pane is active, select the next or previous option in the task pane.	Tab or Shift+Tab
Display the full set of commands on the task pane menu.	Ctrl+Down Arrow
Move among choices on a selected submenu; move among certain options in a group of options in a dialog box.	Down Arrow or Up Arrow
Open the selected menu, or perform the action assigned to the selected button.	Spacebar or Enter
Open a shortcut menu; open a drop-down menu for the selected gallery item.	Shift+F10
When a menu or submenu is visible, select the first or last command on the menu or submenu.	Home or End
Scroll up or down in the selected gallery list.	Page Up or Page Down
Move to the top or bottom of the selected gallery list.	Ctrl+Home or Ctrl+End

Use Dialog Boxes

Action	Keyboard shortcut
Move to the next option or option group.	Tab
Move to the previous option or option group.	Shift+Tab
Switch to the next tab in a dialog box.	Ctrl+Tab
Switch to the previous tab in a dialog box.	Ctrl+Shift+Tab
Move between options in an open drop-down list, or between options in a group of options.	Arrow keys
Perform the action assigned to the selected button; select or clear the selected check box.	Spacebar
Open the list if it is closed and move to that option in the list.	First letter of an option in a list
Select an option; select or clear a check box.	Alt+ the underlined letter in an option
Open a selected drop-down list.	Alt+Down Arrow
Close a selected drop-down list; cancel a command and close a dialog box.	Esc
Perform the action assigned to a default button in a dialog box.	Enter

Use Edit Boxes Within Dialog Boxes

An edit box is a blank in which you type or paste an entry, such as your user name or the path of a folder.

Action	Keyboard shortcut
Move to the beginning of the entry.	Home
Move to the end of the entry.	End
Move one character to the left or right.	Left Arrow or Right Arrow
Move one word to the left.	Ctrl+Left Arrow
Move one word to the right.	Ctrl+Right Arrow
Select or cancel selection one character to the left.	Shift+Left Arrow
Select or cancel selection one character to the right.	Shift+Right Arrow
Select or cancel selection one word to the left.	Ctrl+Shift+Left Arrow
Select or cancel selection one word to the right.	Ctrl+Shift+Right Arrow
Select from the cursor to the beginning of the entry.	Shift+Home
Select from the cursor to the end of the entry.	Shift+End

Index

restricting data
  via data types, 144. *See also* data types
  to default value, 167
  via field size property, 150
  to list values, 167, 168
  via relationships, 172
restricting databases, 309–313, 323
restricting editing in forms, 300
results datasheets, 361
revealing hidden fields, 62
ribbon
  button appearance, xvi
  collapsing, 13
  commands on, xv
  commands on, adding/removing, 349
  customizing, 346–347, 350
  decreasing width of, xvi
  defined, 361
  dynamic nature of, xvi
  expanding, 7, 352
  groups, 6, 359
  groups, adding/removing, 348
  hiding, 352
  hiding commands, 7
  minimizing, 7, 352
  overview of, xv, 6
  resetting to original configuration, 350
ribbon tabs, 6
  defined, 361
  removing, 347
  renaming, 349
Rich Text data type, 145, 283
right-aligning labels, 94
rounding values in Number fields, 151
Row Height dialog box, 62
row selectors, 361
rows, 16
  in forms, selecting, 96
  inserting, 153
  resizing, 61, 62
rulers, turning on/off, 247
rules for formatting reports, 134–135
rules, validation. *See also* expressions
  asterisks in, 162
  creating, 159, 160
  data types compatible with, 159
  defined, 362
  in Design view, 163
  entering manually, 160
  error messages for, 160, 163

  field-level, 159
  overview of, 159
  record-level, 159, 164
  wildcard characters in, 162
Run button, 32, 215, 219
running Access 2010, 4, 8
running queries, 29–32, 213, 215, 219

S

Save As dialog box, 57, 147
Save As Query dialog box, 119
Save button, 6, 54, 71
Save & Publish page, 324
Saved Imports button, 267
saving
  forms, 84, 92
  queries, 29
  records, 54–55
  tables, 54, 57, 71
  themes, 85
schemas, XML, 272, 361
ScreenTips
  customizing display of, 7
  overview of, xxv
  viewing, 7
searching Help, xxviii
searching wildcard character, 113, 115
sections, report, 246
secure passwords, 361
security, 315
security warnings, 8, 14, 361
Select All button, 90, 96, 134
Select button, 238
Select Column button, 94
select queries, 29, 209
  converting to action queries, 231
  converting to delete queries, 236
  converting to update queries, 233
  creating, 211
  defined, 361
  setting up, 210
  wizards for, 210
Select Row button, 96
selecting
  adjacent fields, 62, 63
  controls, 80, 185
  controls, all, 90, 96, 134
  fields, 65, 164

About the Authors

Joyce Cox

Joyce has 30 years' experience in the development of training materials about technical subjects for non-technical audiences, and is the author of dozens of books about Office and Windows technologies. She is the Vice President of Online Training Solutions, Inc. (OTSI).

As President of and principal author for Online Press, she developed the *Quick Course* series of computer training books for beginning and intermediate adult learners. She was also the first managing editor of Microsoft Press, an editor for Sybex, and an editor for the University of California.

Joan Lambert

Joan has worked in the training and certification industry for more than a decade. As President of OTSI, Joan is responsible for guiding the translation of technical information and requirements into useful, relevant, and measurable training and certification tools.

Joan is a Microsoft Office Master (MOM), a Microsoft Certified Application Specialist (MCAS), a Microsoft Certified Technology Specialist (MCTS), a Microsoft Certified Trainer (MCT), and the author of more than two dozen books about Windows and Office (for Windows and Mac).

The Team

This book would not exist without the support of these hard-working members of the OTSI publishing team:

- Jan Bednarczuk
- Rob Carr
- Susie Carr
- Jeanne Craver
- Kathy Krause
- Marlene Lambert
- Jaime Odell
- Jean Trenary
- Elisabeth Van Every

We are especially thankful to the support staff at home who make it possible for our team members to devote their time and attention to these projects.

Devon Musgrave provided invaluable support on behalf of Microsoft Learning.

The content of this book and its practice files is based on the content of *Microsoft Office Access 2007 Step by Step*, by Steve Lambert, Dow Lambert, and Joan Lambert Preppernau.

Online Training Solutions, Inc. (OTSI)

OTSI specializes in the design, creation, and production of Office and Windows training products for information workers and home computer users. For more information about OTSI, visit:

www.otsi.com